Death Penalties

The Supreme Court's Obstacle Course

Death Penalties

The Supreme Court's Obstacle Course

Raoul Berger

Harvard University Press
Cambridge, Massachusetts
and London, England
1982

Library of Congress Cataloging in Publication Data
Berger, Raoul, 1901–
　Death penalties.

　Bibliography: p.
　Includes indexes.
　1. Capital punishment—United States. 2. United States.
Supreme Court. I. Title.
KF9227.C2B47　　　345.73′0773　　　82-3054
ISBN 0-674-19426-8　　　347.305773　　AACR2

To the memory
of my parents

Contents

Death Penalties

The Supreme Court's Obstacle Course

Abbreviations

Ann. Cong.	*Annals of Congress,* vol. 1 (1789; 2d ed. 1834, print bearing running head "History of Congress")
Bedau	Hugo A. Bedau, *The Courts, the Constitution, and Capital Punishment* (1977)
Berger *G/J*	Raoul Berger, *Government by Judiciary: The Transformation of the Fourteenth Amendment* (1977)
Berger, *Congress v. Court*	Raoul Berger, *Congress v. The Supreme Court* (1969)
Bickel	Alexander M. Bickel, *The Supreme Court and the Idea of Progress* (1978)
Blackstone	William Blackstone, *Commentaries on the Laws of England* (1765–1769)
Elliot	Jonathan Elliot, *Debates in the Several State Conventions on the Adoption of the Federal Constitution* (2d ed., 1836)
Farrand	Max Farrand, *The Records of the Federal Convention of 1787* (1911)
Federalist	*The Federalist* (Modern Lib. ed., 1937)
Furman	*Furman v. Georgia,* 408 U.S. 238 (1972)
Globe	*Congressional Globe* (39th Congress, 1st Session 1866)
McGautha	*McGautha v. California,* 402 U.S. 183 (1971)
Perry	Michael Perry, "Interpretivism, Freedom of Expression and Equal Protection," 43 Ohio State Law Journal 261 (1981)
Poore	Ben P. Poore, *Federal and State Constitutions, Colonial Charters* (1877)

Italics. Italics throughout are those of the author, except where noted "Italics in the original."

1

Introduction

All authority that is not approved by true reason seems weak. But true reason, since it rests on its own strength, needs no reinforcement by any authority.

Johannes Scotus Erigena
A.D. 867*

ONE hundred eighty-one years after the adoption of the Bill of Rights a sadly divided Supreme Court, in *Furman v. Georgia,* discovered that the sovereign power of the States over death penalties had been curtailed by the Eighth Amendment's "cruel and unusual punishments" clause.[1] Prior to June 1972 an

---

* Will Durant, *The Age of Faith* 477 (1950). "What makes a thing true is not who says it, but the evidence for it." Sidney Hook, *Philosophy and Public Policy* 121 (1980). Chief Justice Taney declared that the Court's "judicial authority" should "depend altogether on the force of the reasoning by which it is supported." The Passenger Cases, 48 U.S. (7 How.) 283, 470 (1849), dissenting opinion.

1. 408 U.S. 238 (1972); hereinafter cited as Furman. "The presumption is powerful that such a far-reaching, dislocating construction . . . was not uncovered by judges, lawyers and scholars for seventy-five years because it was not there." Romero v. International Terminal Operating Co., 358 U.S. 354, 370–371 (1959), Frankfurter, J., concurring opinion.

1

unbroken string of cases, including *McGautha v. California*[2] only fourteen months earlier, had "unswervingly"[3] recognized the States' power. *Furman* was a case, said Justice White, in which "we strongly disagree among ourselves."[4] A plurality of three ruled against discretionary jury sentencing and was joined by Justices Brennan and Marshall, who flatly held death penalties unconstitutional. The reasons for the judgment, Justice Powell noted, "are stated in five separate opinions, expressing as many different rationales";[5] four dissenting opinions were better attuned; and the whole required 232 pages of explication. Justice Douglas, one of the *McGautha* dissenters, considered that a 5 to 4 decision "meant it barely passed muster as a constitutional procedure."[6] Still less does such a decision afford solid footing for repu-

2. 402 U.S. 183 (1971), hereinafter cited as McGautha.

3. Justice Powell referred to "the unswerving position that this Court has taken in opinions spanning the last hundred years. On virtually every occasion that any opinion has touched on the question . . . it has been asserted affirmatively, or tacitly assumed, that the Constitution does not prohibit the penalty." Furman 428; and see id. 417, dissenting opinion. "The several concurring opinions" in Furman, said Justice Blackmun, "acknowledge, as they must, that until today capital punishment was accepted and assumed as not unconstitutional per se under the Eighth Amendment or the Fourteenth Amendment." Id. 407, dissenting opinion. It cannot be controverted that, as Chief Justice Burger stated, "In the 181 years since the enactment of the Eighth Amendment, not a single decision of this Court has cast the slightest shadow of a doubt on the constitutionality of capital punishment." Id. 380, dissenting opinion.

4. Furman 314. Chief Justice Burger remarked, "The widely divergent views of the Amendment expressed in today's opinions reveal the haze that surrounds this constitutional command." Id. 376.

5. Id. 414. Justice Powell alluded to "the shattering effect this collection of views has on the root principles of *stare decisis,* federalism, judicial restraint and—most importantly—separation of powers." Id. 417. This was scarcely the "mighty counterthrust" that activist Hugo Bedau considered would "be required to alter the direction of those decisions." Hugo A. Bedau, *The Courts, the Constitution, and Capital Punishment* 35 (1977), hereinafter cited as Bedau.

6. McGautha 231.

diation of long-standing precedent rooted in historical fact[7] and well-nigh universal approval by the State legislatures. It is a paradox, moreover, that despite their own divided counsels and resultant uncertainty, the five should condemn the uncertainty allegedly arising from the absence of *standards* to govern jury sentencing.

"The immediate effect of *Furman*," wrote Hugo Bedau, a leader in the movement to abolish death penalties, "was to overturn the entire prevailing system of capital punishment in this country." Out of a total of "fifty-two criminal jurisdictions . . . only five . . . had totally abolished capital punishment for all crimes." "No death sentence had ever been voided as a violation of due process, equal protection," or "cruel and unusual punishments." "Most commentators," Bedau observed, "expressed dismay and bewilderment at the close ruling, at the inability of the majority Justices to join in any one rationale for their decision, and at the resulting uncertainty over the modes of capital punishment that might still be constitutionally imposed."[8] "Predictably," Chief Justice Burger later wrote, "the variety of opinions supporting the judgment in *Furman* engendered confusion as to what was required in order to impose the death penalty in accord with the Eighth Amendment."[9]

This constitutional earthquake resulted from the labors of a

7. "Unfortunately, the decision beclouds more than it clarifies regarding the constitutionality of capital punishment per se and the scope of the eighth amendment in general."—Malcolm Wheeler, "Toward a Theory of Limited Punishment II: The Eighth Amendment After Furman v. Georgia," 25 Stan. L. Rev. 62 (1972).

8. Bedau 81–83. Justice Thurgood Marshall wrote in his concurring opinion that "41 States, the District of Columbia, and other federal jurisdictions authorize the death penalty for at least one crime." Furman 341. Justice Powell observed, "The capital punishment laws of no less than 39 States and the District of Columbia are nullified." Furman 417. See also Chief Justice Burger, Furman 385.

9. Lockett v. Ohio, 438 U.S. 586, 599 (1978). "The signals from the Court," Chief Justice Burger remarked, "have not, however, been easy to decipher." Id. 602.

small band of dedicated abolitionists, led by a few top-flight lawyers in the service of the NAACP—fully one-half of the occupants
on death row are blacks.[10] "Until fifteen years ago," Bedau wrote,
"save for a few mavericks, no one gave any credence to the possibility of ending the death penalty by judicial interpretation of
constitutional law." "Save for a few eccentrics and visionaries," he
remarked, the death penalty was "taken for granted by all men . . .
as a bulwark of the social structure."[11] The abolitionists, however,
enjoyed a priceless advantage: they appealed to Justices who "ab-
horred" death penalties,[12] among them Justice Douglas, who was
"a visible and unswerving opponent of the death penalty,"[13]
joined by the no less committed Justices Brennan and Thurgood
Marshall. The campaign had the aura of a moral crusade; opponents were not merely ill-advised, they yielded, in the words of
Justice Douglas, to "deep-seated sadistic instincts."[14] He relied
rather on his own "gut reactions," disclosing in a burst of autobi-
ographical candor that "the 'gut' reaction of a judge at the level of
constitutional adjudication, dealing with the vagaries of due process . . . and the like, was the main ingredient of his decision."[15]

10. For a résumé of this crusade, see Bedau 78–90; for black occupancy,
see Furman 364, Marshall, J., concurring opinion.

11. Bedau 118, 12.

12. E. B. Prettyman, Jr., *Death and the Supreme Court* 308 (1961).

13. Bedau 109.

14. McGautha 242. This is but another of what Sidney Hook terms
Douglas' "slap-dash characterizations." He instances, "We must realize
that today's Establishment is the new George III," and comments on "the
preposterous comparison between our democratic political system and the
brutal tyranny of George III. Actually the only branch of the American
government whose powers in certain respects are comparable to the despotism of the British crown is the judicial despotism." Sidney Hook, *Philosophy and Public Policy* 31, 34, 35 (1980). See also infra Chapter 4, note 48.

15. He recounts that when he came on the bench, Chief Justice Hughes
"made a statement to me which at the time was shattering but which over
the years turned out to be true: 'Justice Douglas, you must remember one
thing. At the constitutional level . . . ninety percent of any decision is
emotional. The rational part of us supplies the reasons for supporting our
predilections' . . . I knew that judges had predilections . . . But I had never

Why, one wonders, should millions of Americans prefer his "gut reactions" to their own attachment to death penalties.

When the Court, faced by an immediate "backlash against judicially imposed abolition,"[16] strayed from the abolitionist path in *Gregg v. Georgia*,[17] though undertaking to supervise the sentencing process, Bedau lamented that the Justices "have put aside their personal scruples against the death penalty in the name of federalism, judicial restraint, legislative deference,"[18] an astonishingly topsy-turvy view of the judicial role. "Federalism," basic to our constitutional structure,[19] ought to yield to the "personal

---

been willing to admit to myself that the 'gut' reaction of a judge at the level of constitutional adjudications dealing with the vagaries of due process . . . was the main ingredient of his decision. The admission of it destroyed in my mind some of the reverence for immutable principles." W. O. Douglas, *The Court Years, 1939–1975* 8 (1981). Earlier in the century such after-the-fact rationalizations were characterized as "wishful thinking." Max Isenbergh justly comments that this passage "accounts for, if it does not explain, the intellectual nihilism of his worst opinions." Max Isenbergh, "Thoughts on William O. Douglas' *The Court Years:* A Confession and Avoidance," 30 Amer. U. L. Rev. 415, 422 (1981). Compare Douglas' statement in Zorach v. Clauson, 343 U.S. 306, 314 (1952): "Our individual preferences, however, are not the constitutional standard." Compare also Hughes's explanation with his statement quoted infra, text accompanying note 29.

Douglas erroneously attributed the "vagaries" of the Justices to due process. He knew better, see infra Chapter 4, note 46. Alexander Bickel, discussing the Court's treatment of "obscenity," adverted to "The vagaries of the subjective individual judgments that the Justices were pressing into service as the law of the Constitution." Bickel 51.

16. Bedau 111.

17. Gregg v. Georgia, 428 U.S. 153 (1976).

18. Bedau 119. Bedau also stated: "Hidden beneath the *veneer* of constitutional argument is that the Court has proved itself arbitrary and discriminatory in its defense of the death penalty." Bedau 118. The "veneer of constitutional argument" is an unacceptable substitute for *Bedau*'s predilections!

19. Reflecting the views of Justice Frankfurter, Louis Henkin wrote, "federalism matters . . . because the history of this country has proved its

scruples" of the Justices! Nevertheless, the ongoing abolitionist campaign, as past performance indicates, is not to be taken lightly. A phalanx of counsel for the NAACP and the Civil Liberties Union, who for years have served as architects of the new order and created a "death-row logjam," appear in selected death penalty cases. By one stratagem or another they have succeeded in keeping convicted murderers, guilty beyond a doubt and under State law subject to the death penalty, alive for ten years.[20] In Bedau's words, they regard *Gregg,* for example, as opening up "a virgin field of argument . . . for defense lawyers to explore in future cases . . . new possibilities that with imaginative and resourceful litigation may avoid or nullify many death penalties."[21]

The abolitionist arguments, picked up by the Court, I propose to show, are spun out of thin air; they are evangelistic and hortatory, substituting ringing condemnation of an "attitude of vengeance"[22] for constitutional analysis. What passes for analysis seeks to pour into the terms "cruel and unusual punishments" what the abolitionist would make them mean today for the defeat of capital punishment.[23] It is largely woven from disputed empiri-

---

validity as a principle of progressive government." It remains "important to render unto the states the respect and responsibility that can and ought to remain theirs." In Wallace Mendelson, ed., *Felix Frankfurter: The Judge* 70, 71 (1964).

20. Bedau 83–84. Bedau hazarded the prediction, "we will not see another execution in this nation in this century." Id. 90. The "death row population has reached an all-time high of more than 780 convicted murderers. Resourceful defense lawyers, through protracted appeals, have so far prevented the execution of all but four of those condemned since the 1972 decision." *New York Times,* June 14, 1981, p. 28. Justice Rehnquist charged that the Court has "made it virtually impossible for states to enforce with reasonable promptness their constitutionally valid capital punishment statutes," that "the existence of the death penalty in this country is virtually an illusion." Coleman v. Balkcom, *New York Times,* April 28, 1981, p. D23, dissenting from a denial of certiorari.

21. Bedau 116.

22. Id. 76.

23. Justice Blackmun concluded: "Although personally I may rejoice at the Court's result, I find it difficult to accept or justify as a matter of his-

cal considerations plus stray utterances from a few inapposite cases that themselves are open to question. The counterconstitutional arguments have not in my judgment been adequately explored; and that exploration needs to be placed in the larger setting of what Louis Lusky admiringly describes as the Court's "assertion of the power to revise the Constitution, bypassing the cumbersome procedure prescribed by Article V."[24] As if the Court is absolved of compliance with the Constitution because it is "cumbersome!" By that logic, a burglar may defend a break-in through a window because the door was barred. Of course there must be room

---

tory, of law, or of constitutional pronouncement . . . It has sought and achieved an end." Furman 414. Bedau states, however, that if our interest in the " 'original intent of the framers' . . . is to be more than an exercise in historical scholarship," it "must take its dominant cues from the constitutional (structural, fundamental) needs of our society and our ideals and aspirations as they are understood today." Bedau 14. This is double-talk for a discard of the "original intent of the framers" in favor of "our aspirations" of "today." But, he wrote in 1976, "the public pulse, as measured by all the opinions of the last few years, indicates that the American people still want the death penalty, and that all the evidence and arguments against it . . . have not significantly changed this attitude." Bedau 102. "According to a Gallup poll published in March [1981], two-thirds of all Americans, the highest percentage in 28 years, favor the death penalty for murder." *New York Times,* June 14, 1981, p. 28. More significantly, the majority of the States speedily repudiated Furman by reenacting death penalties in what they thought would be acceptable terms. See infra Chapter 6, text accompanying notes 60–61. Bedau wrote in 1968 that death penalties "are not unconstitutional under the Eighth Amendment because however cruel and unusual they may now be, they are *not more* 'cruel' and *not more* 'unusual' than were those that prevailed in England and the colonies two or three hundred years ago. An unbroken line of interpreters has held that it was the original understanding and intent of the framers of the Eighth Amendment . . . to proscribe as 'cruel and unusual' only such modes of execution as compound the simple infliction of death with added cruelties or indignities . . . Similarly, even if the death penalty was imposed by statute for a trifling offense, it is doubtful that it would be 'cruel and unusual' according to the 'original understanding.' " Bedau 35, italics in the original. For proof of these historical conclusions, see infra Chapter 3.

24. Louis Lusky, Book Review, 6 Hastings Con. L. Q. 403, 406 (1979).

for change, but the "real issue," as Willard Hurst perceived in 1954, is "who is to make the policy choices in the twentieth century: judges or the combination of legislature and electorate that makes constitutional amendments"?[25] The veritable "stampede of state reenactments of the death penalty" on the heels of *Furman*[26] evidences with unmistakable clarity that the issue is nothing less than the right of the people to govern themselves.[27]

The Court's revision of the "cruel and unusual punishments" clause is but one more arrogation of power under the aegis of the Fourteenth Amendment, but another chapter in the tale of judicial make-believe. Back in 1937, in the midst of Franklin Roosevelt's Court-Packing Plan, Professor Felix Frankfurter wrote to him, "People have been taught to believe that when the Supreme Court speaks it is not they who speak but the Constitution,whereas, of course, in so many vital cases, it is *they* who speak and *not* the Constitution. And I verily believe that that is what the country needs most to understand."[28] It is a lesson the people have yet to learn. Thirty years later a sober scholar, Paul Kauper, wrote respecting the "stuffy and bland cliche that what the Court is doing is 'required' by the Constitution. Such statements, however, cannot obscure or conceal that these texts mean just what the Court makes them mean and that Charles Evans Hughes went

25. Willard Hurst, "Discussion," in Edmond Cahn, ed., *Supreme Court and Supreme Law* 75 (1954).

26. J. H. Ely, *Democracy and Distrust* 65 (1980); Bedau 93.

27. Justice Powell considered that "the sweeping action undertaken today reflects a basic lack of faith and confidence in the democratic process . . . impatience with the slowness, and even the unresponsiveness, of legislators is no justification for judicial intrusion upon their historic powers." Furman 465. See infra Chapter 5.

28. Max Freedman, ed., *Roosevelt and Frankfurter: Their Correspondence, 1928–1945* 383 (1967), italics in the original. Shortly before Solicitor General Robert H. Jackson became a Justice, he wrote, "This political role [acting as a "continuing constitutional convention"] of the Court has been obscure to laymen—even to most lawyers." R. H. Jackson, *The Struggle for Judicial Supremacy* xi (1941).

to the heart of the matter when he said that . . . the Constitution is what the judges say it is."[29]

It is the purpose of this study to show that there is a wide gap between what the Justices say the "cruel and unusual punishments" clause "requires" and the limited purpose the Framers meant it to serve. Control of death penalties and of the sentencing process, it may confidently be asserted, was left by the Constitution to the States. Once the people realize that they are wrongfully being deprived of the right to decide for themselves whether or not to enact death penalties, they will not be at a loss for corrective measures.

29. Paul G. Kauper, "The Supreme Court: Hybrid Organ of State," 21 S.W.L. Rev. 573, 579 (1967). My own elaborate exposition of this view, Raoul Berger, *Government by Judiciary: The Transformation of the Fourteenth Amendment* (1977), hereinafter cited as Berger *G/J*, touched off a controversy with academicians who sought to defend the Court's *results,* never mind the means. Some of the polemics are listed in Michael Perry, "Interpretivism, Freedom of Expression and Equal Protection," 42 Ohio St. L. J. 261, 285 n. 100 (1981).

Contrast with Judge Irving R. Kaufman's naive recapitulation of "stuffy and bland cliches" as if they were Holy Writ ("Congress v. the Court," *New York Times Magazine,* Sept. 20, 1981, p. 44) Michael Perry's conclusion, after evaluating the ongoing debate: "There is no plausible textual or historical justification for constitutional policymaking by the judiciary—no way to avoid the conclusion that noninterpretive review, whether of state or federal action, cannot be justified by reference either to the text or to the intention of the Framers of the Constitution." Perry, supra at p. 275. See also L. A. Alexander, "Modern Equal Protection Theories: A Metatheoretical Taxonomy and Critiques," 42 Ohio St. L. J. 3, 4 (1981). For activist acknowledgment, see infra Chapter 9.

2

Incorporation of the Bill of Rights: En Bloc or Selective

T HE threshold question, before inquiring into the meaning of the Eighth Amendment's "cruel and unusual punishments" clause, is by what warrant is the Bill of Rights made applicable to the States? For 135 years, Justices Harlan and Stewart reminded the Court, every Member had agreed that the Founders exempted the States from the Bill of Rights.[1] This, as Louis Henkin observed, was "the consistent, often reaffirmed, and almost unanimous jurisprudence of the Court."[2] The latest decision to the contrary is not like a pancake all the better for being hot off the griddle.[3] For the Founders, precedents carried great weight.

1. Duncan v. Louisiana, 391 U.S. 145, 173 (1968).
2. Louis Henkin, " 'Selective Incorporation' in the Fourteenth Amendment," 73 Yale L. J. 74, 76 (1963).
3. Justice Henry Baldwin observed early on, "There is no more certainty that a last opinion is more correct than the first." Livingston's Executrix v.

Without the common law, that is, the precedents, Chancellor Kent declared, "the courts would be left to a dangerous discretion to roam at large in the trackless field of their own imaginations,"[4] as has been abundantly illustrated in our times. Hamilton also stressed that "to avoid arbitrary discretion in the courts, it is indispensable that they should be bound down by strict rules and precedents, which serve to define and point out their duty in every particular case that comes before them."[5]

These admonitions are even more weighty when the early decisions are closer in time to the Framers, for it is a canon of interpretation that contemporaneous constructions carry great weight.[6] Instead, Professor Kurland observed, "The list of opin-

---

Story, 36 U.S. (11 Pet.) 351, 400 (1837), dissenting opinion. With thinly veiled irony Justice Powell questioned in Furman 431, whether "the ultimate wisdom as to the appropriateness of capital punishment . . . has somehow been revealed," the assumption "contrary to a century of precedent, that we now know the answer for all time to come." Justice Frankfurter, in a similar case, refused "to say that everybody on the Court has been wrong for 150 years and that which has been deemed part of the bone and sinew of the law should now be extirpated." Green v. United States, 356 U.S. 165, 193 (1958), concurring opinion.

4. 1 James Kent, *Commentaries on American Law* 373 (9th ed., 1858).

5. *The Federalist,* No. 78 at 504, 510 (Mod. Lib. ed., 1937), hereinafter cited as Federalist. Current contempt for "rules and precedents" overlooks Jean Monnet's sage advocacy of "rules of action" for the Common Market—they "substitute an enduring collective memory for fleeting and fragmented . . . experience" (Jean Monnet, *Memoirs* (457 [1977]), of individual judges often distorted by "gut reactions."

6. In 1454 Chief Justice Prisot explained, "the judges who gave these decisions in ancient times were nearer to the making of the statute than we now are, and had more acquaintance with it," Windham v. Felbridge, Y.B. 33 Hen. 4, f. 38, 41 pl. 17, quoted in Sir C. K. Allen, *Law in the Making* 193 (6th ed., 1958). Justice William Johnson referred in 1827 to the presumption that the contemporaries of the Constitution have claims to our deference "because they had the best opportunity of informing themselves of the understanding of the framers of the constitution, and of the sense

ions destroyed by the Warren Court reads like a table of contents from an old constitutional casebook"; the Burger Court, too, "has left its precedents in shambles."[7] In any event, the authority of a decision is a function of its reasoning, and it is always open to questioning on first principles.[8] Indeed, the 1780 Massachusetts Constitution, paralleled by four other early State constitutions, advised that "A frequent recurrence to the fundamental principles of the constitution . . . [is] absolutely necessary to preserve the advantages of liberty and to maintain a free government . . . The people have a right to require of [their representatives] an exact and constant observance of them."[9] Such provisions evidence what Willard Hurst considers to be "a very basic principle of our constitutionalism . . . a distrust of official power."[10]

We start with the terms of the First Amendment because they flash the interpretive clue: "*Congress* [not a State] shall make no law . . . abridging the freedom of speech." For the Bill of Rights

---

put upon it by the people when it was adopted by them." Ogden v. Saunders, 25 U.S. (12 Wheat.) 212, 290. See also Stuart v. Laird, 5 U.S. (1 Cranch) 299, 309 (1803).

7. Philip Kurland, *Politics, the Constitution and the Warren Court* 90 (1970); Leonard Levy, *Against the Law* 260 (1974).

8. Chief Justice Burger "categorically" rejected the "thesis that what the Court said lately controls over the Constitution," Coleman v. Alabama, 399 U.S. 1, 22–23 (1970). Justice Douglas wrote: a judge "remembers above all else that it is the constitution which he swore to support and defend, not the gloss which his predecessors may have put upon it." W. O. Douglas, "Stare Decisis," 49 Colum. L. Rev. 735, 736 (1949). Justice Frankfurter considered that "the ultimate touchstone of constitutionality is the Constitution itself and not what we have said about it." Graves v. N.Y. ex rel. O'Keefe, 306 U.S. 466, 491–492 (1939), concurring opinion.

9. Article XVIII, 1 Ben P. Poore, *Federal and State Constitutions, Colonial Charters* 959 (1877), hereinafter cited as Poore. New Hampshire (1784), Article 38, 2 Poore 1283; North Carolina (1776), Article XXI, 2 Poore 1410; Pennsylvania (1776), Article XIV, 2 Poore 1542; Vermont (1777), Article XVI, 2 Poore 1860.

10. "Discussion," in Edmond Cahn, ed., *Supreme Court and Supreme Law* 75 (1954).

was "dictated by the jealousy of the States as further limitations upon the power of the Federal Government."[11] In 1833 Chief Justice Marshall, who had been a delegate to the Virginia Ratification Convention, explained in *Barron v. Baltimore* that "Had Congress engaged in the extraordinary occupation of improving the constitutions of the several States by affording the people additional protection from the exercise of power by their own governments in matters which concerned themselves alone, they would have declared this purpose in plain and intelligible language."[12] Marshall's conclusion is confirmed in the debates of the First Congress, draftsmen of the Bill of Rights. In proposing the First Amendment, Madison urged that it be extended to the States because "the State governments are as liable to attack these invaluable privileges as the General Government is, and therefore ought to be cautiously guarded against."[13] But the view that prevailed was that of Thomas Tucker: "It will be much better, I apprehend, to leave the State Governments to themselves,"[14] and Madison was voted down by the House. Egbert Benson explained that all

11. Davidson v. New Orleans, 96 U.S. 97, 101 (1877). The Court explained: "so far from the States which insisted upon these amendments contemplating any restraints or limitations by them on their own powers, the very cause which gave rise to them was a strong jealousy on their part of the power which they had granted in the Constitution." Holmes v. Jennison, 39 U.S. (14 Pet.) 540, 587 (1840). Jefferson wrote: "I hope that a Declaration of Rights will be drawn up to protect the people against the Federal government, as they are already protected in most cases against the State governments." H. D. Hazeltine, "The Influence of Magna Carta on American Constitutional Development," in H. E. Malden, ed., *Magna Carta, Commemoration Essays* 180, 216 n. 1 (1917). Patrick Henry stated in the Virginia Ratification Convention, "you have a bill of rights to defend you against the state government ... and yet you have none against the Congress." 3 Jonathan Elliot, *Debates in the Several State Conventions on the Adoption of the Federal Constitution* 446 (2d ed., 1836), hereinafter cited as Elliot.

12. 32 U.S. (7 Pet.) 243, 250 (1833).

13. 1 *Annals of Congress* 441 (Gales & Seaton, 1834, print bearing running head "History of Congress") hereinafter cited as *Ann. Cong.*

14. Id. 755.

the Committee of Eleven, to whom the Amendments had been referred, "meant to provide against was their being infringed by the [federal] Government."[15] Such was the understanding of Jefferson. In a letter to Abigail Adams, September 11, 1804, he wrote that

> The power . . . is fully possessed by the several state legislatures. It was reserved to them, and was denied to the general government. . . . While we deny that Congress have a right to controul the freedom of the press, we have ever asserted the right of the states, and their exclusive right to do so.[16]

So too, "Among the proposed amendments adopted by the House of Representatives in 1789 and submitted to the Senate was Article Fourteen: 'No State shall infringe the right of trial by jury in criminal cases . . .' The Senate deleted this article in adopting the amendments which became the Bill of Rights."[17] After quoting this history, the Supreme Court, per Justice Byron White, commented, "This relatively clear indication that the framers of the Sixth Amendment did not intend its jury trial requirement to bind the States is, of course, of little relevance in interpreting the Due Process Clause of the Fourteenth Amendment, adopted specifically to place limitations upon the States."[18]

15. Id. 732.

16. Dennis v. United States, 341 U.S. 494, 522 n. (1951), Frankfurter, J., concurring opinion. Dissenting in Beauharnais v. Illinois, 343 U.S. 250, 296 (1952), Justice Jackson said, "as the opinion of this Court now points out, the Jeffersonians' objection to the federal sedition prosecutions was largely fear of federal usurpation of state powers over the subject." Leonard Levy explains: "the prohibition on Congress was motivated far less by a desire to give immunity to political expression than by a solicitude for states' rights and the federal principle. The primary purpose of the First Amendment was to reserve to the states an exclusive authority, as far as legislation was concerned, in the field of speech and press." Levy, "Liberty of the Press from Zenger to Jefferson," in Leonard W. Levy, *Judgments: Essays in American Constitutional History* 115, 136 (1972).

17. Quoted in Duncan v. Louisiana, 391 U.S. 145, 153 n. 20 (1968).

18. Id.

THE EFFECT OF THE FOURTEENTH AMENDMENT

Was the Fourteenth Amendment designed to place State criminal trials under federal control? The Justices have relied on two
theories for the answer. Justice Black's theory, based on some remarks by John A. Bingham and Senator Jacob M. Howard in the
1866 debates, is that the Bill of Rights was incorporated in the
Fourteenth Amendment in toto.[19] He acknowledged, however,
that "this view, although often urged in dissents, has never been
accepted by a majority of this Court."[20] It was thoroughly discredited by Charles Fairman in a careful study,[21] of which Justice
Harlan justly said, "The overwhelming historical evidence mar-
shalled by Professor Fairman demonstrated, to me conclusively,
that the Congress and state legislators who wrote, debated and
ratified the Fourteenth Amendment did not think they were 'in-
corporating' the Bill of Rights."[22] My own study of the 1866 debates confirmed Fairman's findings;[23] even activists now concur
that the Framers did not intend such incorporation.[24]

The other theory, *"selective incorporation,"* contemplates piece-

19. Adamson v. California, 332 U.S. 46, 68 (1947).

20. Betts v. Brady, 316 U.S. 455, 474 (1942). "From the beginning,"
Professor Henkin wrote, "the Court has rejected the claim that the four-
teenth amendment subjected the states to all the limitations in the Bill of
Rights." Henkin, supra note 2 at 74–75. Among the landmark cases are
Hurtado v. California, 110 U.S. 516 (1884); Twining v. New Jersey, 211
U.S. 78 (1908); Palko v. Connecticut, 302 U.S. 319 (1937); Adamson v.
California, 332 U.S. 46 (1947).

21. Charles Fairman, "Does the Fourteenth Amendment Incorporate
the Bill of Rights?" 2 Stan. L. Rev. 5 (1949).

22. Duncan v. Louisiana, 391 U.S. 145, 174 (1968).

23. Raoul Berger *G/J* 134–156; Raoul Berger, "Incorporation of the Bill
of Rights in the Fourteenth Amendment: A Nine-Lived Cat," 42 Ohio St.
L. J. 435 (1981). In McGrain v. Daugherty, 273 U.S. 135, 161 (1927), the
Court looked to the practice of Parliament to hold that the investigatory
power was an attribute of the power to legislate.

24. For citations see Michael Perry, "Interpretivism, Freedom of Expression and Equal Protection," 42 Ohio St. L. J. 261, 286 n. 105 (1981),
hereinafter cited as Perry.

meal incorporation by the Court, a course to which Justice Black vehemently objected, although in the end, as he himself noted, "the selective incorporation process" has "already worked to make most of the Bill of Rights' protections applicable to the States."[25] It represented, in the words of Justice White, "a new approach,"[26] departing from the Court's long course and not purporting to rest on historical warrant. Some articles of the Bill of Rights, Justice Cardozo had explained, were "brought within the Fourteenth Amendment by a process of absorption," a process that "had its source in the belief [whose?] that neither liberty nor justice would exist if they were sacrificed." The "specific pledges of particular amendments *have been found* to be implicit in the concept of *ordered liberty,* and thus, through the Fourteenth Amendment, became valid as against the States."[27] Not the faintest trace of "ordered liberty" is to be "found" in the history of the Fourteenth; the "absorption" manifestly is a judicial construct. In what remains the most searching study of "selective incorporation," Louis Henkin wrote, "Selective incorporation finds no support in the language of the amendment, or in the history of its adoption," and it is truly "more difficult to justify than Justice Black's position that the Bill of Rights was wholly incorporated."[28] Henkin observes, "It is hardly possible to see" in the due process clause "some purpose to select some specifics of the Bill of Rights" and not the whole."[29] "Ordered liberty," he justly

25. Duncan v. Louisiana, 391 U.S. 145, 171 (1968).
26. Id. 149, n. 14.
27. Palko v. Connecticut, 302 U.S. 319, 325–326 (1938). Justice Byron White regards the concept of "ordered liberty" as merely a means whereby a majority of the Court can impose "its own philosophy and predilections upon State legislatures or Congress." Robinson v. California, 370 U.S. 660, 689 (1962), dissenting opinion.
28. Henkin, supra note 2 at 77: "There is some evidence that some persons associated with the adoption of the amendment contemplated that it might apply to the states. There is no evidence, and it is difficult to conceive, that anyone thought or intended that the amendment should impose on the states a selective incorporation."
29. Id. at 78.

states, is an "uncertain, debateable, changeable touchstone,"[30] and therefore lends itself to unlimited judicial manipulation. Of Cardozo's touchstone, "the conscience of mankind,"[31] Henkin remarks, "There is no relation—historical, linguistic or logical—between that standard and the specific provisions, or any specific provision of the Bill of Rights."[32] It reduces to how "the Court reads that conscience,"[33] a most unreliable guide as we shall see in the very frame of death penalties. Its unreliability is further illustrated by Cardozo himself: "The right to trial by jury ... [is] not of the very essence of a scheme of ordered liberty"[34]—this about an institution held "sacred" by the Founders, to be kept forever "inviolate"[35] and, in contrast to "selective incorporation," twice specifically provided for in the Constitution.[36] Thirty years later a different set of Justices held that "trial by jury in criminal cases is fundamental to the American scheme of justice."[37]

In fine, as Judge Henry Friendly wrote, "it appears undisputed that the selective incorporation theory" has no "historical support

30. Id. at 79.
31. Palko v. Connecticut, 302 U.S. 319, 325 (1938).
32. Henkin, supra note 2 at 78.
33. Id. at 75; see also Ely, infra Chapter 6, text accompanying note 46. Robert Bork pointed out that when the Court "chooses fundamental values," it "makes rather than implements value choices," and that "cannot be squared with the suppositions of a democratic society." R. J. Bork, "Neutral Principles and Some First Amendment Problems," 47 Ind. L. J. 1, 10–11 (1971). In 1947 Justice Frankfurter, alluding to the controversy "as to the historic meaning of 'cruel and unusual punishments,' " said that a State does not deny due process to a person "when it treats him in a mode about which opinion is fairly divided." Louisiana ex rel. Francis v. Resweber, 329 U.S. 459, 470, concurring opinion. Later the Court held that where there was "wide disagreement among those who have studied" legal insanity, "it is clear that adoption of the irresistible impulse test is not 'implicit in the concept of ordered liberty.' " Leland v. Oregon, 343 U.S. 790, 801 (1952).
34. Palko v. Connecticut, 302 U.S. 319, 325 (1938).
35. Infra Chapter 6, text accompanying notes 99–104.
36. Article III, §2(3); Sixth Amendment.
37. Duncan v. Louisiana, 391 U.S. 145, 149 (1968).

... [T]he present Justices feel that if their predecessors could arrange for the absorption of some such provisions in the due process clause, they ought to possess similar absorptive capacity toward other provisions equally important in their eyes,"[38] an excellent illustration of Charles Evans Hughes's dictum: "The Constitution is what the Court says it is."[39] Justice Black, however, found it "impossible ... to believe that such unconfined power is given to judges in our constitution that is a written one in order to limit governmental power."[40]

DUE PROCESS

Because "selective incorporation" purportedly derives from the due process clause, and because the clause supremely illustrates the Court's manipulation of a clear text for its own purposes, a glance at its history will aid in understanding the technique applied by the Court to the "cruel and unusual punishments" clause. The due process clause has been so befogged by the Court as to confuse even as clear-eyed a judge as Justice Harlan. He approached "selective incorporation" by way of the words "liberty" and "due process of law," but considered it is "difficult" to define the "very broad and general" words due process. "Where," he asked, "does the Court properly look to find the specific rules that define and give content to the terms?"[41] Given that they are borrowed from the common law and had a long-settled meaning, the Court time and again has in such case looked to English and colonial law.[42]

---

38. H. J. Friendly, "The Bill of Rights as a Code of Criminal Procedure," 53 Calif. L. Rev. 929, 934, 935 (1965).

39. *Addresses of Charles Evans Hughes* 185 (2d ed., 1916); see also supra Chapter 1, note 29.

40. Duncan v. Louisiana, 391 U.S. 145, 168 (1968), concurring opinion; see also Chief Justice Marshall, infra Chapter 5, text accompanying note 10.

41. Duncan v. Louisiana, id. at 174–176.

42. For details see infra Chapter 4.

Summarizing 400 years of that law, Hamilton stated on the eve of the Convention that

> The words "due process" have a *precise technical* import, and are *only* applicable to the process and proceedings of courts of justice; *they can never be referred to an act of the legislature.*[43]

Consequently, the Court may not in the name of due process invalidate a *statute,* for example, an enactment of death penalties. For as the Court, per Justice Miller, declared in *Davidson v. New Orleans,* the Barons did not by Magna Carta's "law of the land" intend to protect themselves against the enactment of laws by the Parliament.[44] They sought protection against arbitrary deprivations by King John without the shelter of judicial proceedings under standing law.[45] Charles P. Curtis, whose *Lions Under the Throne* is a paean to the Justices, said that the meaning of "due process of law" in the Fifth Amendment "was as fixed and definite as the common law could make a phrase . . . It meant a procedural process."[46]

---

43. 4 *The Papers of Alexander Hamilton,* ed. Syrett and Cooke 35 (1962). Raoul Berger, " 'Law of the Land' Reconsidered," 74 Nw. U. L. Rev. 311 (1979). Judge William Lawrence, a member of the 39th Congress and the scholarly adviser to the Managers of the House in the impeachment of Andrew Johnson, quoted the Hamilton definition in 1871, *Congressional Globe,* 41st Cong., 3d Sess., 1245 (1871).

44. Davidson v. New Orleans, 96 U.S. 97, 102 (1877).

45. Raoul Berger, " 'Law of the Land' Reconsidered," 74 Nw. U. L. Rev. 1, 3–4 (1979), and id. text accompanying n. 45.

46. C. P. Curtis, "Review and Majority Rule," in Edmond Cahn, ed., *Supreme Court and Supreme Rule* 170, 177 (1954).

Sanford Kadish dismisses the historical data on the ground that "due process" is "drained of any independent *integrity* as a governing normative principle. It becomes merely a vehicle for delaying the implementation of a change in procedural law until it is accepted by the conscience of a sufficient number of relevant segments of the community." Quoted in Arthur Goldberg and Alan Dershowitz, "Declaring the Death Penalty Unconstitutional," 83 Harv. L. Rev. 1773, 1779 (1970). For Kadish the "conscience of the community" which weighed so heavily with Cardozo must yield to the "integrity" of the words. But respect for that "integrity" requires that the word be given the meaning it had for those who used it. "Integrity" is

When due process was embodied in the Fourteenth Amendment it did not change color; the phrase, said the Court, "was used in the same sense and to no greater extent,"[47] as appears from the legislative history. The framers were anxious to secure judicial protection for the freeman; they were concerned lest he be "denied a remedy in the courts," because theretofore he had been "denied process of law to enforce the right and avenge the wrong."[48]

---

defined as "unimpaired or uncorrupted state; original condition." *Oxford English Dictionary.* It is not merely integrity of the words "due process" but integrity of construction that is at stake. Intellectual conscience requires fairness with the facts. For this it suffices to quote an activist paladin, Paul Brest: "suppose that the Constitution required that some acts were to be performed 'bi-weekly.' At the time of the framing of the Constitution, this meant only 'once every two weeks'; but modern dictionaries, bowing to pervasive misuse, now report 'twice a week' (i.e. semi-weekly) as an acceptable definition. To construe the definition now to mean semi-weekly would certainly be a change of meaning (and an improper one at that)." Paul Brest, *Processes of Constitutional Decisionmaking: Cases and Materials* 146 n. 38 (1975). See also Berger, *G/J* 370–371. Writing to Henry Lee, June 25, 1824, Madison said, "What a metamorphosis would be produced in the code of law if all its ancient phraseology were to be taken in its modern sense!" 3 Max Farrand, *The Records of the Federal Convention of 1787* 464 (1911), hereinafter cited as Farrand. See also infra Chapter 4, text accompanying notes 33–39.

47. Hurtado v. California, 110 U.S. 516, 535 (1884). That identity again underlines the artificial nature of "selective incorporation." For "due process" is associated in the Fifth Amendment with provisions for grand jury indictments, just compensation, double jeopardy, self-incrimination—now "selectively incorporated" in the due process of the Fourteenth. When the Framers explicitly provided for indictments and just compensation cheek by jowl with due process, they obviously postulated that those provisions were not embraced by due process. After an elaborate survey of the historical materials Justice Moody concluded that the privilege against self-incrimination "was not conceived to be inherent in due process of law, but on the other hand a right separate, independent and outside of due process. Congress, in submitting the amendments to the several States, treated the two rights as exclusive of each other." Twining v. New Jersey, 211 U.S. 78, 110 (1908). One hundred years ago the Court held that if they were contained within due process, they were superfluous. Hurtado v. California, 110 U.S. 516, 534 (1884).

48. *Globe* 1263, 1265; see Berger *G/J* 201–206.

"Let him be heard in court," pleaded Senator Charles Sumner.[49] John Bingham, draftsman of the clause, said that its meaning had been settled "long ago" by the courts,[50] and that meaning, but for what John Hart Ely justly labels a couple of aberrational cases,[51] was universally procedural. James Garfield, a framer who had re-studied the debates of the 39th Congress in 1871, considered that the Amendment's due process clause secured "an impartial trial according to the law of the land,"[52] meaning State law. Nowhere in the Reconstruction debates from 1865 through 1875 did I encounter a wider definition; there is not the slightest intimation that the framers meant to confer judicial power to displace policy-making by State legislatures. That long-settled meaning entitles us to require, in the words of Chief Justice Marshall that "to establish a principle never before recognized [it] should be expressed in plain and explicit terms,"[53] all the more when the Court lays claim to powers long exercised by the States and reserved to them by the Tenth Amendment.[54]

The main concern of the Fourteenth's framers was to prevent *discrimination* against blacks with respect to certain *enumerated* rights,[55] not to empower Congress—much less the federal courts—[56] to regulate those rights. Senator Lyman Trumbull, Chairman of the Senate Judiciary Committee, explained that if a State did not discriminate, the Civil Rights Bill (which was

49. *Globe* 675.

50. Id. 1089.

51. J. H. Ely, *Democracy and Distrust* 16, 18 (1980).

52. *Congressional Globe,* 42d Cong., 1st Sess., App. 153 (1871).

53. United States v. Burr, 25 F. Cas. 55, 165 (C. C. D. Va. 1807) (No. 14,693).

54. Infra text accompanying notes 80–81; and Chapter 5, text accompanying notes 153–154.

55. See infra Chapter 5, text accompanying notes 73–82; and Appendix A, text accompanying note 13.

56. Section 5 of the Fourteenth Amendment provides, "The Congress shall have power to enforce by appropriate legislation the provisions of this article." In Ex parte Virginia, 100 U.S. 339, 345 (1879), the Court stressed that "It is not said the judicial power . . . shall extend" to such enforcement. For discussion see infra Chapter 7, text accompanying notes 57–76.

"identical" with and incorporated in the Amendment)[57] "has no operation whatever in the State."[58] Thaddeus Stevens, leader of the radicals, defended the prototype Bingham Amendment as only conferring "power to *correct such discrimination*"; the Fourteenth Amendment, he said "allows Congress to correct the unjust legislation of the States, *so far* that the law which operates on one shall operate equally upon all."[59] In short, Congress, and a fortiori the Court, was not meant to determine what rights a State must supply, but only to bar discrimination against blacks *if* certain rights were given to whites. Let that be admitted, it may be countered, does not governance of jury sentencing fall within "procedural" due process[60] and therefore entitle the court to lay down "standards?" To this there are two answers. First, the Court declared in *Owenbey v. Morgan:* "A procedure customarily employed, long before the Revolution, in . . . England, and generally accepted by the states . . . cannot be deemed inconsistent with due process of law."[61] Jury sentencing discretion was an established practice at the adoption of the Constitution.[62] Second, the con-

57. See infra Chapter 5, note 76.

58. *Globe* 600. Trumbull reiterated that it "in no manner interferes with the municipal regulations of any State which protects all alike in their rights of person and property." Id. 1761. The Bill, Samuel Shellabarger explained, does "not confer or regulate rights"; that would "be an assumption of the reserved rights of the States and the people"; its "whole effect is . . . to require that whatever of these enumerated rights and obligations are imposed by State laws shall be for all citizens alike." It secures "Equality of protection in those enumerated civil rights which the States may deem proper to confer upon any races." Id. 1293.

59. Id. 1063, 2459. For additional citations, see Raoul Berger, "Ely's 'Theory of Judicial Review,' " 42 Ohio St. L. J. 87, 105–106 n. 159 (1981).

60. For the common law powers of the jury, see infra Chapter 6, text accompanying notes 106–124.

61. 256 U.S. 94, 111 (1921). Speaking of the traditional power to exclude indigent migrants, the Supreme Court declared in New York v. Miln, 36 U.S. (11 Pet.) 102, 132 (1837), that since the power "undeniably existed at the formation of the Constitution," it was not "taken from the States" by the Commerce paragraph.

62. Infra Chapter 6, text accompanying notes 108–121.

temporaneous view of the Fourteenth Amendment by the Court was: "It is not possible to hold that a party has, without due process of law, been deprived of property when . . . he has *by the laws of the State,* a fair trial in a court of justice, according to the modes of proceeding applicable to such a case."[63] In other words, the standard is state-wide, not national.[64] All that is required, as English and colonial law attest, is that the trial conform to customary procedure under a standing law of the State.[65]

It begs the question simply to maintain, as does Justice White, that "the Due Process Clause of the Fourteenth Amendment [was] adopted specifically to place limitations upon the States."[66] What limitations? It is now widely accepted—the "one person, one vote" doctrine notwithstanding—that suffrage was excluded from the Fourteenth Amendment and left to the States, as the subsequent enactment of the Fifteenth Amendment to fill the gap alone should demonstrate. Justice Harlan reminded the Court that the reapportionment decisions were "made in the face of irrefutable and still unanswered history to the contrary."[67] Louis Lusky, an activist, refers to Harlan's "irrefutable and unrefuted

63. Davidson v. New Orleans, 96 U.S. 97, 165 (1877).

64. Speaking of the equal protection clause, Dean Phil C. Neal wrote: "the equality ordained is a statewide equality, encompassing the persons 'within its jurisdiction' and not a nationwide or external equality." Phil C. Neal, "Baker v. Carr: Politics in Search of Law," 1962 S. Ct. Rev. 252, 293. See also Daniel Polsby, "The Death of Capital Punishment?: Furman v. Georgia," 1972 S. Ct. Rev. 1, 28. "The Fourteenth Amendment does not profess to secure to all persons in the United States the benefit of the same laws and the same remedies. Great diversities in these respects may exist in two States separated by an imaginary line. On one side of the line there may be a right of trial by jury, and on the other side no such right. Each State prescribes its own mode of judicial proceedings." Missouri v. Lewis, 101 U.S. 22, 31 (1879), per Justice Bradley. See also supra, text accompanying note 54.

65. See Raoul Berger, " 'Law of the Land' Reconsidered," 74 Nw. U. L. Rev. 1, 8–9 (1979).

66. Supra, text accompanying note 18.

67. Griswold v. Connecticut, 381 U.S. 479, 501 (1965). For historical details, see Berger *G/J* 30, 52–68.

demonstration" to that effect,[68] and more and more activists concur.[69] The evidence for the exclusion of segregation is little less clear. Nathaniel Nathanson, himself an activist, wrote that Alexander Bickel "conclusively" proved that the Amendment "would not require school desegregation" and that "Berger's independent research and analysis confirms and adds weight to those conclusions."[70] To be sure, the court has held to the contrary, but its desegregation decision is confuted by the historical evidence.[71]

Nowhere has the Court pointed to evidence that the States intended in 1866 to turn control of their criminal administration over to Congress or the Court. The fact is that the framers were attached to State sovereignty. Roscoe Conkling, a member of the Joint Committee on Reconstruction of both Houses, stated: "The proposition to prohibit States from denying civil or political

68. Louis Lusky, Book Review, 6 Hastings Con. L. Q. 403, 406 (1979).

69. For citations, see Perry, supra note 24 at 285 n. 100.

70. Nathaniel Nathanson, Book Review, 56 Tex. L. Rev. 579, 581 (1978). For activist concurrence, see Dean Alfange, "On Judicial Policy-making and Constitutional Change: Another Look at the 'Original Intent' Theory of Constitutional Interpretation," 5 Hastings Con. L. Q. 603, 622 (1978); see also id. 601–607. "Could it reasonably be claimed that segregation had been outlawed by the Fourteenth when the yet more basic emblem of citizenship—the ballot—had been withheld from the Negro under that Amendment?" Richard Kluger, *Simple Justice* 635 (1976). See also Randall Bridwell, Book Review, 1978 Duke L. J. 907, 913. H. Abraham, Book Review, 6 Hastings Con. L. Q. 467 (1979). M. L. Benedict notes that the "Supreme Court shocked the nation with its decision in *Brown v. Board of Education,* the greatest judicial intrusion into policymaking since its obstruction of New Deal legislation in the early 1930s." M. L. Benedict, "To Secure These Rights: Rights, Democracy and Judicial Review in the Anglo-American Constitutional Heritage" 42 Ohio St. L. J. 69 (1981).

71. Berger *G/J* 100–101, 117–133; Berger, supra note 43 at 311, 326–329. The "legislative history of the fourteenth amendment clearly discloses that the Framers did not mean for the amendment to have any effect on segregated public schooling or on segregation generally." Perry, supra note 24 at 292. To have upended segregated schools "would have exposed the [Civil Rights] bill to active opposition in the North." 6 Charles Fairman, *History of the Constitution of the United States* 1177 (1971).

rights to any class of persons encounters a great objection on the threshold. It trenches upon the principle of existing local sovereignty." Interference with suffrage, he said, "meddles with a right reserved to the States . . . and to which they will long cling before they surrender it."[72] Numerous statements testify to this attachment. While James W. Patterson of New Hampshire was "opposed to any law discriminating against [blacks] in the security of life, liberty, person, [and] property"; "beyond this," he said, "I am not prepared to go."[73]

Where is the evidence that measures designed to safeguard blacks from certain discriminations were suddenly transformed into an instrument for control of local criminal administration[74]—and this in many Northern areas where a black presence was negligible or absent? To the contrary, Chairman James Wilson emphasized during the debates on the Civil Rights Bill, "We are not making a general criminal code for the States,"[75] a reassurance addressed to a suspicious audience. Justice Miller, who had been active in Iowa politics,[76] and whose political antennae had not atrophied in Washington, held in the *Slaughter-House Cases:*

72. *Globe* 391, 358.

73. Id. 2699.

74. There is evidence to the contrary: Giles W. Hotchkiss of New York was willing to provide that "no State shall discriminate" but refused to "authorize Congress to establish uniform laws . . . [for] the protection of life, liberty, and property." Id. 1095. For similar expressions, see Berger *G/J* 186–187. Even with respect to the narrow scope of the Civil Rights Bill, Samuel Shellabarger, a vigorous proponent, declared, that if the Bill "did in fact *assume to confer* or define or regulate these civil rights, which are named by the words contract, sue . . . then it would, it seems to me, be an assumption of the reserved rights of the States and the people." But the Bill, he emphasized, did not "confer or regulate rights"; it "require[d] that whatever of these enumerated rights and obligations are imposed by State laws shall be for and upon all citizens alike." *Globe* 1293. The framers had a jealous regard for the reservations to the States expressed in the Tenth Amendment.

75. *Globe* 1120.

76. Charles Fairman, *Mr. Justice Miller and the Supreme Court* 26–39 (1939).

"we do not see in these amendments any purpose to destroy the main features of the general system . . . our statesmen have still believed that the existence of the States with power for domestic and local government . . . was essential."[77] In 1907 the Court declared:

> It is within the power of a State to enact laws creating and defining crimes against its sovereignty . . . prescribing the character of the sentence . . . In these respects the State is supreme and its powers absolute, and without any limits other than those prescribed by the Constitution of the United States.[78]

There are numerous statements to the same effect by a diverse group of Justices,[79] who depart, however, from their own wise counsels when the spirit moves them.

77. Slaughter-House Cases, 83 U.S. (16 Wall.) 36, 82 (1872). The "commitment to traditional state-federal relations meant," wrote Alfred Kelly, an apologist for the Warren Court, that "the radical Negro reform program could be only a very limited one." Kelly, "Comment on Harold M. Hyman's Paper" in H. M. Hyman, ed., *New Frontiers of the American Reconstruction* 55 (1966).

78. Coffey v. Harlan County, 204 U.S. 659, 662 (1907). At this juncture incorporation of the bill of rights, and interpretation of "cruel and unusual punishments" to limit death penalties were in the womb of the future.

79. Justice Jackson observed: "The use of the due process clause to disable the States in protection of society from crime is quite as dangerous and delicate a use of judicial power as to use it to disable them from social or economic experimentation" (as the laissez-faire Justices had done). Ashcraft v. Tennessee, 322 U.S. 143, 174 (1944), dissenting opinion. Justices Harlan and Stewart protested against "fastening on the States federal notions of criminal justice," saying, "The States have always borne primary responsibility for operating the machinery of criminal justice within their borders, and adapting it to their peculiar circumstances." Duncan v. Louisiana, 391 U.S. 145, 173, 172 (1968). Writing for a plurality in Powell v. Texas, 392 U.S. 514, 533 (1968), Justice Thurgood Marshall, a deeply committed foe of death penalties, decried the Court's making itself "under the aegis of the Cruel and Unusual Punishments Clause, the ultimate arbiter of the standards of criminal responsibility in diverse areas of the criminal law throughout the country" (cited with approval by Chief Justice Burger in Coker v. Georgia, 433 U.S. 584, 612–613 [1977]). In Powell v.

We need to recall Madison's assurance in Federalist No. 39 that the federal "jurisdiction extends to certain enumerated objects only, and leaves to the several States a residuary and *inviolable sovereignty* over all other subjects."[80] He reiterated in Federalist No. 45 that

> The powers delegated by the proposed Constitution to the federal government are few and defined. Those which are to remain in the State governments are numerous and indefinite. The former will be exercised principally on *external objects* as war, peace, negotiation and foreign commerce ... The powers reserved to the several States will extend to all the objects which, in the ordinary course of affairs; concern the lives, liberties, and properties of the people, and the *internal order,* improvement, and prosperity of the State.[81]

Texas, Justices Black and Harlan observed that throughout "the nation remembered that it could be more tranquil and orderly if it functioned on the principle that the local communities should control their own peculiarly local affairs under their own local rules ... This nation is too large, too complex and composed of too great a diversity of people for any one of us to have the wisdom to establish the rules by which local Americans must govern their local affairs." 392 U.S. at 547. Justice Powell shared their sentiment: "This Court has emphasized the importance in a democratic society of preserving local control of local matters." City of Rome v. United States, 446 U.S. 156, notes 11, 12 (1980). Justice Stewart, joined by Justices Clark, Harlan, and White in Townsend v. Sain, 372 U.S. 293, 334 (1963), stated, "Under our Constitution the State of Illinois has the power and duty to administer its own criminal justice," dissenting opinion. Justice Frankfurter considered that "any 'uniform code of criminal procedure federally imposed' would be unfortunate." Alexander M. Bickel, *The Supreme Court and the Idea of Progress* 32 (1978), hereinafter cited as Bickel. Worse, it would be unconstitutional. Frankfurter held that the Fourteenth Amendment "is not the basis of a uniform code of criminal procedure federally imposed." Felix Frankfurter, *Law and Politics* 192–193 (1939). Such considerations were admirably epitomized in Missouri v. Lewis, quoted supra note 64.

80. Federalist at 249.

81. Id. at 303. It was stated in New York v. Miln, 36 U.S. (11 Pet.) 102, 139 (1837), per Barbour, J., that the States might legislate on any subject concerning "the welfare of the whole people of a state, or any individual

Such assurances were calculated to quiet fears lest too much State power be surrendered to the federal newcomer. It is a crowning irony that the Justices should transform the Bill of Rights into an instrument of encroachment on State control of purely local matters in the face of Madison's explanation that the "great object" of the Bill was to *"limit* and qualify the powers of Government, by *excepting* out of the grant of power those cases in which the Government ought not to act, or to act only in a particular mode."[82] That particular mode, in the case of "cruel and unusual punishments," did not contemplate interference with State control of death penalties.

---

within it; whether it respected them as man, or as citizens of the state; whether in their public or private relations; whether it related to the rights of person or of property."

82. 1 *Ann. Cong.* at 437; see also Raoul Berger, "The Ninth Amendment," 66 Cornell L. Rev. 1 (1980).

3

History of the "Cruel and Unusual Punishments" Clause

THE Eighth Amendment provides, "excessive bail shall not be required, nor excessive fines imposed, nor cruel and unusual punishments inflicted." Until the clause was lifted out of obscurity in the very recent past there was little incentive to dig into its historical roots, so that Anthony Granucci correctly wrote in 1969 that it had "never been adequately investigated.[1] His article, a pioneer effort by a young graduate,[2] widely cited by the Justices, became the foundation of the spurious doctrine that the clause, borrowed from the Bill of Rights of 1689, prohibits exces-

1. Anthony Granucci, " 'Nor Cruel and Unusual Punishments Inflicted': The Original Meaning," 57 Calif. L. Rev. 839 (1969), hereinafter cited as Granucci.
2. He obtained his law degree in 1968, id. n*. Justice Marshall cited him as "Professor Granucci." Furman 319, n. 14.

siveness in punishment.[3] Justice Thurgood Marshall also reasoned that because "the 'cruel and unusual' language of the Eighth Amendment immediately follows language that prohibits excessive bail and excessive fines, [t]he entire thrust of the Eighth Amendment is . . . against that which is excessive."[4] But cruel punishment was set off from excessive bail and fines, so that Marshall would deprive the shift from "excessive" to "cruel" of meaning. The terms mean different things—a punishment may be excessive without being cruel, and the choice of different terminology indicates a different, rather than the same, purpose.[5] In fact, the Founders were accustomed to punishments that by our standards would be regarded as "excessive," and gave no inkling of an intention to bar them.

ENGLAND

To make his case that punishment must not be excessive, Granucci begins with the Magna Carta prohibition in Article 20[6] of certain amercements: "A free man shall not be amerced for a trivial offence, except in accordance with the degree of the offence; and for a serious offence he shall be amerced according to its gravity." Amercements were compensation for injuries, not penal fines levied by a court. Prior to the Norman invasion the Anglo-Saxon laws, like those of other primitive peoples, provided for composition of the blood feud by a tariff of payments to the kinsmen of the victim, prescribed according to a man's station

3. For citations to Granucci, see Rummel v. Estelle, 445 U.S. 263, 288–289 (1980); Gregg v. Georgia, 428 U.S. 153, 169 (1976); Furman 242, 274, 318 n. 11, 319 n. 14, 376 n. 2, 419 n. 3; Goldberg and Dershowitz, supra Chapter 2, note 46 at 1785, 1789.

4. Furman 332.

5. Crawford v. Burke, 195 U.S. 176, 190 (1904): "a change in phraseology creates a presumption of a change in intent."

6. Granucci 845. He cites it as chapter 14; I follow the numbering used by William McKechnie, *Magna Carta: A Commentary on the Great Chapter of King John* (1905).

and the injured member—an eye, limb, or loss of life.[7] In time such payments were made to the Crown instead of the kinsmen, the amount being assessed by a group of the culprit's neighbors,[8] for the jury was as yet unknown.[9] Instead of being arbitrarily fixed by the Crown, the amount was settled by impartial assessors, "by the oath of honest men of the neighborhood."[10] This established custom, expressed in Chapters 20, 21, and 22 of Magna Carta, had nothing to do with the penal judgment of a court but constituted compensation for an injury. It was not, therefore, "the equivalent of the modern fine";[11] there was a "fine" of quite different provenance.[12] "The great object" of the several amercement provisions, McKechnie concluded, "was to eliminate the arbitrary element; the Crown must conform to its own customary rules."[13] Under the more familiar Chapter 39, a man could be deprived of life or liberty by judicial proceedings under standing law or custom, there being no intention by the "law of the land" phrase to curtail the lawmaking function, but rather to protect the barons against the king's arbitrariness.[14]

Granucci goes on to say:

A fourteenth century document, which purports to be a copy of the Laws of Edward the Confessor (1042–66), *extended* the policy of the amercements clause to cover physical punishments as well.

We do forbid that a person shall be condemned to death for a

7. McKechnie, id. at 334–335; see also Raoul Berger, "From Hostage to Contract," 35 Ill. L. Rev. 154, 157–158 (1940).

8. McKechnie, id. at 336.

9. Id. at 163.

10. Id. at 339.

11. Granucci 845 n. 27.

12. In contrast to the "punishment of misdeeds" aspect of amercements, "fine" was "used for voluntary offerings made to the king with the object of some concession in return"; the individual "was under no legal obligation to make any offer at all." McKechnie, supra note 6 at 344.

13. Id. 338.

14. Raoul Berger, " 'Law of the Land' Reconsidered," 74 Nw. U. L. Rev. 1, 3 (1979); supra Chapter 2, at text accompanying notes 44–45.

trifling offense. But for the correction of the multitude, extreme punishment shall be inflicted according to the nature and extent of the offense.

Thus by the year 1400, we have the expression of "the long standing principle of English law that the punishment should fit the crime. That is, the punishment should not be, by reason of its excessiveness or, severity, greatly disproportionate to the offense charged."[15]

Boyd Barrington, the authority Granucci cites for the "fourteenth century document," wrote, however, that "there seems to be no doubt at all, in the minds of historians and antiquarians that the whole of the chronicle reputed to have been written by Ingulph was a forgery of the fourteenth century."[16] That document may therefore be dismissed.

The "long standing principle" quotation was borrowed by Granucci from Richard L. Perry, who asserts:

This principle was set forth in a statute in 1553 which stated that the security of the kingdom depended more upon the love of the subject toward the king than upon the dread of laws imposing rigorous penalties and that laws made for the preservation of the commonwealth without great penalties were more often obeyed and kept than laws made with extreme punishment.[17]

Queen Mary professedly was concerned with the undue breadth of treason charges rather than with "rigorous penalties." Her statute refers to "many noble persons ... [who] have of late (for Words only) ... suffered shameful death not accustomed to Nobles";

15. Granucci 846.

16. Boyd Barrington, *The Magna Charta and Other Great Charters of England* 181 (2d ed., 1900). It is this history, although he mistakenly cites Perry, that Justice Powell relies on for his statement "By 1400 the English common law had embraced the principle not always followed in practice, that punishment should not be excessive either in severity or length." Rummel v. Estelle, 445 U.S. 263, 289 (1980).

17. The statute is 1 Mary, Stat. I, c. 1. Richard L. Perry, *Sources of Our Liberties* 236 (1978).

and it enacts that "only such [acts] as were declared and expressed to be treason" by the Treason Acts of 25 Edw. III[18] were to be adjudged treason, to be punished only as provided by that statute. In the second session, stat. I, c. VI, Mary declared *counterfeiting* to be High Treason on "such pains of death" as befits treason. These pains, Blackstone tells us, were "terrible": after hanging, the offender was to be "cut down alive," "his entrails to be taken out and burned, while he was yet alive," and the like.[19] Queen Mary's mercy, such as it was, was fleeting. Having shortly thereafter married the Catholic Philip of Spain, she procured two "ferocious new treason laws" in 1555 against treason by "words,"[20] the very thing she had condemned in 1553. Mary's pious obeisance in 1553 therefore affords scant support for a "long standing principle . . . that the punishment should fit the crime."

To complete his survey of the "common law" Granucci cites *Hodges v. Humkin, Mayor of Liskerret* (1613), wherein "the King's Bench applied chapter 14 [20] of the Magna Carta to a malicious kind of imprisonment."[21] The Mayor had imprisoned one who had made "very unseemly speeches" about him, without "any Bed to lie on, or any bread or meat to eat," thus violating Chapter 14 [20] (the amercement provision of Magna Carta), for "imprisonment ought always to be according to the quality of the offense."[22] This was not a holding by King's Bench but a quotation from one of three opinions, that of Justice Croke. Justices Haughton and Dodderidge did not invoke Chapter 20, possibly because it prohibited excessive amercements, not imprisonment. The "words spoken, was not in the presence of the mayor"[23] and therefore constituted an out-of-court contempt. Croke considered the imprisonment "malicious" because "being so long time after the offence, as in August for an offence in June before." The pun-

18. 1 Mary, 1st Sess. Stat. I c. 1 (1553).

19. 4 William Blackstone, *Commentaries on the Laws of England* 92–93 (1765–1769), hereinafter cited as Blackstone.

20. G. R. Elton, *England Under the Tudors* 219 (1960).

21. Granucci 847. The case is reported in 80 E. R. 1015 (1613).

22. Granucci 847.

23. 80 E. R. 1016.

ishment, he held, "ought to be inflicted for the offence, flagrante crimine, whilest the offence is fresh, the which was not observed here ... the imprisonment here was unjust, being so long time after the offence ... the ready way [was] to bring him into contempt." Croke added that the mayor's return to the habeas corpus petition "is not good, but altogether uncertain and insufficient."[24] Haughton also held that the return was insufficient for lack of specification and stated that the mayor could not "imprison [Hodges] forever"; Dodderidge likewise thought the imprisonment overlong.[25] In these circumstances—belated punishment of an out-of-court contempt—Croke's phrase "imprisonment ought always to be according to the quality of the offence" offers spindly underpinning for Granucci's summation: "prior to the adoption of the Bill of Rights in 1689 England had developed a common law prohibition against excessive punishment in any form."[26] At most *Hodges v. Humkin* stands for the proposition that a mayor is *not authorized* to imprison one for disrespectful words spoken out of court for an overlong term imposed months after the speech.

Certainly Parliament did not feel itself bound by Croke's pronouncement, but enacted a swelling list of capital offenses, so that by about 1800 there were more than 200 capital crimes,[27] many for trifling offenses. As late as 1813 Lord Ellenborough inveighed against repeal of the death penalty for the theft of a few shillings.[28] To be sure, any one who could read was insulated from

24. Id.
25. Id.
26. Granucci 847.
27. Furman 334.
28. Id. 246 n. 9. The bill was "finally enacted in 1827," id. Against this background one marvels that Justices Stewart, Powell, and Stevens should root the doctrine of "excessive" punishment in the "dignity of man," meaning that "the punishment must not be grossly out of proportion to the severity of the crime." Gregg v. Georgia, 428 U.S. 153, 173 (1976). What could be more grossly disproportionate than death for the theft of a few shillings?

Justice Brennan censoriously views Archdeacon William Paley's justification in 1785 of "England's 'Bloody Code' of more than 250 capital

such punishment by "benefit of clergy";[29] and in time death sentences were commuted to transportation to and imprisonment in the colonies.[30] But commutation of a statutory sentence does not nullify the statute. The crowded catalog of statutes decreeing death for trivial offenses explodes the so-called common law "doctrine" that punishment must fit the crime. Granucci himself tells us that a mid-eighteenth-century commentator, Thomas Wood, whose *Institutes of the Laws of England* (1763) was "available in the colonies," gives "a dreary catalogue of the types of punishment in use in the middle of the eighteenth century. Included are all the barbarities which George Mason [of Virginia] seemed to think were forbidden by the Bill of Rights of 1689. Wood's commentary *does not acknowledge any limits on punishment,* either statutory or at common law."[31]

Granucci persuasively argues that the phraseology of the 1689 Bill of Rights was not a response to Lord Justice Jeffreys' Bloody Assize, as is commonly believed,[32] and tellingly points out that "none of the 'cruel' methods of punishment which were employed in the 'Bloody Assize' ceased to be used after the passage of the Bill of Rights."[33] Instead, he looks for "evidence of what the framers of the Declaration of Rights intended to prohibit . . . to

crimes," McGautha 281, overlooking the significance of a high churchman's endorsement of such punishments at the adoption of the Constitution. He would substitute his 1971 view for that entertained by the people in 1789, the latter alone being the index of common law terms. The history is irreconcilable with Brennan's opinion that "a severe punishment may not be excessive. A punishment is excessive under this principle if it is unnecessary." Furman 279.

29. 1 J. F. Stephen, *History of the Criminal Law of England* 458 et seq. (1883).

30. Id. 471.

31. Granucci 860, 862. Dissenting in Weems v. United States, 217 U.S. 349, 393 (1910), Justice Edward White (Justice Holmes joined) declared that "in England it was nowhere deemed that any theory of proportional punishment was suggested by the bill of rights."

32. Granucci 853–856.

33. Id. 855–856.

Titus Oates and the infamous 'Popish Plot' of 1678–1679."[34] The
Oates trial took place in May 1685;[35] the Declaration of Rights
was adopted in February 1689; and the relevant debate on the
Oates trial occurred in June 1689.[36] Its weight as a contemporaneous construction can be evaluated only after consideration of
some additional details.

In the interest of chronology I begin with the legislative history of the Bill of Rights, to which Granucci commendably
turned for the derivation of "cruel and unusual." On February 2,
1689, a spokesman for the drafting committee of the House of
Commons reported,

> The requiring excessive bail of persons committed in criminal
> cases, and imposing excessive fines, and *illegal* punishments, to
> be prevented.

The Commons agreed, sent it to the Lords, whence the final version emerged and was agreed to by the Commons on February 12,
1689, preceded by a significant clause:

> whereas ... excessive fines have been imposed; and *illegal* and
> cruel punishments inflicted,

therefore it is declared

> That excessive bail ought not to be required, nor excessive fines
> imposed; nor cruel and unusual punishments inflicted.[37]

Presumably Granucci found no explanation of the shift from "illegal" to "cruel and unusual" and concluded that "The final
phraseology, especially the use of the word 'unusual,' must be

34. Id. 856.
35. 10 *Howell's State Trials* 1322 (Cobbett's Collection, 1809–1826).
36. 9 Anchitell Gray, *Debates of the House of Commons, 1667–1674* 287 et
seq. (1763).
37. Granucci 854–855.

laid simply to chance and sloppy draftsmanship."[38] If there was any reference to the Oates trial in this legislative history, it was not cited by Granucci.

Oates was a minister of the Church of England, whose perjured testimony about a Catholic plot to assassinate the King had led to the execution of fifteen Catholics for treason. He was sentenced to (1) a fine of 2,000 marks; (2) life imprisonment; (3) whipping; (4) pillorying four times a year; and (5) to be defrocked. Granucci relates that Oates's petition to both Houses of Parliament to be released from the judgment was rejected by the House of Lords.[39] For light on the original meaning of the words "cruel and unusual" Granucci turns to a dissent by a minority of the Lords. In brief, the dissent stated that (1) it is "wholly out of [the] power" of a temporal court to divest Oates of his "priestly habit," that "belonging to the ecclesiastical courts only"; (2) the judgments are "barbarous, inhuman and unchristian; and there is *no precedent* ... [for] whipping and committing to prison for life, *for the crime of perjury"*; ... and (4) it was contrary to Parliament's recent declaration (in the Bill of Rights) that "excessive bail ought not to be required, nor excessive fines imposed, nor cruel and unusual punishments inflicted."[40] Defrocking by a temporal court was "unusual" because that was the office of an ecclesiastical court. Granucci comments that life imprisonment "probably would not be considered excessive in a case of perjury which had resulted in erroneous executions. Whipping did not constitute a cruel method of punishment in England at the time of Oates' conviction."[41]

That comment overlooks that "at the common law there was not any course of law to punish perjury."[42] The relevant statute, 5

38. Id. 855.
39. Id. 857–858.
40. Id. 858.
41. Id. 859.
42. 3 Stephen, supra note 29 at 245. "Temporal" penalties were first imposed upon the offence by the statute of 32 Hen. 8, c. 9, s. 3 (1540), which "punished subornation of perjury in certain cases by a fine of £10, but

Eliz. c. 9 (1562), provided that if the offender could not pay the fine, there was to be "six months imprisonment and pillory . . . besides certain incapacities."[43] The dissenting Lords justly maintained, therefore, that "there is no precedent . . . [for] whipping and committing to prison for life, for the crime of perjury."[44] The House of Commons agreed with the dissenting Lords on the ground that a minister of the Church of England may not be "degraded of his priestly and canonical habit" by a temporal court.[45] Granucci concluded that "In the context of the Oates case, 'cruel and unusual' seems to have meant a mere punishment unauthorized by statute and not within the jurisdiction of the court to impose."[46] That was the view of the Commons, but it was not

---

left perjury itself unpunished . . . This was followed in 1562 by 5 Eliz. c. 9, which punishes subornation in certain special cases and courts with a penalty of £40, and perjury itself with a penalty of £20." Id. 244.

As late as 1828, 5 Eliz. apparently remained the governing statute. It is the sole entry under "perjury" in 1 Joseph Chitty, *Collection of Statutes* 289 (1828). For history of perjury, see 4 W. S. Holdsworth, *History of English Law* 515–519 (3d ed., 1923).

43. 3 Stephen, id. 244.

44. The dissenting Lords stated, 5: "Because sir John Holt, sir Henry Pollfexen, the two chief justices and sir Robert Atkins, chief baron, with six judges more (being as that were then present), for these and many other reasons, did before us, solemnly deliver their opinions, and unanimously declare that the said judgments were contrary to law and ancient practice and therefore erroneous, and ought to be reversed." Granucci 858. Sir Robert Howard repeated in the House of Commons, "The Judges all present in the Lords' House gave their opinion: 'That the judgment against *Oates* was contrary to law.' " 9 Gray, supra note 36 at 287.

45. See statements by Howard and Sir William Williams, 9 Gray, id. at 287, 291.

46. Granucci 859. Justice Brennan cites this statement for "as we now know, the English history of the clause reveals a particular concern with the establishment of a safeguard against arbitrary punishments." "Indeed," he asserts, "the very words 'cruel and unusual punishments' imply condemnation of the arbitrary infliction of severe punishments." Furman 274–275 n. 14. Yet Granucci noted that the existing *barbarous* punishments continued to be inflicted. Supra text accompanying note 31; see also infra note 52.

shared by the Lords. The case, tried by Chief Justice Jeffreys, had been removed to the House of Lords by writ of error; judgment was affirmed. Oates then petitioned the Lords to be released from the judgment, but they affirmed.[47] In the Commons, Sir Robert Howard acknowledged that the Lords were the "Supreme Judicature in Parliament," reasoned that there was *legislative* power to repeal the judgment, and asked for a Bill to reverse it.[48] On June 11, 1689, the Commons "Resolved, That Bills be brought in to reverse the judgments against Mr. Oates . . . as cruel and illegal";[49] the Commons passed a bill to reverse on July 2, 1689, but it failed of passage in the Lords.[50]

In sum, the debate on the *Oates* trial came several months after adoption of the Bill of Rights in February 1689; the Commons echoed the conjunction of "cruel and illegal" met in the legislative history of the Bill of Rights.[51] But the judgment of the Lords, the Supreme Court of Judicature, sentencing Oates to whipping, pillorying, and lengthy imprisonment for perjury, was left standing. With the dissenters' invocation of the "cruel and unusual punishments" clause before them the Lords in effect decided that whipping, pillorying, and excessive imprisonment were not within the clause. Moreover, the existing barbarous punishments (let alone death penalties), as Granucci noted, continued to be inflicted after the Bill of Rights.[52] And for better than one

47. Supra note 35.

48. 9 Gray, supra note 36 at 287.

49. Id. at 294.

50. 10 *Howell's State Trials,* supra note 35 at 1329.

51. Hawley proposed that the "judgment against *Oates* be called a cruel and illegal judgment" and was joined by Williams, 9 Gray, supra note 36 at 290, 293.

52. "[N]one of the 'cruel' methods of punishment which were employed in the 'Bloody Assize' ceased to be used after the passage of the Bill of Rights. Executing male rebels by drawing and quartering continued with all its embellishments, until 1814 when disembowelling was *eliminated by statute.*" Granucci 855–856. See also supra text accompanying note 31. During a debate in the House of Lords in 1965, the Lord Chancellor said: "When we abolished the punishment for treason that you should be

hundred years trifling offenses could be visited with capital punishment, a construction by Parliament which refutes Granucci's conclusion that the Bill of Rights "reiterat[ed] the English policy against disproportionate penalties."[53] Justice Powell's reliance on Granucci for the proposition that "The principle of disproportionality is deeply rooted in English constitutional law"[54] is

---

hanged, and then cut down while still alive, and then disembowelled while still alive . . . we took the view that it was a punishment no longer consistent with our own self-respect." 268 Parl. Deb. H. L. (5th series) 703 (1965). This indicates that to fall within the "cruel and unusual punishments" clause a punishment had to be both cruel (barbarous) *and* "unusual," that is, a departure from the customary. And it shows that the penalty had not become obsolete but required abolition by an Act of Parliament.

Justice Marshall transformed this reference to a barbarous punishment to "*Capital* punishment is a 'punishment no longer consistent with our own self-respect' and therefore violative of the Eighth Amendment." Furman 315. If it did not violate the 1689 clause, it did not violate the Eighth Amendment; abolition, at any rate, was for Parliament, not the courts. Justice Marshall's unreliability is again demonstrated by his deduction from the statement in Wilkerson v. Utah, 99 U.S. 130, 135–136 (1878): "punishment of *torture* . . . and all other *in the same line* of unnecessary cruelty, are forbidden," the proposition that "the Court found that unnecessary cruelty was no more permissible than torture," Furman 322, thereby assimilating death by crucifixion to hanging for robbery. So too, his statement that "the Eighth Amendment itself was adopted to prevent punishment from becoming synonymous with vengeance," Furman 343, is entirely a figment of his imagination. Again, Marshall flatly stated that capital punishment "violates the Eighth Amendment because it is morally unacceptable to the people of the United States at this time in their history," Furman 360, a pronouncement the people speedily repudiated. See infra Chapter 6, text accompanying notes 60–61.

Contrast with the historical evidence Justice Douglas' sweeping statement, citing Granucci, that the Bill of Rights of 1689 "was concerned primarily with selective or irregular imposition of harsh penalties and its aim was to forbid arbitrary and discriminating penalties of a severe nature," Furman 242, which he then describes as "the English proscription against selective and irregular use of penalties." Id. 245.

53. Granucci 860.

54. Rummel v. Estelle, 445 U.S. 263, 288 (1980). Justice Edward White concluded that the prevailing English practice up to the American Revolu-

therefore misplaced. It is a principle of very recent and dubious vintage. Powell tells us that "The principle that grossly disproportionate sentences violate the Eighth Amendment was first enunciated in this Court by Mr. Justice Field in *O'Neil v. Vermont,* 144 U.S. 323 (1892)"[55]—in a dissenting opinion. Field assumed, rather than demonstrated, that "proportionality" was rooted in the common law, a fragile assumption on which to rest the overthrow of the clear common (and statutory) law to the contrary.

Thus far our focus has been on the word "cruel," but the punishment must be *both* "cruel *and* unusual." After canvassing the history of the 1689 clause Granucci concluded that the use of "unusual" was inadvertent, substituted without explanation for "illegal," leading him to suggest that it meant "illegal."[56] "Unusual" was not and is not a synonym for "illegal"; more than speculation is required to persuade that the draftsmen assimilated the terms. A simpler explanation is at hand, as Chief Justice Warren perceived: "If the word 'unusual' is to have any meaning apart from the word 'cruel' . . . the meaning should be the ordinary one, signifying something different from that which is ordinarily done." His mistake was to conclude that "Denaturalization as a punishment certainly meets this test,"[57] wrenching "denaturalization" from the time frame of 1689 and 1789, at which time denaturalization in the form of expatriation and banishment was "usual." On the other hand, certain punishments such as crucifixion or boiling in oil were no longer customary in 1689 and therefore were *both* "cruel and unusual." Although the punishment for treason—disembowelment while alive—was horrible, it survived until it was abolished by Parliament in 1814.[58] Thus Parliament,

---

tion left no room for "any theory of proportional punishment suggested by the bill of rights or that a protest was thereby intended against the severity of punishments." Weems v. United States, 217 U.S. 349, 393 (1910) dissenting opinion, Holmes, J., concurring.

55. Rummel v. Estelle, id. at 289 n. 5.

56. The "use of the word 'unusual' must be laid simply to chance and sloppy draftsmanship." Granucci 855. Chief Justice Burger and Justice Marshall echoed this view, Furman 376 n. 2, 318.

57. Trop v. Dulles, 356 U.S. 86, 100 (1958).

58. Supra note 52.

creator of the 1689 Bill of Rights, indicated that what was customary in 1689 was not "unusual," and that "cruelty" alone did
not ban the punishment; it also had to depart from what was customary in 1689. No historical evidence compels a reading contrary
to the natural conjunctive interpretation.

Following in Warren's footsteps, Justice Stewart concluded in
Furman that "these sentences are 'unusual' in the sense that the
penalty of death is infrequently imposed for murder,"[59] substituting his own meaning for that of the Framers. And seduced—not
for the first time[60]—by his own rhetoric, he added, "These death
sentences are cruel and unusual in the same way that being struck
by lightning is cruel and unusual."[61] Lightning strikes the innocent without warning, whereas a murderer was on notice that his
offense courted a death penalty, though there was the possibility
that a merciful jury might spare his life, a contingency of which
he may scarcely complain. Justice Douglas delivered himself of an
even more vulnerable statement: "It would seem to be incontest-
able that the death penalty inflicted on one defendant is 'unusual'
if it discriminates against him by reason of his race, religion,
wealth, social position, or class."[62] Yet the "benefit of clergy,"
which exempted any one who could read from the death penalty,
"incontestably" discriminated against the uneducated on the basis
of "class,"[63] and it persisted long after the 1689 Bill of Rights.
Douglas himself recounts that "In those days the target was not
the blacks or the poor, but the dissenters . . . who opposed government's recurring efforts to foist a particular religion on the people

59. Furman 309.

60. His famous phrase "I cannot define hard core pornography, but I
know it when I see it" is, like the Chinese emperor's mandate from heaven,
unknowable until he pronounces it, a poor guide to the perplexed. Bickel
adverted to "the erratic and apparently inarticulable subjectivity of the
Court's obscenity decisions." Bickel 77.

61. Furman 309.

62. Id. 242.

63. The point was made by Chief Justice Burger, id. 377 n. 2; see also 1
Stephen, supra note 29 at 459 et seq.

... One cannot read this history without realizing that the desire for equality was reflected in the ban against 'cruel and unusual punishments' contained in the Eighth Amendment."[64] This is wishful thinking: "At the convention of 1689, Macaulay exults, 'the assertors of liberty said not a word about the natural equality of men.' "[65] The fact that the First Congress thought it necessary by the Act of April 30, 1790, to prohibit resort to "benefit of clergy" as an exemption from capital punishment[66] attests it did not consider that the Bill of Rights outlawed discriminatory punishment. Here as elsewhere Douglas identified his own predilections with constitutional mandates.

One thing is clear beyond peradventure: the "cruel and unusual punishments" clause left death penalties untouched. Writing seventy years after the appearance of the clause in the 1689 Bill of Rights, Blackstone said of "deliberate and wilful murder, a crime at which human nature starts," that it is "punished almost universally throughout the world with death,"[67] striking testimony by the great commentator that the death penalty was not affected by the clause.

UNITED STATES

Whether there was in fact no "causal connection between the 'Bloody Assize' and the cruel and unusual punishments clause"[68]

64. Furman 255.

65. William Dusinberre, *Henry Adams: The Myth of Failure* 159 (1980). Nor were the Framers dedicated to "equality." General C. C. Pinckney told the South Carolina convention, "Another reason weighed particularly with the members from this state, against the insertion of a bill of rights. Such bills generally begin with declaring that all men are by nature born free. Now, we should make that declaration with a very bad grace, when a large part of our property consists in men who are actually born slaves." 4 Elliot 316.

66. §21 (1st Cong., 2d Sess.), 1 Stat. 117.

67. 4 Blackstone 194.

68. Granucci 856.

is of no moment if the Founders thought there was. "It matters not," Charles Evans Hughes wrote, "whether they were accurate in their understanding of the Great Charter, for the point is . . . what the colonists thought it meant" in framing their own constitutional provisions.[69] The records refer only to barbarous punishments, not to jurisdictional limitations.[70] Although the several references to "cruel and unusual" are equivocal and were washed out by subsequent *actions,* no historical account may fail to notice them, particularly because in some quarters they have been given undue weight.

This much is certain: "barbarous" punishment did not to the minds of the Founders include death penalties. At the adoption of the Constitution there were in the colonies "from ten to eighteen capital offenses," including "piracy, arson, rape, robbery, burglary and sodomy."[71] In the Virginia Ratification Convention, Patrick Henry protested against the absence of the Virginia provision "that excessive bail ought not to be required, nor excessive fines imposed, nor cruel and unusual punishments inflicted." He emphasized that "our ancestors . . . would not admit of tortures or cruel and barbarous punishments" and feared that Congress "may introduce the practice of . . . torturing to extract a confession of the crime . . . in order to punish with still more relentless severity."[72] From this Justice Thurgood Marshall deduced that Henry "wished to insure that 'relentless severity' would be prohibited by the Constitution."[73] Uttered in the context of "tortures" and "barbarous" punishments, Henry scarcely meant by "relentless severity" to strike down the death penalties which obtained throughout the colonies and in his own State. As Justice Brennan noted, "When this country was founded . . . the practice of pun-

69. C. E. Hughes, *The Supreme Court of the United States* 186 (1928).

70. See supra text accompanying note 46.

71. Woodson v. North Carolina, 428 U.S. 280, 289 n. 16; see also Furman 335. In 1897 Congress "reduced the number of federal capital offenses from 60 to 3 (treason, murder, rape)." Furman 339.

72. Quoted by Justice Marshall in Furman 320–321.

73. Furman 321.

ishing criminals by death was widespread and by and large accept-able to society."[74]

In the Massachusetts Convention, Holmes stated that Congress "are nowhere restrained from *inventing* the most cruel and *unheard* of punishments."[75] Manifestly Holmes feared the invention of "unheard of" punishments. Justice Brennan considers that it does not follow from the Holmes-Henry remarks that the Framers were "exclusively concerned with prohibiting torturous punishments," and that both "focussed wholly upon the necessity to restrain the legislative power."[76] Of course crimes are defined and their pun-ishments declared by the legislature. Holmes's and Henry's insis-tence that "Congress must be limited in its power to punish" does not answer the question: did they mean to deny to Congress a power then exercised by every State legislature—the power to pre-scribe death penalties? A departure from accepted practice cannot rest on mere speculation. As Chief Justice Marshall said: "an opinion which is . . . to establish a principle never before recog-nized, should be expressed in plain and explicit terms."[77]

The interchange in the First Congress, which drafted the Bill of Rights, between William L. Smith of South Carolina and Samuel Livermore is little more enlightening. Both were opponents of the clause, which on established canons deprives their remarks of any weight as legislative history.[78] Smith objected that the import of "cruel and unusual punishment" was "too indefinite"; Livermore commented, "it is sometimes necessary to hang a man, villains often deserve whipping, and perhaps having their ears cut off; but are we in future to be prevented from inflicting these punish-

74. Id. at 305. Justice Blackmun observed, "The several concurring opinions acknowledge, as they must, that until today capital punishment was accepted and assumed as not unconstitutional *per se* under the Eighth Amendment or the Fourteenth Amendment." Id. 407.

75. Quoted by Justice Brennan, id. 258–259.

76. Id. 260.

77. United States v. Burr, 25 F. Cas. 55, 165 (C. C. D. Va. 1807) (No. 14,693); see also Pierson v. Ray, 386 U.S. 547, 554–555 (1967).

78. For citations, see Berger *G/J* 157 n. 2, 160 n. 13.

ments because they are cruel?"[79] Justice Brennan reads Livermore
to object that "the clause might someday prevent the legislature
from inflicting what were then quite common and in his view
'necessary' punishments—death, whipping and ear cropping. The
only inference to be drawn from Livermore's statement is that the
'considerable majority' was prepared to run that risk." And Brennan concludes "we cannot know *exactly* what the Framers
thought 'cruel and unusual punishments' were."[80] For present
purposes it suffices that the face of the Bill of Rights itself discloses that death penalties were contemplated, thereby disposing
of the "risk" that "cruel and unusual punishments" might someday be construed to preclude death penalties. The Fifth Amendment guarantees that "No person shall be held to answer for a
capital [punishable by death] . . . crime, unless on a presentment
or indictment," or "be twice put in jeopardy of life" for the same
offense, or "be deprived of life . . . without due process of law."
These provisions premise that one may be deprived of life.[81] The
"cruel and unusual punishments" clause must be read together
with these provisions; obviously the First Congress was not out-
lawing by the Eighth Amendment the right to impose death penalties it simultaneously recognized in the Fifth. Justice Brennan
acknowledges that from the Fifth Amendment we can "infer that
the Framers recognized the existence of what was then a common
punishment. We cannot, however, make the further inference
that they intended to exempt this particular punishment from the
express prohibition of the Cruel and Unusual Punishments
Clause."[82] A contrary inference, that the Framers meant to bar
State employment of a "common punishment," one, in Brennan's
words, that "has been employed throughout our history,"[83]

79. Quoted by Justice Brennan, Furman 262.
80. Id. 263.
81. Citing the above materials, a plurality of three concurring Justices
concluded that "It is apparent from the text of the Constitution itself that
the existence of capital punishment was accepted by the Framers." Gregg v.
Georgia, 428 U.S. 153, 177 (1976).
82. Furman 283.
83. Id. 282.

requires explanation; Brennan offers none. In a comparable case the Court declared, "So-called petty offenses were tried without juries both in England and the Colonies and have always been held to be exempt from the otherwise comprehensive language of the Sixth Amendment's jury trial provisions. There is no substantial evidence that the Framers intended to depart from this established common law practice."[84] At common law it was presumed that common law terms were to be given their common law meaning. That presumption is not to be displaced by speculation based on equivocal legislative history. The Framers knew how to abjure an undesirable common law meaning. Aware, for example, that "numerous and dangerous excrescences" had disfigured the English law of treason, they redefined and limited it.[85] Their omission similarly to exclude death penalties speaks volumes.

Then, too, special safeguards in application of the death penalty were provided by the Fifth Amendment precisely because the Framers postulated that the death penalty was unaffected by the Eighth Amendment. Not to infer, as Brennan maintains, that the Framers meant to "exempt this particular punishment [death penalties] from the express prohibition of the Cruel and Unusual Punishments Clause," is to render those safeguards useless. For in the absence of death penalties there was no need for the safeguards. The continued vitality of death penalties is further attested by the Act of April 30, 1790, enacted by the selfsame First Congress, the best interpreter of what it meant by the "cruel and unusual" clause it adopted. That Act made murder, forgery of public securities, robbery, and rape punishable by death, incontrovertible evidence that the Framers did not intend "cruel and unusual" to exclude death penalties.[86] To this may be added the

84. Duncan v. Louisiana, 391 U.S. 145, 160 (1968); see also Chief Justice Marshall, supra text accompanying note 77.

85. 2 James Wilson, *Works,* ed. R. G. McCloskey 663, 665 (1967); 2 Farrand 347.

86. Ch. 9, 1 Stat. 115. In the face of this 1790 death penalty for robbery imposed by the draftsmen of the Bill of Rights, that is, the First Congress, Justice Marshall maintains that "a penalty is unconstitutional whenever it is unnecessarily harsh or cruel. This is what the *Founders* of this country in-

statement of Justice James Wilson, a leading Framer, in his 1791 Philadelphia Lectures: "In England, in the United States, in Pennsylvania, and almost universally throughout the world, the crime of wilful and premeditated murder is and has been punishable with death. Indeed it seems agreed by all, that, if a capital punishment ought to be inflicted for any crime, this is unquestionably a crime for which it ought to be inflicted."[87] Wilson, "commonly accepted . . . as the most learned and profound legal scholar of his generation,"[88] was hardly oblivious of the "cruel and unusual punishments" clause, framed, as it were, under his nose only two years earlier. Justice Brennan comments on the 1790 Act: "Obviously concepts of justice change; no immutable moral order requires death for murderers and rapists."[89] He relies for the change in "concepts of justice" on society's "virtually total" rejection of the death penalty,[90] an assessment that society speedily proved "totally wrong."[91] Be it assumed that "concepts of justice" have

---

tended; this was what their fellow citizens believed the Eighth Amendment provided." Furman 332.

Bedau, a leading opponent of death penalties, felt constrained to concede, "even if the death penalty was imposed by statute for a trifling offense, it is doubtful that it would be 'cruel and unusual' according to the 'original understanding.' " Bedau 35. Nevertheless, Justice Brennan asserts, *"We know* that the Framers did not envision 'so narrow a role [torture, etc.] for this basic guaranty of human rights,' " citing Goldberg and Dershowitz. Furman 268.

87. 2 Wilson, supra note 85 at 661. "In his masterful study of the original understanding of the first amendment," Leonard Levy likewise looked to the beliefs of "the generation which adopted the constitution and the Bill of Rights." Perry 287–288.

88. Id. 2. 1 James Wilson, *Works,* ed. R. G. McCloskey 2 (1967).

89. Furman 304.

90. Id. 305. Brennan also states, "We know 'that the words of the [clause] are not precise, and that their scope is not static.' We know, therefore, that the clause 'must draw its meaning from the evolving standards of decency that mark the progress of a maturing society.' . . . A punishment is 'cruel and unusual,' therefore, if it does not comport with human dignity." Furman 269, 270. For analysis of this concept, see infra Chapter 6, text accompanying notes 21–34.

91. Infra Chapter 6, text accompanying notes 60–61.

changed, that does not endow the Court with power to effectuate the change. The 1790 Act testifies that the *Constitution* does not bar death penalties, and a "change" requires an amendment by the people under Article V, not by the Court. In the midst of his defense of judicial review in Federalist No. 78, Hamilton assured the Ratifiers that

> Until the people have, by some solemn and authoritative act, annulled or changed the established form, it is binding . . . and no presumption, or even knowledge of their sentiments, can warrant their representatives in a departure from it, prior to such an act.[92]

Brennan's analysis tacitly posits that the Justices may rewrite the Constitution despite the Framers.

An indefatigable abolitionist, Hugo Bedau, acknowledges that resort to the due process and cruel and unusual punishment clauses could not be "supported by historical research into the original intention of the Congress or the states in proposing and ratifying these amendments." He likewise recognized that "An unbroken line of interpreters has held that it was the original understanding and intent of the framers of the Eighth Amendment to proscribe as 'cruel and unusual' only such modes of execution as compound the simple infliction of death with added cruelties," for example, "burning at the stake, crucifixion."[93] Those interpretations are reinforced by the fact, emphasized by Louis Henkin, that "Prohibitions of the Constitution . . . are limitations on the freedom to govern. They are therefore to be narrowly construed. . . . As concerns the States, in particular, the Constitution leaves them large freedom to do what they like—and what the Justices may not like—subject only to the *clearest and narrowest*

92. Federalist 509. In the First Congress, Madison stated, "My idea of the sovereignty of the people is, that the people can change the Constitution if they please, but while the Constitution exists, they must conform to its dictates." 1 *Ann. Cong.* 739. See also infra Chapter 5, text accompanying note 9.

93. Bedau 14, 35.

limitation.''[94] Quite clearly the Framers did *not* mean to limit State control of death penalties.

Did the Fourteenth Amendment work any change in this respect? Let it be assumed *arguendo* that the Eighth Amendment was "absorbed" in the Fourteenth, and it remains to prove that the 1866 framers intended to cut down the established State death penalties. Justice Douglas cited John Bingham's statement that "cruel and unusual punishments have been inflicted under State laws within this Union,"[95] but at best this is an argument for incorporation of the Eighth Amendment; it does not indicate which punishments were "cruel and unusual." Moreover, to borrow from Chief Justice Marshall, an intention "to establish a principle never before recognized should be expressed in plain and explicit terms,"[96] a canon repeated by Justice Miller, who refused to "em-

94. Henkin, in Wallace Mendelson, ed., *Felix Frankfurter: The Judge* 96 (1964). See also Madison, supra Chapter 2, text accompanying notes 80–82. Chief Justice Burger commented that the "widely divergent views of the amendment expressed in today's opinions reveal the haze that surrounds this constitutional command," and referred to the "enigmatic character of the command." Furman 376. The enigma is solved when one looks to the centuries of English and colonial practice, the index of meaning for common law terms. But if the command is indeed "enigmatic," the rights reserved to the States by the Tenth Amendment are not to be cut down under cover of vague language. See infra Chapter 5, text accompanying notes 153–157.

95. Furman 241. Charles Fairman remarks on "the disconcerting way in which Bingham would pluck a constitutional phrase and toss it in at some point to which it had no relevance." 6 Charles Fairman, *History of the Supreme Court of the United States* 1289 (1971). The framers' aim was to prevent discrimination with respect to narrowly enumerated rights, not to incorporate the Bill of Rights in whole or in part. Supra Chapter 2; infra Chapter 5, text accompanying notes 73–99.

96. Supra note 77. Such an intention is rebutted by Thomas Cooley, Chief Justice of the Michigan Supreme Court and eminent commentator on the Constitution, who wrote in the midst of the Reconstruction era: "any punishment, declared by statute for an offense which was punishable in the same way at common law could not be regarded as cruel and unusual punishment in the constitutional sense." Quoted by Justice Edward White in Weems v. United States, 217 U.S. 349, 357 (1910), dissenting opinion.

brace a construction" of the Fourteenth Amendment that would subject the States' local concerns to "the control of Congress . . . in the absence of language which expressed such a purpose too clearly to admit of doubt."[97] My own immersion in the history of the Fourteenth Amendment leads me to concur with Professor Henkin's observation that the Amendment "did not . . . withdraw from the states the principal administration of criminal justice."[98] Justice Powell, joined by Chief Justice Burger and Justices Blackmun and Rehnquist, therefore stood on solid ground in stating, "The Court rejects as not decisive the clearest evidence that the Framers of the Constitution and the authors of the Fourteenth Amendment believed that those documents posed no barrier to the death penalty."[99] That rejection substituted the will of the five Justices for that of the Framers. And it proceeded in the teeth of the Court's own canon: "A procedure customarily employed, long before the Revolution, in . . . England, and generally adopted by the States . . . cannot be deemed inconsistent with due process of law."[100] It remains to be said that in *Gregg v. Georgia* (1976), a

97. Slaughter-House Cases, 83 U.S. (16 Wall.) 36, 78 (1872). Justice Frankfurter said of this case, it "has the authority that comes from contemporaneous knowledge of the purposes of the Fourteenth Amendment." Louisiana ex rel. Francis v. Resweber, 329 U.S. 459, 466 (1947), concurring opinion. See also supra Chapter 2, note 6.

98. Henkin, in Wallace Mendelson, ed., *Felix Frankfurter: The Judge* 99 (1964); see also supra Chapter 2, note 79.

99. Furman 417.

100. Owenbey v. Morgan, 256 U.S. 94, 111 (1921). See also supra Chapter 2, note 61.

That the Court thus proceeds in the teeth of its own statements to the contrary does not astonish Court-watchers. On most occasions it selects from its own opposing pronouncements one that fits the desired result. It was faithful to the canon in Betts v. Brady, 316 U.S. 455, 465 (1942), rejecting the argument that the Fourteenth Amendment incorporated the Sixth's "fundamental" right to counsel, saying: "Relevant data on the subject are afforded by constitutional and statutory provisions subsisting in the colonies and the States prior to inclusion of the Bill of Rights in the national Constitution, and in the constitutional, legislative, and judicial history of the States to the present date. These are the most authoritative

plurality of the Court, Justices Stewart, Powell, and Stevens, found that the Framers "were primarily concerned with proscribing 'tortures' and other 'barbarous' methods of punishment" and held that "the punishment of death does not *invariably* violate the Constitution,"[101] thus reserving the right to pull the string on

---

sources for ascertaining the considered judgment of the citizens of the States upon the question." Betts was overruled in Gideon v. Wainright, 372 U.S. 335 (1963). But that did not spell the demise of the canon, which was again invoked in Duncan v. Louisiana, 391 U.S. 145, 152–153 (1968). After noting English and colonial attachment to trial by jury, its reaffirmation by the First Continental Congress and in the Declaration of Independence, and expressions in the constitutions of the thirteen States and in the Sixth Amendment, the Court declared that "Even such skeletal history is impressive support for considering the right of trial by jury trial in civil cases to be fundamental to our system of justice." By the same token, the attachment to death penalties of the English, colonists, Thirteen States, and the great preponderance of the States up to the present time equally constitutes "impressive support" for regarding the States' right to cling to that long-established practice as "fundamental." The Court's high-handed disregard of its own canons testifies to the thoroughly subjective nature of its lawmaking, which embodies the Justices' predilections rather than an inescapable response to a *requirement* of the Constitution.

101. 428 U.S. 153, 170, 169 (1976). The plurality, however, does not moor itself to the "original meaning," but states: "Considerations of federalism, as well as respect for the ability of a legislature to evaluate the moral consensus concerning the death penalty and its social utility as a sanction, require us to conclude, in the absence of more convincing evidence, that the infliction of death as a punishment for murder is not without justification and thus is not unconstitutionally severe." Id. at 186–187.

Acknowledging that opposition to death penalties could not rest on the original meaning of "cruel and unusual," that to argue for the prohibition "would be to confuse possible legislative desirability with constitutional requirements," Bedau nevertheless delivers himself of the extraordinary statement "our interest today in the 'original intent of the framers' if it is to be more than an exercise in historical scholarship, must take its dominant cues from the (structural, fundamental) needs of our society and our ideals and aspirations as they are understood today." Bedau 35, 36, 14. "Interest in the original intent" is scuttled in favor of "our aspirations" of "today." In fact, he called for judicial revision of the Constitution, and his

death penalties. Justices White and Rehnquist and Chief Justice
Burger in a concurring opinion disagreed that the "death penalty,
however imposed and for whatever crime," is "cruel and unusual
punishment."[102] History places this beyond controversy.

It has been noted that Justice Douglas considered that "the idea
of equal protection of the laws . . . is implicit in the ban on 'cruel
and unusual punishments.' "[103] Of Chief Justice Warren's similar
attempt to read the equal protection of the Fourteenth Amendment back into the Fifth, his worshipful disciple John Hart Ely
said, it is "gibberish both syntactically and historically."[104] That
does not, however, dispose of the effect of the "equal protection"
clause itself. Douglas rang the changes on the alleged selective application of death penalties "to minorities whose numbers are few,
who are outcasts of society, and who are unpopular, but whom
society is willing to see suffer though it would not countenance
general application of the same penalty across the board."[105] But
Douglas conceded that "We cannot say from facts disclosed in
these records that these defendants were sentenced to death because they are black."[106] Justice Stewart also concluded that "racial discrimination has not been proved,"[107] as did Chief Justice
Burger;[108] even Justice Marshall remarked that "it is difficult to
ascertain the degree to which the death penalty is discriminatorily
imposed."[109] Now comes Hans Zeisel, who submits on the basis

---

identification of his "aspirations" with "our ideals" was quickly repudiated
by the adoption of fresh death penalty statutes in 35 States on the heels of
Furman v. Georgia. Infra Chapter 6, text accompanying notes 60–61.

102. 428 U.S. at 226.

103. Furman 257; supra text accompanying note 62.

104. J. H. Ely, *Democracy and Distrust* 32 (1980).

105. Furman 245; see also id. 248 n. 10, 255–256.

106. Id. 253.

107. Id. 310.

108. Burger found "no empirical basis for concluding that juries have
generally failed to discharge in good faith the responsibility . . . of choosing
between life and death in individual cases according to the dictates of community values." Id. 389.

109. Id. 368.

of a study of racial discrimination in Florida that its existence has been established.[110] But discrimination in Florida does not constitute proof of discrimination in Oregon or Vermont. What, asks Ely, "would a showing of invidious discrimination in Arkansas have to do with the constitutionality of the death penalty, say, in Montana?"[111] Moreover, as Phil Neal pointed out, "the equality ordained is a Statewide equality, encompassing the persons 'within its jurisdiction' and not a nationwide or external equality."[112] For it is the "laws" of the States severally, not jointly, that are required to afford "equal protection." Nevertheless, Zeisel, moving from the proposition that "differential sentencing based on race is obviously the ultimate affront to evenhandedness, the clearest example of arbitrariness in a legal sense," concludes that "There is simply no way to ensure the evenhanded administration of the death penalty. That alone should be sufficient reason for its abolition."[113] His draconian remedy overshoots the mark. He does not, be it noted, level his criticism at the *jury,* which, he earlier wrote (with Harry Kalven), "is highly sensitive to equality of treatment and inequality of role when the death penalty is in issue."[114] Instead, he "concentrates on the role of the prosecutor . . . because the prosecutor has overpowering control over the flow of offenders to death row."[115] Unlike jurors, however, prosecutors are continuing public officials who are susceptible to influence by publicity and public opinion and, as Zeisel himself has shown, can ameliorate discrimination.[116] Abolition of the death penalty is not therefore the only alternative.

110. Hans Zeisel, "Race Bias in the Administration of the Death Penalty: The Florida Experience," 95 Harv. L. Rev. 456 (1981).

111. J. H. Ely, *Democracy and Distrust* 173 (1980).

112. Phil C. Neal, "Baker v. Carr: Politics in Search of Law," 1962 S. Ct. Rev. 252, 293. See also Missouri v. Lewis, quoted supra Chapter 2, note 64.

113. Zeisel, supra note 110 at 457, 468.

114. Harry Kalven and Hans Zeisel, *The American Jury* 317 (1966).

115. Zeisel, supra note 110 at 466. "Prosecutors can change the character of the death row population at will," id. at 468.

116. Id. 464–466.

Since Justices Douglas and Marshall insisted that jury sentencing discriminates against racial defendants,[117] and since activist counsel are likely further to press the view that it violates "equal protection," I shall assume that such discrimination is nationwide and venture a few comments. It is by no means obvious that racial discrimination in jury sentencing amounts to a denial of equal protection. A key to the framers' thinking was furnished by Thaddeus Stevens: "Whatever law punishes a white man for a crime shall punish the black man precisely in the same way." He referred to the Black Codes, saying, "I need not enumerate these partial and oppressive laws."[118] Such statutes, Kenneth Stampp wrote, "made certain acts felonies when committed by Negroes but not when committed by whites . . . they assigned heavier penalties to Negroes than to whites convicted of the same offense."[119] Senator Edgar Cowan of Pennsylvania remarked, "If a cruel and unusual punishment were to be inflicted upon a negro, an exceptional punishment, one which discriminated against him,"[120] he would be protected. Like the men of 1689, the 1866 framers were concerned with the nature of the punishment, not the sentencing process.

All intendments militate against tampering with that process. The common law prized the discretion of the jury and shielded its verdicts from judicial inquiry.[121] As an "attribute" of "trial by jury," these perquisites have constitutional stature.[122] It should take more than the "indeterminate," "vague and ambiguous" words "equal protection"[123] to persuade that the framers meant

117. Id. 456.
118. *Globe* 2459.
119. Kenneth Stampp, *The Peculiar Institution* 210 (1956).
120. *Globe* 500.
121. See infra Chapter 6, text accompanying notes 85–125.
122. Infra Chapter 6, text accompanying note 108.
123. Ely considers that like the "quite inscrutable" privileges or immunities clause, the equal protection clause "is also unforthcoming with details." J. H. Ely, *Democracy and Distrust* 98 (1981). "Taken literally and alone, it may be that the equal protection clause is too obscure for judicial enforcement." Wallace Mendelson, Book Review, 6 Hastings Con. L. Q.

thereby to abandon so important and valued an attribute. Even in the face of unmistakably comprehensive terms—"every person"— the Supreme Court held that an intention to curtail the established common law immunity of judges required specific provision.[124] An intention to interfere with a State's control of its jury system is further negated by repeated assurances that Negroes would not sit on juries. A prominent advocate of their rights, William Lawrence of Ohio, said of the Civil Rights Act of 1866, progenitor of the Fourteenth Amendment, it "does not affect the right to sit on juries. That it leaves to the States to be determined each for itself."[125] Given a bar against Negro participation in the jury process, the best possible safeguard against discrimination,[126]

437, 451 (1979). Because "of its indeterminacy, the clause does not offer much guidance even in resolving particular issues of discrimination based on race." Paul Brest, "The Misconceived Quest for the Original Understanding," 60 B.U.L. Rev. 204, 232 (1980). See also Brest, infra chapter 5, note 160.

124. In Pierson v. Ray, 386 U.S. 547, 554–555 (1967), the Court, after adverting to the common law immunity of judges from suits for acts performed in their official capacity, stated: "We do not believe that this settled principle was abolished by §1983, which makes liable 'every person' who under color of law deprives another of his civil rights . . . The immunity of judges [is] well established and we presume that Congress would have specifically so provided had it wished to abolish the doctrine." Earlier, Chief Justice Marshall held, "an opinion which is . . . to establish a principle never before recognized should be expressed in plain and explicit terms." United States v. Burr, 25 F. Cas. (No. 14,693) 55, 165 (C.C.D. Va. 1807).

125. *Globe* 632, 1832. For additional citations see Berger *G/J* 163. Dissenting in Ex parte Virginia, 100 U.S. 339, 362–363 (1879), Justice Field correctly stated that provision for Negro jurors was "a change so radical . . . [as] was never contemplated by the recent amendments. The people in adopting them did not suppose they were altering the fundamental theory of their dual system of government."

126. Currently a trial of a black for murder, Wayne Williams, is taking place in Atlanta, Georgia, before a black judge and 8 black jurors out of 12. *New York Times,* Jan. 5, 1982, A-11. One dissenting black juror will suffice to bring about a hung jury. If Williams is sentenced to death by such a jury, he can hardly complain of racial discrimination. Zeisel has shown that a broader jury panel can be secured by publicity. Zeisel, supra note 110 at 464–466.

it is difficult to assume that the framers provided for even more far-reaching intervention in the States' sentencing processes, particularly when in many States the Negro presence was negligible.[127] Then too, the notion that the States would be required to abolish the death penalty if their juries did not evenhandedly sentence blacks runs counter to the framers' narrowly ameliorative aims.[128] They sought to ensure access to the Courts, to a *fair trial,* so that an innocent black would not be railroaded to death. But to assume that they also meant to save an undoubtedly guilty black murderer from the death penalty because a jury had sentenced a white to life imprisonment is to ignore the racism that ran deep in the North in 1866.[129]

We must be wary of reading our sentiments back into the minds of the framers.[130] Well aware of the anti-Negro sentiments of his Ohio constituency,[131] John Bingham, draftsman of the

127. David Donald wrote, "Disturbed by the revolutionary changes Sumner hoped to bring about in the South, Republican Congressmen were horrified that he proposed to extend them to the North as well." David Donald, *Charles Sumner and the Rights of Man* 299 (1970). For additional citations, see Berger *G/J* 71 n. 6.

128. For these aims see infra Chapter 5, text accompanying note 70–99.

129. For citations see Berger, *G/J,* index "Racism"; and see Raoul Berger, "The Fourteenth Amendment: Light from the Fifteenth," 74 Nw. U. L. Rev. 311, 314–316 (1979). "Negrophobia . . . played a part in Reconstruction incompleteness." H. M. Hyman, *A More Perfect Union* 447 (1973). For further discussion of the equal protection clause, see infra Chapter 5, text accompanying notes 151 et seq., and Appendix A.

130. Eminent British historians caution, "We must learn, not from modern theorists, but from contemporaries of the events we are studying"; we should not impose "upon the past a creature of our own imaginings." H. G. Richardson and G. O. Sayles, "Parliament and Great Councils in Medieval England," 77 L. Q. Rev. 213, 224 (1961). It is a "historical fallacy" to "appraise a former historical era by the criteria of values that have become important since." A. S. Miller and R. F. Howell, "The Myth of Neutrality in Constitutional Adjudication," 27 U. Chi. L. Rev. 661, 673 (1960).

131. Senator John Sherman of Ohio said, "we do not like Negroes. We do not conceal our dislike." Quoted by C. V. Woodward, "Seeds of Failure in Radical Race Policy," in H. M. Hyman, ed., *New Frontiers of the American Reconstruction* 128 (1966). In the election of April 1867, Ohio "overwhelmed a negro suffrage amendment by 40,000." Woodward at 137.

Fourteenth Amendment, defended the omission of Negro suffrage from the new Tennessee Constitution, while expressing re-
gret that "justice for all is not to be secured in a day."[132] It is open
to this generation to give effect to nobler and more generous sentiments, but by Article V that power of amendment is reserved to
the people, not given to the Courts to exercise under the guise of
"interpretation." The anti-discriminationists are not so much
concerned with curing discrimination, which Zeisel, for example,
considers incurable, as with total abolition of the death penalty.[133]
The Court has acknowledged that the people cling to the death
penalty;[134] and were the issue submitted to the people, they would
not, I hazard, abandon the penalty because a black murderer,
found guilty beyond a reasonable doubt after a fair trial, is sentenced to death, whereas from time to time a white murderer is
not. Nothing in the Constitution, in my judgment, authorizes
the Court to abolish the death penalty.

132. *Globe* 3979.
133. For similar statements by Justice Brennan and Marshall, see infra
Chapter 6, text accompanying note 132. Justice Powell pointed out that
the "same discriminatory impact argument could be made with equal force
and logic with respect to those sentenced to prison terms," Furman 447,
for our jails are crammed with black prisoners. He justly observes, "The
root causes of the higher incidence of criminal penalties on 'minorities and
poor' will not be cured by abolishing the system of penalties. Nor, indeed,
could any society have a viable system of criminal justice if sanctions were
abolished or ameliorated because most of those who commit crimes happen
to be underprivileged. The basic problem results not from the penalties
imposed for criminal conduct but from social and economic factors that
have plagued humanity since the beginning of recorded history." Furman
447.
134. See infra Chapter 6, text accompanying notes 60–61.

4

Common Law Terms in the Constitution

AT the root of the Court's transformation of the "cruel and unusual punishments" clause lies the assumption that the Court is empowered to revise the Constitution, discreetly expressed as "adaptation" to changing conditions.[1] Such claims are garbed in jewels of obfuscation; for example, the proscription of cruel and unusual punishments "is not fastened to the obsolete but may *acquire* meaning as public opinion becomes enlightened

1. Myres McDougal and Asher Lans, "Treaties and Congressional-Executive or Presidential Agreements: Interchangeable Instruments of National Policy," 54 Yale L. J. 185, 585 (1945), argued for legitimation of Executive Agreements in place of treaties on the basis of "adaptation by usage," explaining that "the process of amendment is politically difficult, other modes of change have emerged." Id. 293. The emergence is undeniable, but that does not settle the question whether there is any power of amendment outside Article V.

by a humane justice"[2]—a veiled excuse for judicial midwifery. This is like telling a child that babies are brought by the stork.[3] Judicial soundings of public opinion call for the arts of a sooth-sayer and, as will appear, are as little reliable. A similar and oft-cited statement is found in *Hurtado v. California:* "to hold that such a characteristic [that it was immemorially the actual law] is essential to due process of law, would be to deny every quality of the law but its age, and to render it incapable of progress or im-provement."[4] Such rhetoric has the inestimable advantage of making critics appear as foes of progress, prey to a "mechanical, filiopietistic theory," devotees of "artifacts of verbal archeology."[5] But recognition of the need to adapt to change is not equivalent to a grant of power to do so. The only such constitutional grant is that of Article V, which confers power on the people, not the Court.[6] For the moment let it suffice that Chief Justice Marshall,

2. Weems v. United States, 217 U.S. 349, 378 (1910). Compare *Parlia-ment's* repeal of the disembowelment penalty. Supra Chapter 3, note 52. The Weems dictum is cited by Justice Douglas in Furman 242, by Chief Justice Burger, dissenting in Furman 383, and by Justices Stewart, Powell, and Stevens in Gregg v. Georgia, 428 U.S. 153, 171 (1976).

3. Justice Douglas acknowledged that the *Court* "has been reading" the "evolving gloss of civilized standards" into the Bill of Rights. McGautha 241. Apparently oblivious to the self-conferred nature of this practice, Jus-tice Marshall stated: "Perhaps the most important principle in analyzing 'cruel and unusual' punishment questions" is that this language " 'must draw its meaning from the evolving standards of decency that mark the progress of a maturing society.' Thus a penalty that was permissible at one time in our Nation's history is not necessarily permissible today." Furman 329. When what was "permissible" at the adoption of the Constitution furnishes the constitutional standard, who is to substitute a new one—the people by amendment or the Court?

4. 110 U.W. 516, 529 (1884).

5. McDougal and Lans, supra note 1 at 262, 291.

6. In the First Congress, Elbridge Gerry, erstwhile President of the Con-tinental Congress and a leading Framer, said: "The people have" directed a "particular mode of making amendments, which we are not at liberty to depart from . . . Such a power [to alter the Constitution] would render the most important clause of the Constitution nugatory." 1 *Ann. Cong.* 503.

who first recited that the Constitution must "be adapted to the various crises of human affairs,"[7] emphatically disclaimed judicial power "to change that instrument."[8] The Founders resorted to a written Constitution the more clearly to limit delegated power, to create a fixed Constitution;[9] and an important means for the accomplishment of that purpose was their use of common law terms of established and familiar meaning. The significance of the Framers' employment of common law terms has gone unnoticed by the abolitionists, on and off the Court.

The Framers "were born and brought up in the atmosphere of the common law and thought and spoke in its vocabulary." Hence, the Court stated in 1925, "when they came to put their conclusions into the form of fundamental law in a compact draft, they expressed them in terms of the common law, confident that they could be shortly and easily understood."[10] As said in 1797 by a contemporary of the Convention, James Bayard, on behalf of the Managers of the House in the impeachment of Senator William Blount: the common law was "the first source from which all the colonies originally derived the principles of their law, [it] was the only point of resort to which it could be expected that all [the

---

See also Hamilton, supra Chapter 3, text accompanying note 92. For a similar expression in Washington's Farewell Address see 35 George Washington, *Writings,* ed. J. C. Fitzpatrick 228–229 (1940), adding, "let there be no change by usurpation, for though this, in one instance, may be the instrument of good, it is the customary weapon by which free governments are destroyed." See also infra note 56.

In his *Commentaries on the Constitution of the United States* (vol. 1, §426 at 325, 5th ed., 1905), Justice Story wrote that if a constitutional restriction "be mischievous, the power of redressing the evil lies with the people by an exercise of the power of amendment. If they choose not to apply the remedy, it may fairly be presumed the mischief is less than would arise from a further extension of the power, or that it is the least of two evils."

7. McCulloch v. Maryland, 17 U.S. (4 Wheat.) 315, 415 (1819).

8. Gerald Gunther, ed., *John Marshall's Defense of McCulloch v. Maryland* 118 (1969).

9. Infra Chapter 5, text accompanying note 6.

10. Ex parte Grossman, 267 U.S. 87, 109 (1925).

States] would have recourse. We accordingly find many terms which cannot be understood, and many regulations which cannot be executed without the aid of the common law of England."[11]

Many a term was shorthand for a congeries of rights. To express all that was implicated by "trial by jury," for example, would have required prolix detail unsuited to a Constitution. So, when anxious delegates inquired whether they would have the prized right to challenge jurors, they were assured that it was an "attribute" of "trial by jury."[12] Presumably the Framers were aware of the long-settled rule of construction expressed in Bacon's *Abridgment:* "If a Statute make use of a Word the meaning of which is well known at the common law, the Word shall be understood in the same sense it was understood at the Common Law."[13] In the Convention, John Dickinson referred to Blackstone for the definition of ex post facto laws; and James Wilson said felony was "sufficiently defined by common law."[14] Madison noted in the Virginia Ratification Convention that *"Felony* is a word . . . to be found in the British laws."[15] So completely did the Framers assume that the terms they employed would be accompanied by their common

11. Francis Wharton, *State Trials of the United States* 264 (1849). For additional citations, see Raoul Berger, *Impeachment: The Constitutional Problems* 144 n. 101 (1973).

12. 3 Elliot 467–468, 546, 557–559. Justice Bushrod Washington declared, "The right of challenge was a privilege highly esteemed, and anxiously guarded, at the common law . . . the common law rule must be pursued." United States v. Johns, 26 F. Cas. 616, 617 (C. C. D. Pa. 1806) (No. 15, 481).

13. 4 Matthew Bacon, *A New Abridgment of the Law* 647 ("Statute" (1) (4)); (3d ed., 1768). "A lot of American law came out of Bacon's and Viner's Abridgments." Julius Goebel, "Ex Parte Clio," 54 Colum. L. Rev. 450, 455 (1954). Justice Story wrote: "Bacon's Abridgment, Statute I, contains an excellent summary of the rules for construing statutes." 1 Joseph Story, *Commentaries on the Constitution of the United States* 283 (1833). In Gibbons v. Ogden, 22 U.S. (9 Wheat.) 1, 190 (1824), Chief Justice Marshall stated that if a word was understood in a certain sense "when the Constitution was framed . . . the convention must have used it in that sense," and it is that sense "which is to be given judicial effect."

14. 2 Farrand 448, 316.

15. 3 Elliot 531, emphasis in the original.

law meaning that they defined treason narrowly in order to restrict its excessive scope at common law.[16] So too, by the Act of April 30, 1790, the First Congress provided for capital punishment without "benefit of clergy," as did a number of earlier State statutes, in order to insure that the English exculpation would not apply.[17] The common law was the mapped world; to depart therefrom was to venture into the unknown. How better secure the cherished "rights of Englishmen"[18] than by adhering to the terms in which they were enshrined? Consider the almost slavish adherence to common law phraseology exemplified by the Framers' repetition almost word-for-word of the 1689 formula, "That excessive bail ought not to be required, nor excessive fines imposed, nor cruel and unusual punishments inflicted," only substituting "shall" for "ought not to be" required. Consequently, as Justice Story stated in 1820, the common law "definitions are necessarily included, as much *as if they stood in the text* of the Constitution."[19]

Chief Justice Marshall and other early judges repeatedly turned to the common law for the meaning of constitutional terms borrowed therefrom,[20] and a string of Supreme Court decisions followed in their wake. To learn whether a summary proceeding violated due process, the Court decided in 1856, per Justice Curtis, "we must look to those settled usages and modes of proceeding

16. Supra Chapter 3, text accompanying note 85.

17. For citations see Raoul Berger, "Bills of Attainder: A Study of Amendment by the Court," 63 Cornell L. Rev. 355, 362 n. 52 (1978).

18. Alfred Kelly, "Clio and the Court: An Illicit Love Affair," 1965 S. Ct. Rev. 119, 154–155. For example, the First Continental Congress resolved on October 14, 1774, that the "colonies are entitled to the common law of England" and to the privilege of being tried "according to the course of that law." Quoted in Duncan v. Louisiana, 391 U.S. 145, 152 (1968).

19. United States v. Smith, 18 U.S. (5 Wheat.) 153, 160 (1820). Justice Brennan goes down a false trail in saying, "We have very little evidence of the Framers' intent in including the Cruel and Unusual Punishments Clause." Furman 258. The established presumption is that they used the terms because they intended them to have their common law meaning, which required no explanation.

20. For citations see Berger, supra note 17 at 361, 362-363 n. 55.

existing in the common and statute law of England prior to the emigration of our ancestors."[21] Citing Kent's *Commentaries*, the Supreme Court stated in 1904: "In ascertaining the meaning of the phrase taken from the Bill of Rights it must be construed with reference to the common law from which it was taken."[22] Such learning was reiterated by the Court in 1925.[23] These decisions reflect a fundamental purpose: common law terms *served to delimit* delegated power. Schooled in the repeated overthrow of democracies in the past, the Founders feared the greedy expansiveness of power, "its endlessly propulsive tendency to expand itself beyond legitimate boundaries."[24] Since, said Madison, "power

21. Murray's Lessee v. Hoboken Land & Improvement Co. 59 U.S. (18 How.) 272, 276–277 (1855). Justice Douglas flailed a straw man in saying, "none of us ... would conclude that (apart from constitutional specifics) *any* notice, *any* procedure, *any* form of hearings, *any* type of trial prescribed by any legislature would pass muster under procedural due process." McGautha 236 n. For due process secures the pre-Constitution "settled usages and modes of proceeding."

22. Kepner v. United States, 195 U.S. 100, 125 (1904); see also United States v. Wong Kim Ark, 169 U.S. 649, 658 (1898).

23. Supra note 10. In McGrain v. Daugherty, 273 U.S. 135, 161 (1927), the Court looked to the practice of Parliament to hold that the investigatory power was an attribute of the power to legislate. In Schick v. Reed, 419 U.S. 256, 261 (1974), the issue was whether the President, in commuting a death sentence to a life sentence, was authorized to condition the commutation on no parole. The Court stated, "At the time of the drafting and adoption of our Constitution it was considered elementary that the prerogative of the English Crown could be exercised upon condition."

24. Bernard Bailyn, *The Ideological Origins of the American Revolution* 56–57 (1967). Thomas Burke, a delegate from North Carolina to the Continental Congress, wrote to Governor Richard Caswell, March 11, 1777: "Power of all kinds has an irresistible propensity to increase a desire for itself. It gives the passion of ambition a velocity which increases on its progress; & this is a passion which grows in proportion as it is gratified ... [T]he delusive intoxication which power naturally imposes on the human mind ... inevitably lead to an abuse & corruption of power, & is in my humble opinion the proper object of vigilance & jealousy." 6 *Letters of Delegates to Congress, 1774–1789,* P. H. Smith, ed. 427 (1980). The nascent nation did not have to wait for Lord Acton to learn that "power corrupts."

is of an encroaching nature . . . it ought to be effectively restrained from passing the limits assigned to it."[25] In the Virginia Ratification Convention, George Mason stated, "considering the natural lust of power inherent in man, I fear the thirst of power will prevail to oppress the people."[26] Washington adverted in his Farewell Address to the "love of power and proneness to abuse it."[27] Hence the Founders resorted to a written Constitution in order, Chief Justice Marshall explained, that the delegated powers be defined and limited,[28] a fact that he had learned at first hand as a participant in the Virginia Ratification Convention. Justice James Iredell, who led the struggle for adoption of the Constitution in the North Carolina Convention, earlier wrote that the Framers sought "to define with precision the objects of the legislative power, and to restrain it within *marked and settled* boundaries."[29] In Jefferson's graphic phrase, "It is jealousy and not confidence which prescribes limited Constitutions to *bind down* those whom we are obliged to trust with power"; they should be bound "down from mischief by the chains of the Constitution."[30] The means the Founders employed to forge the "chains," to fashion a "fixed and permanent" Constitution, were words, common law terms of established meaning. If the Justices may jettison the meaning those terms had for the Framers in favor of their own contradictory meaning, then are the "chains" of the Constitution converted to ropes of sand.[31]

25. Federalist No. 48 at 321.

26. 3 Elliot 32.

27. 1 James O. Richardson, *Compilation of the Messages and Papers of the Presidents, 1789–1897* 219 (1897).

28. Marbury v. Madison, 5 U.S. (1 Cranch) 137, 176 (1803).

29. Calder v. Bull, 3 U.S. (3 Dall.) 386, 399 (1798).

30. 4 Elliot 543.

31. Willard Hurst wrote, "If the idea of a document of superior authority is to have meaning, terms which have a precise, history-filled content to those who draft and adopt the document must be held to that precise meaning." Hurst, "Discussion on The Process of Constitutional Construction" in Edmond Cahn, ed., *Supreme Court and Supreme Law* 75 (1954).

Constitutions, Justice William Paterson, who had been a leading Framer, explained, were "reduced to written exactitude and
precision . . . The Constitution is certain and *fixed;* it contains the
permanent will of the people . . . and can be revoked or altered only
by the authority that made it,"[32] that is, by amendment under
Article V. The Declaration of Independence bears witness to the
creation of a government by "consent of the governed." In the
Federalist Hamilton repeated that the "fabric of American empire
ought to rest on the solid basis of the Consent of the People."[33]
The conditions of that consent are spelled out in the Constitution. "The people," averred Iredell, "have chosen to be governed
under such and such principles. They have not chosen to be governed or promised to submit upon any other."[34] The Framers
expressed their consent in well-understood common law terms.
Substitution by the Court of its own meaning for that of the
Framers changes the scope of the people's consent, displaces the
Framers' value choices, and violates the basic principle of government by consent of the governed. The subsisting statutory provisions for death penalties in about forty States, overturned by *Furman,* testify that the people are content to be governed by the
original intention of the Framers. As said by Chief Justice Warren, "the provisions of the Constitution" are "the rules of government."[35] By changing the meaning of the words the Court
changes the rules. Chief Justice Taney declared: "If in this Court
we are at liberty to give the old words new meanings when we
find them in the Constitution, there is no power which may not
by this mode of construction, be conferred on the general govern-

32. VanHorne's Lessee v. Dorrance, 2 U.S. (2 Dall.) 303, 308 (C. C. D.
Pa. 1795). See also supra note 6, and infra Chapter 5.
33. Federalist No. 22 at 141.
34. 2 G. J. McRee, *Life and Correspondence of James Iredell* 146
(1857–1858). "As a nation, we are committed to the idea that government,
to be ethically defensible, requires the consent of the governed." Terrance
Sandalow, "Judicial Protection of Minorities," 75 Mich. L. Rev. 1162, 1178
(1977).
35. Trop v. Dulles, 356 U.S. 86, 103 (1958).

ment and *denied to the States.*[36] In this he echoed Madison: if "the sense in which the Constitution was accepted and ratified by the Nation . . . be not the guide in expounding it, there can be no security . . . for a faithful exercise of its powers."[37] Jefferson was of like mind.[38] And it remained the view of the Reconstruction Congress. In January 1872 a unanimous Senate Judiciary Committee Report, signed by Senators who had voted for the Fourteenth Amendment, stated: "A construction which should give the phrase . . . a meaning different from the sense in which it was understood and employed by the people when they adopted the Constitution, would be as unconstitutional as a departure from the plain and express language of the Constitution."[39] No expres- to the contrary in the several Conventions came to my attention, and activists have pointed to none. Instead they customarily rely on Chief Justice Marshall's reference in *McCulloch v. Maryland* to a "constitution intended to endure for ages to come, and consequently to be adapted to the various crises of human affairs."[40] When the decision came under attack, he defended that he was pleading for elasticity in Congress' "choice of *means"* to execute existing powers and denied any "constructive assumption of powers never meant to be granted." Again and again he repudiated any claim for "extension by construction" and flatly disclaimed a judicial "right to change that instrument."[41] It is pre-

36. The Passenger Cases, 48 U.S. (7 How.) 283, 478 (1849). Justice Black repeatedly inveighed against a conception of due process "whereby the supreme constitutional law becomes the Court's view of 'civilization' at a given moment." D. Hutchinson, "Unanimity and Desegregation Decision-making in the Supreme Court, 1948–1958," 68 Geo. L. J. 1, 48 (1979).

37. 9 James Madison, *Writings* 191, ed. G. Hunt (1900–1910).

38. Jefferson pledged as President to administer the Constitution "according to the safe and honest meaning contemplated by the plain understanding of the people at the time of its adoption." 4 Elliot 446. That was likewise Chief Justice Marshall's guide, supra note 13.

39. S. Rep. No. 21, 42d Cong., 2d Sess. 2 (1872), reprinted in Alfred Avins, *The Reconstruction Amendments' Debates* 2, 571–572 (1967).

40. 17 U.S. (4 Wheat.) 316, 407–408 (1819).

41. The details are set forth in Berger *G/J* 373–378.

cisely that power which Douglas and like-minded Justices now claim in veiled rhetoric. No grant of power to do so, as will appear, can be located in the Constitution; and for that reason an ardent admirer of the Court's self-assumed revisory role has rent the veil and maintains that the Justices "are not bound by the Constitution."[42]

When the Court, in *McGautha v. California* (1971), rejected the argument that a jury's untrammeled discretion to pronounce a death sentence was violative of the Constitution, Justice Douglas dissented, saying that "The Court has history on its side—but history alone,"[43] as if that were solely of interest to antiquarians. On the other hand, Justice Horace Gray, one of the most scholarly Justices, considered that "all questions of constitutional construction" are "largely a historical question."[44] For history *records* the Framers' intention to limit the powers delegated, not least to judges;[45] therefore, it may not be offhandedly dismissed. Mark how Douglas treats due process:

> We need not read procedural due process as designed to satisfy man's deep-seated sadistic instincts. We need not in deference to

42. Raoul Berger, "Paul Brest's Brief for an Imperial Judiciary," 40 Md. L. Rev. 1 (1981). Robert Cover likewise thrusts aside "the self-evident meaning of the Constitution" in favor of an "ideology" framed by the Court, because "we" have decided to "entrust" the judges with measuring legislative action by that "ideology." Cover, Book Review, *New Republic,* Jan. 14, 1978, 26, 27. Of where "we" so decided he speaketh not.

43. McGautha 241.

44. Sparf and Hansen v. United States, 156 U.S. 51, 169 (1895), dissenting opinion.

45. Infra Chapter 5, text accompanying notes 6–12. Abolitionist confusion on this score is illustrated by Bedau's explanation that "our interest in the 'original intent of the framers' if it is to be more than an exercise in historical scholarship, must take its dominant cues from the constitutional (structural, fundamental) needs of our society and our ideals and aspirations as they are understood today." Bedau 14. In plain talk, this is a call for judicial revision of the Constitution. Who else is to divine "our aspirations as they are understood today"? The Court itself has confessed that it misread "our aspirations" with respect to capital punishment. Infra Chapter 6, text accompanying notes 60–61.

those sadistic instincts say we are bound by history from defining procedural due process so as to deny men fair trials [by leaving sentencing in jury discretion].[46]

Denunciation of sadism cannot free him from the "chains" of the Framers' intention. Nor can men like Montesquieu, Kant, Locke, Rousseau, Mill, and Sir James Fitzjames Stephen be tarred as "sadists."[47] Douglas never learned from Cardozo that "Not all precepts of conduct precious to the hearts of many of us are immutable principles of justice";[48] he could not separate his "gut

46. McGautha 242. But compare his dissent in Hannah v. Larche, 363 U.S. 420 (1960): "Due process under the prevailing doctrine is what the judges say it is; and it differs from judge to judge, from court to court. This notion of due process makes it a tool of the activists who respond to their own visceral reactions in deciding what is fair, decent, or reasonable." Id. 505. "[O]ne who tries to rationalize the cases on cold logic or reason fails. The answer turns on the personal predilections of the judge . . . This is a serious price to pay for adopting a free-wheeling concept of due process." Id. 506. He also rejected "canons of decency" because judgment would turn on "the idiosyncrasies of the judges," infra Chapter 6, text accompanying note 34. Douglas blew both hot and cold, as the particular result demanded. In a subsequent opinion, Justice White wrote: "It will not do to denigrate these legislative judgments as some form of vestigial savagery . . . for they are solemn judgments, reasonably based, that imposition of the death penalty will save the lives of innocent persons." Roberts v. Louisiana, 428 U.S. 325, 355 (1976), dissenting opinion. Douglas was among those who "arrogantly imply that none but fools or knaves can disagree with them." Sidney Hook, *Philosophy and Public Policy* 14 (1980).

47. Walter Berns, *For Capital Punishment* 21, 22 (1979); see also infra Chapter 8, text accompanying notes 1–4. The retributive "theory has been defended by secular saints like G. E. Moore and Immanuel Kant, whose dispassionate interest in justice cannot reasonably be challenged." Hugo Bedau, *The Death Penalty in America* 148 (1967). See also Jacques Barzun, id. 154. For Locke, Rousseau, Montesquieu, and Mill, see Berns, *For Capital Punishment* 22.

48. Snyder v. Massachusetts, 291 U.S. 97, 122 (1934). "It is a misfortune," Justice Holmes said, "if a judge reads his conscious or unconscious sympathy with one side or another into the law, and forgets that what seems to him to be first principles are believed by half his fellow men to be wrong." O. W. Holmes, *Collected Legal Papers* 295 (1920). In Otis v.

reactions" from constitutional dogma,[49] and he ignored that it is not deference to "sadistic instincts" but due respect for the will of the Founders, for government by consent of the governed, that leads us to inquire what did the words "due process" mean to them. At the adoption of the Constitution they were not deemed to preclude death penalties or jury sentencing discretion; consequently, the latter do not fall afoul of due process.[50]

The "wooden position of the Court," Douglas remarked in *McGautha,* "cannot be reconciled with the *evolving gloss* of civilized standards which this Court . . . *has been reading into* the procedural due process safeguards of the Bill of Rights."[51] What

---

Parker, 187 U.S. 606, 608 (1903), the Court, per Justice Holmes, stated that laws are not void because "based on conceptions of morality with which [the Justices] may disagree."

In Jones v. Mayer Co., 392 U.S. 409, 449 n. 6 (1968), Douglas protested against "allowing the legal mind to draw lines and make distinctions that have no place in the jurisprudence of a nation striving to rejoin the human race," this about the Court's *revision* of the Civil Rights Act of 1866, a fact demonstrated by Charles Fairman in great detail. 6 Charles Fairman, *History of the Supreme Court of the United States* 1207–1259 (1971). Bickel commented, "Few would quite adopt this emotional, not to say anti-intellectual tone." Bickel 97–98. Worse, Douglas' decisions time and again disclose a conviction that he alone had access to the truth. See supra Chapter 1, note 14. Sidney Hook concluded that Douglas was "willing to sacrifice democratic due process for some specific desideratum," and commented that "whoever places greater emphasis upon the product rather than the process . . . upon an all-sanctifying end rather than upon the means of achieving it, is opening the door to anarchy." Hook, *Philosophy and Public Policy* 34–35, 36 (1980).

49. "As history amply proves, the judiciary is prone to misconceive the public good by confounding private notions with constitutional requirements." A.F. of L. v. American Sash & Door Co., 335 U.S. 538, 542 (1949), Frankfurter, J., concurring opinion. Referring to the "hard core," "liberal" wing of the Court, Frankfurter wrote to Judge Learned Hand that "Their common denominator is a self-righteous power-lust." H. N. Hirsch, *The Enigma of Felix Frankfurter* 181 (1981).

50. Supra Chapter 2, text accompanying note 61.

51. McGautha 241.

Douglas disparages as "frozen"[52] the Founders prized as "fixed."[53] He relies on *Hurtado* for the proposition that "this flexibility and capacity for growth and adaptation is the peculiar boast and excellence of the common law."[54] Such "excellence" derived from the fact that Parliament left to the courts, subject to being overruled, the development of the *private* law of contracts, torts, and the like. But the enforcement of a Constitution is in the domain of *public* law, law limiting the powers of all three branches. Here judicial decisions cannot be overruled by the legislature; adaptation of the Constitution emphatically was *not* left to the courts, but reserved to the people themselves; it invades the powers the Tenth Amendment reserves to the States.[55] It cannot, therefore, be justified by the private law practice that knew no judicial reversal of the will of Parliament nor of sovereign States. More than "unfreezing" rhetoric is required to justify a judicial takeover of undelegated power, jealously reserved.

Justice Black, more faithful to the intention of the Framers, rejected the notion that due process is "a phrase with no permanent meaning, but one which is bound to shift from time to time in accordance with judges' predilections and understandings of what is best for the country . . . It is impossible for me to believe that such unconfined power is given to judges in our Constitution that is a written one in order to limit governmental power."[56] It

52. Supra, text accompanying note 46.
53. Infra Chapter 5, text accompanying notes 6–12.
54. McGautha 243.
55. Infra Chapter 5, text accompanying notes 153–157. When a particular ruling displeased him, Douglas denounced it as "such a serious invasion of state sovereignty protected by the Tenth Amendment that it is in my view not consistent with our constitutional federalism." Maryland v. Wirtz, 392 U.S. 183, 201 (1968), dissenting opinion.
56. Duncan v. Louisiana, 391 U.S. 145, 168 (1968), concurring opinion. The Court would do well to ponder on what it said, per Chief Justice Fuller in McPherson v. Blacker, 146 U.S. 1, 36 (1892): "we can perceive no reason for holding that the power confided to the States by the Constitution has ceased to exist because the operation of the system has not fully realized the hopes of those by whom it was created. Still less can we recog-

does not follow that the Constitution is "frozen"; the improvement sought by Douglas & Co. may be sought from the people by way of an amendment giving Congress or the Court power to control death penalties. Against a fancied "freezing" the Tenth Amendment opposes the explicit reservation to the States of undelegated power. Judicial unfreezing aims to deprive the States of sovereignty over matters of local interest reserved to them by that Amendment.[57] The "unfreezing" that today confers a boon on occupants of death row may tomorrow construe away the protection of habeas corpus. The Court itself has taught us that power may be malign as well as benign.[58]

Weems v. United States, the bible of death penalty abolitionists, argued that "Time works changes, brings into existence new conditions and purposes. Therefore a principle to be vital must be of

---

nize the doctrine, that because the Constitution has been found in the march of time sufficiently comprehensive to be applicable to conditions not within the minds of the framers, and not arising in their time, it may, therefore, be wrenched from the subjects expressly embraced within it, and amended by judicial decision without action by the designated organs in the mode by which alone amendments can be made." For amplification of such considerations, see infra Chapter 5.

57. For discussion of the Tenth Amendment, see infra Chapter 5, text accompanying notes 151–156, and supra Chapter 2, text accompanying notes 80–82. Justice Powell rightly maintained that Furman "encroaches upon an area squarely within the historic prerogative of the legislative branch—both state and federal—to protect the citizenry through the designation of penalties for prohibitable conduct." Furman 418. Such considerations are dismissed by Bedau, 36, as "an appeal to an implausibly reactionary notion of legislative experimentation and judicial restraint"!

58. The record, Henry Steele Commager wrote with respect to the pre-1937 Court, reveals "that the Court has effectively intervened, again and again, to defeat Congressional attempts to free the slave, to guarantee civil rights to Negroes, to protect working men, to outlaw child labor, to assist hard-pressed farmers, and to democratize the tax system." Commager, "Judicial Review and Democracy," 19 Va. Q. Rev. 417, 428 (1943). Leonard Levy considered that "millions of Negroes suffered lives of humiliation for five or more decades . . . because the Court betrayed the intent of the Reconstruction Amendments." Levy, ed., *Judicial Review and the Supreme Court* 35 (1967).

wider applications than the mischief that gave it birth."[59] This confuses application of a principle to new facts with the Court's replacement of a constitutional principle by its own. Of course the Fourth Amendment "search and seizure" principle, for example, goes beyond physical searches to comprehend current wiretaps and electronic surveillance. They are analogous to what was prohibited and illustrate the application of a principle to similar facts. Very different is the abolitionist reading of the cruel and unusual punishments clause—that clause did not prohibit death penalties either in England or the colonies. Nor was a ban on disproportionate penalties a part of the common law. Consequently, *Weems* was not giving a "wider application" to an accepted principle but *replacing the principle* with its own opposite.[60]

Consider the *Weems* dictum "Time works changes, brings into existence new conditions and purposes" in light of the Court's journey from pole to pole in the fourteen months that elapsed between *McGautha* and *Furman,* leading Justice Blackmun to observe that the Court was "evidently persuaded that somehow the passage of time has taken *us* to a place of greater maturity and outlook," though there was "nothing that demonstrates a significant movement of any kind in these brief periods."[61] It is changes in the Justices rather than in conditions that generally explain

59. 217 U.S. 349, 372 (1910).

60. For the Court's own emphasis on the distinction, see McPherson v. Blacker, supra note 56. See also Perry, supra Chapter 1, note 29 at 281.

61. Furman 408, dissenting opinion. The grip of the Weems analysis is illustrated by Chief Justice Burger's dissent in Furman, 382: "the Eighth Amendment prohibition cannot fairly be limited to those punishments thought excessively cruel and barbarous at the time of the adoption of the Eighth Amendment. A punishment is inordinately cruel . . . chiefly as perceived by the society so characterizing it. The standard of extreme cruelty is not merely descriptive, but necessarily embodies a moral judgment. The standard itself remains the same, but its applicability must change as the basic mores of society change." A standard that "remains the same" cannot by a shift in rhetoric to "applicability" "change," as is the fact when the standard permitted death penalties and now would not.

seismic shifts in doctrine.[62] One need not be a devotee of stare
decisis to doubt that the latest Bench, like Paul of Tarsus en route
to Damascus, has been given a blinding vision that was denied to
its predecessors,[63] particularly when the latter are firmly rooted in
historical fact. The Justices need ever to bear in mind Justice
Jackson's caution: "We are not final because we are infallible; we
are infallible because we are final."[64]

Weems' verbal legerdemain reflects a persistent judicial trait, illustrated by Justice Douglas' fascinating reference to the "vagaries

62. The triumph of libertarian impulses on the bench, Archibald Cox
wrote, was in part due to "the fate which puts one man upon the Court
rather than another." Cox, *The Role of the Supreme Court in American Government* 35 (1976). When the Four Horsemen were replaced by Justices Black,
Douglas, and Warren, they brought about a constitutional revolution.
Surveying the field in 1975, Bedau wrote, "Since Justice Douglas has been
a visible and unswerving opponent of the death penalty, his participation
. . . is critical. Three years ago, Furman v. Georgia was decided by a five to
four majority. Without the vote of Justice Douglas, Fowler v. North
Carolina could well fail to be decided in a fashion favorable to abolition by
even that slender margin." Bedau 109. Paul Kauper observed that "changes
in interpretation often result from the appointment of a new Justice who
aligns himself with a position previously taken only by a minority of a
closely divided Court. Here the subjective element of constitutional interpretation stands out in bold relief." Kauper, "The Supreme Court: Hybrid
Organ of State," 21 S. W. L. Rev. 573, 581 (1967).

63. Justice Henry Baldwin, who sat on the bench with Chief Justice
Marshall, observed, "There is no more certainty that a last opinion is correct than the first." Livingston's Executrix v. Story, 36 U.S. (11 Pet.) 351,
400 (1837), dissenting opinion. Justice Frankfurter rejected the notion
that the Court may "say that everybody on the Court has been wrong for
150 years and that that which has been deemed part of the bone and sinew
of the law should now be extirpated . . . It is not for the Court to fashion a
wholly novel constitutional doctrine . . . in the teeth of an unbroken and
judicial history from the foundation of the Nation." Green v. United
States, 356 U.S. 165, 192 (1958), concurring opinion. In Federalist No. 78
at 510, Hamilton wrote, "To avoid an arbitrary discretion in the courts, it
is indispensable that they should be bound down by strict rules and precedents."

64. Brown v. Allen, 344 U.S. 443, 540 (1953), concurring opinion.

of due process."[65] "Vagary" is defined as a wild fancy or extravagant notion.[66] Nothing was further from the minds of the Founders than to employ words that would allow "wild fancies."[67] They were acutely conscious that every power conferred on the federal government correspondingly diminished that of the States in which they put their trust.[68] "Vague and uncertain words, more especially Constitutions," Samuel Adams wrote, "are the very instruments of slavery."[69] Chief Justice Taney noted that "Every word appears to have been weighed [by the Founders] with the utmost deliberation, and its force and effect to have been fully understood."[70] Let one example suffice. The impeachment clause came to the floor of the Convention referring only to "Treason & bribery."[71] George Mason observed that "Treason as defined in the constitution will not reach many great and dangerous offenses ... Attempts to subvert the Constitution may not be

65. Supra Chapter 1, text accompanying note 15.

66. *Funk and Wagnall's Desk Standard Dictionary.*

67. For Hamilton, due process had a "precise technical import." Supra Chapter 2, text accompanying note 43.

68. For the Founders' attachment to State sovereignty, see infra Chapter 5, text accompanying notes 61–66.

69. 3 Samuel Adams, *Writings,* ed. H. A. Cushing 262 (1904). Rufus King, one of the Framers, told the Massachusetts Ratification Convention that the Federal Convention desired "to use those expressions that were most easy to be understood and least equivocal in their meaning ... We believe that the powers are clearly defined, the expression as free from ambiguity as the Convention could make them." 3 Farrand 268; see also Caleb Strong, id. at 248. Madison wrote, "it exceeds the possibility of belief, that the known advocates in the Constitution for a jealous grant and certain definition of federal powers, should have silently permitted the introduction of words or phrases in a sense rendering fruitless the restrictions and definitions elaborated by them." 3 Farrand 488.

70. Holmes v. Jennison, 39 U.S. (14 Pet.) 540, 571 (1840). In 1826 Martin van Buren declared in the Senate, "We know with what jealousy— with what watchfulness—with what scrupulous care its minutest provisions were examined, discussed, resisted and supported, by those who opposed, and those who advocated its ratification." 2 Cong. Deb. 418 (1826).

71. 2 Farrand 495.

Treason as above defined—As bills of attainder which have saved
the British Constitution are forbidden, it is the more necessary to
extend the power of impeachment." Mason therefore moved to
add "or maladministration," but Madison objected that "So vague
a term will be equivalent to a tenure during the pleasure of the
Senate." Thereupon Mason proposed "other high crimes & misdemeanors,"[72] the traditional impeachment catch-all which had a
familiar "technical meaning too limited."[73] That such fastidious
draftsmen would employ "due process" because it would give free
rein to judicial fancies is not merely unthinkable but, as will appear, it is contrary to historical fact. When the Founders put due
process into the Fifth Amendment, wrote Charles P. Curtis, "It
had been chiselled into the law so incisively that any lawyer . . .
could read and understand it." Who "made it a large generality,"
he asked, and answered, "Not they [the Framers]. We [the
Court] did."[74]

Justly did Justice Black say that "any broad unlimited power to
hold laws unconstitutional because they offend what this Court
conceives to be the 'conscience of our people' . . . was not given
by the Framers, but rather has been bestowed on the Court by the
Court."[75] Translated into our death penalty context, the Court
has twisted a common law term of settled meaning—"cruel and
unusual punishments" did not bar jury sentencing discretion or
punishments contrary to "human dignity"—[76] into a bar of what
the common law permitted, defying the adherence of the American people to that common law usage for 181 years.

72. Id. 550.
73. Id. 442.
74. Curtis, supra Chapter 2, note 46 at 177.
75. Griswold v. Connecticut, 381 U.S. 479, 520 (1965), dissenting opinion.
76. For discussion of this catch phrase, see infra Chapter 6, text accompanying notes 25–33.

5

The Role of the Court

"WHEN a question arises with respect to the legality of any power," Lee reassured the Virginia Ratifiers, the question will be, *"Is it enumerated in the Constitution?* . . . It is otherwise arbitrary and unconstitutional."[1] Considering the awesome power the Court exercises, it is surprising that the Constitution does not specifically empower the Court

1. 3 Elliot 186; Chief Justice Marshall stated in McCulloch v. Maryland, 17 U.S. (4 Wheat.) 315, 405 (1819), "This government is acknowledged by all, to be one of enumerated powers . . . it can exercise only the powers granted to it." Earlier Justice Chase said the Constitution "is the source of all the jurisdiction of the national government; so that the departments of the government can never assume any power, that is not expressly granted by that instrument." United States v. Worrall, 2 U.S. (2 Dall.) 384, 393 (C. C. D. Pa. 1798).

to set aside legislation by Congress or the States,[2] let alone to revise, change the meaning of, the Constitution itself, that function
being reserved to the people by the Article V process for amendment.[3] All grants of power are to be viewed against the Founders'
pervasive dread of "despotic government";[4] fearful of power, they
resorted to a written Constitution in order to define and limit it.[5]
Their presuppositions are well summarized by Philip Kurland:

> The concept of the written constitution is that it defines the au-
> thority of government and its limits, that government is the
> creature of the Constitution and cannot do what it does not au-
> thorize ... *A priori,* such a constitution could only have a fixed
> and unchanging meaning, if it were to fulfill its function. For
> changed conditions, the instrument itself made provision for
> amendment which, in accordance with the concept of a written
> Constitution, was expected to be the only form of change.[6]

First and last, the "limited" Constitution was meant to "bind
down" our delegates "from mischief by the chains of the Constitution."[7] Even the legislature, darling of the Founders—in contrast to the judiciary which, Hamilton assured the Ratifiers, "was

2. Respected scholars regard the evidence that judicial review was contemplated as inconclusive. Archibald Cox, *The Role of The Supreme Court in
American Government* 16 (1970); Leonard Levy, ed., *Judicial Review and the
Supreme Court* 2 (1967). Bickel observed that Judge Learned Hand was "unwilling to rest on the historical evidence." A. M. Bickel, *The Least Dangerous Branch* 46 (1962). For a comment on the evidence, see Berger *G/J*
335–366.

3. See supra Chapter 4, note 6. So restrained a judge as Justice Harlan
referred to the Court's "exercise of the amending power." Reynolds v.
Sims, 377 U.S. 533, 591 (1964).

4. Henry Adams, *John Randolph* 38, 18 (1882).

5. Supra Chapter 4, text accompanying notes 24–30.

6. Philip Kurland, *Watergate and the Constitution* 7 (1978). Justice William Paterson declared, "The Constitution is certain and fixed ... and can
be revoked or altered only by the authority that made it." Van Horne's
Lessee v. Dorrance, 2 U.S. (2 Dall.) 303, 308 (C. C. D. Pa. 1795).

7. Supra Chapter 4, text accompanying note 30.

next to nothing," and was in fact regarded with "aversion"[8]—could not change it, for, as Madison said, "it would be a novel and dangerous doctrine that a Legislature could change the Constitution under which it held its existence."[9] Very early Chief Justice Marshall, who had been a protagonist of judicial review in the Virginia Ratification Convention, declared that a written Constitution was designed to define and limit power; he asked, "To what purpose are powers limited . . . if these limits may, at any time, be passed by those intended to be restrained," among whom he included the courts,[10] later specifically disclaiming a judicial "right to change the instrument."[11] Even Chief Justice Warren professed to share these views: "We cannot push back the limits of the Constitution. We must apply those limits *as the Constitution prescribes them,*"[12] apparently unaware that at that very moment he was engaged in rewriting those limits to accommodate his own desires.[13]

8. Hamilton in Federalist No. 78 at 504 n. In his 1791 Lectures, Justice James Wilson said that the judicial power, being derived from a "foreign source," and directed to foreign purposes . . . were objects of aversion and distrust . . . But it is high time that we chastise our prejudices." 1 James Wilson, *Works,* ed. R. G. McCloskey 292–293 (1967).

9. 2 Farrand 92, 93. The Massachusetts House wrote to the Earl of Shelburne in 1768, "the constitution is fixed; it is from thence, that the legislative derives its authority; therefore it cannot change the constitution without destroying its own foundation." H. S. Commager, *Documents of American History* 65 (7th ed., 1963).

10. Marbury v. Madison, 5 U.S. (1 Cranch) 137, 176 (1803). The Constitution was to be a "rule for the government of the courts, as well as of the legislature." Id. at 179–180. Shortly after adoption of the Fourteenth Amendment the Supreme Court declared, "The theory of our government . . . is opposed to the deposit of unlimited power anywhere. The executive, the legislative and the judicial branches . . . are all of limited and defined power." Loan Assn. v. Topeka, 87 U.S. (20 Wall.) 655, 663 (1874).

11. Supra Chapter 4, text accompanying note 41.

12. Trop v. Dulles, 356 U.S. 86, 104 (1958).

13. Such self-delusion recalls Justice Holmes's statement: "Judges are apt to be naif, simple-minded men" who need "to learn to transcend [their] own convictions." O. W. Holmes, *Collected Legal Papers* 295 (1920).

Another factor militated against the grant of a roving commission to the courts to right all "wrongs"[14] by giving the Constitution a "new look." This was the Founders' "profound fear of judicial discretion,"[15] given colorful utterance in 1767 by Chief Justice Hutchinson of Massachusetts: "the *Judge* should never be the *Legislator:* Because then the Will of the Judge would be the Law: and this tends to a State of Slavery."[16] It is now fashionable in academe to regard the separation of powers as passé, but Madison stated in the First Congress, "If there is a principle in our Constitution . . . more sacred than another, it is that which separates the legislative, executive and judicial powers."[17] Spelled out in the Massachusetts Constitution of 1780, it required that "the judicial shall never exercise the legislative and executive powers."[18] Law-making, as Chief Justice Hutchinson understood, was for the Legislator; the Judge was to expound, construe the law.[19] In the Convention, Elbridge Gerry stated that "making the

14. Chief Justice Marshall remarked, "The wisdom and the discretion of congress . . . are the restraints on which the people must often rely solely, in all representative governments." Gibbons v. Ogden, 22 U.S. (9 Wheat.) 1, 97 (1824).

15. Gordon Wood, *The Creation of the American Republic, 1776–1787,* at 299, 304 (1969); see also Harry W. Jones, "The Common Law in the United States: English Themes and American Variations," in *Political Separation and Legal Continuity* 103 (1976).

16. Quoted in Morton Horwitz, "The Emergence of an Instrumental Conception of American Law, 1780–1820" in 5 *Perspectives in American History* 287, 303 (1971). Hutchinson echoed Montesquieu, who was to be the oracle of the several constitutional conventions, and who had written that if Judges were to be the Legislators, the "life and liberty of the subject would be exposed to arbitrary control." 1 Charles Montesquieu, *The Spirit of the Laws* bk. 11, ch. 6 at 181 (Philadelphia, 1802).

17. 1 *Ann. Cong.* 581.

18. Article XXX, 1 Poore 960. For the same utterance by Madison, see 1 *Ann. Cong.* 435–436. It "is a breach of the National fundamental law if Congress gives up its legislative power and transfers it . . . to the judicial branch." Buckley v. Valeo, 424 U.S. 1, 121–122 (1976); see infra note 54. The breach is all the greater when the Court takes over legislative power.

19. For numerous citations, see Raoul Berger, *Congress v. The Supreme Court* (1969) index, "Expounding the Law," and 55–56, hereinafter cited as Berger, *Congress v. Court.*

Expositors of the Laws, the Legislators ... ought never to be done."[20] Corwin summed up, "the function of judicial review is almost invariably related by Members of the Convention to the power of judges as 'expositors of the law.' "[21]

Such utterances are underscored by the Framers' categorical rejection of judicial participation in legislative policymaking. It had been proposed to make the Justices members of a Council of Revision that would assist the President in exercising the veto power on the ground that "laws may be dangerous, unwise ... and yet not so unconstitutional as to justify a judge in refusing to give them effect."[22] Mark the distinction, later repeated by Chief Justice Marshall: an unwise law is not necessarily unconstitutional.[23] But Gerry objected, "it was quite foreign from the nature of ye office to make them judges of the policy of public measures."[24] Nathaniel Gorham chimed in that judges "are not presumed to possess a peculiar knowledge of public measures," and Rufus King objected that judges "ought not to be legislators."[25] As Corwin stated, "The first important step in the clarification of the Convention's ideas with reference to the doctrine of judicial review is marked by its rejection of the Council of Revision idea on the basis of the principle ... 'that the power of *making* ought to be kept distinct from that of *expounding* the laws.' "[26] The perva-

20. 2 Farrand 75.

21. Edward Corwin, *The Doctrine of Judicial Review: Its Legal and Historical Bases* 43–44 (1963).

22. 2 Farrand 73.

23. "The peculiar circumstances of the moment may render a measure more or less wise, but cannot render it more or less unconstitutional." Gerald Gunther, ed., *John Marshall's Defense of McCulloch v. Maryland* 190–191 (1969). "The criterion of constitutionality," said Justice Holmes, "is not whether we believe the law to be for the public good." Adkins v. Children's Hospital, 261 U.S. 525, 570 (1923) dissenting opinion.

24. 1 Farrand 97–98.

25. 2 Farrand 73; 1 Farrand 108. For further details, see Berger *G/J* 300–304.

26. Corwin, supra note 21 at 42. In the Chinese Exclusion Case (Chae Chan Ping v. United States), 130 U.S. 581, 603 (1889), a unanimous Court held per Justice Field, "The province of the court is to pass upon the validity of laws, not to make them."

siveness of this view is attested by *Kamper v. Hawkins,* a landmark assertion of the power of judicial review, wherein Judge Henry of the General Court of Virginia declared that

> The judiciary from the nature of the office ... could never be designed to determine upon the equity, necessity or usefulness of a law; that would amount to an express interference with the legislative branch ... Not being chosen immediately by the people, nor being accountable to them ... they do not, and ought not, to represent the people in framing or repealing any law.[27]

A leading activist, Charles Black, confirms that for the colonists "the function of the judge was thus placed in sharpest antithesis to that of the legislator," who alone was concerned "with what the law ought to be."[28]

Michael Perry, who more than most apologists for an activist Court faces up to unpalatable facts,[29] reduces my many-faceted

27. 3 Va. (1 Va. Cas.) 20, 47 (1793). Henry reflected the prevailing view, articulated by Montesquieu: "The national judges are no more than the mouth that pronounces the words of the law, mere passive beings, incapable of moderating either its force or its rigor." Montesquieu, supra note 16 at 188. It was said in Trustees of the University of N. Carolina v. Foy and Bishop, 1 Murphy 58, 88 (N.C. 1805), "for the judiciary are only to expound and enforce the law and have no discretionary powers enabling them to judge of the propriety or impropriety of laws. They are bound, whether agreeable to their ideas of justice or not, to carry into effect the acts of the legislature as far as they ... do not contravene the constitution."

28. Charles Black, *The People and the Court* 160 (1960). Perry 268 quotes William Nelson: "Contemporary commentators were almost unanimous in assuming that it was 'the duty of judges to conserve the law, not to change it ...' They had no power to repeal, to amend, to alter ... or to make new laws [for] in that case they would become legislators ... the role of the Supreme Court under the Constitution would be 'to ascertain its meaning,' not to fit it to new conditions as they arose."

29. To illustrate his view that "the implications of interpretivism are so severe" as to counsel "rejecting the theory," Perry instances my "failure to call for the overruling of Brown [v. Board of Education]," as showing that "even Berger can't bring himself to accept all the implications" of inter-

argument to the Framers' rejection of "a proposal that the judicial branch ... participate in a Council of Revision."[30] This he dismisses because "noninterpretive review"—"the determination of constitutionality by reference to a value judgment other than the one constitutionalized by the Framers"[31]—"need not constitute such an all-purpose veto, and if it does not, if instead its character is more circumscribed, and if further the Framers did not even contemplate noninterpretive review thus circumscribed, of course it cannot be said that the Framers intended the judiciary not to

---

pretivism. Perry, supra Chapter 3, note 87 at 292-294. Such reasoning would legitimate judicial revision because it is a fait accompli and, viewed realistically, irreversible; it would insulate judicial usurpation and obliterate judicial limits in favor of "desirable" consequences—the end justifies the means.

Nor am I one to draw back from logical inferences, be they ever so painful. I had written: "It would ... be ... probably impossible to undo the past ... But to accept thus far accomplished ends is not to condone the continued employment of the unlawful means ... [T]he difficulty of a rollback cannot excuse the *continuation* of such unconstitutional practices." Berger *G/J* 412-413. When a critic pounced on this passage, I replied, "It is not a failure of analysis to acknowledge that eggs cannot be unscrambled." Quoted in Perry 294. Perry comments, "But judicial precedents *can* be unscrambled—overruled." Emphasis in the original. Decisions can be unscrambled, but *events* cannot. Events, like poured concrete, had hardened, so that overruling Brown could not restore the status quo ante; blacks cannot be forced back into a ghetto. "The past," said the Court, "cannot always be unfrozen." Chicot County Drainage Dist. v. Baxter State Bank, 308 U.S. 371, 374 (1940). "Go and sin no more" represents just such recognition, and it counsels against continued application of an unconstitutional doctrine in ever-expanding fashion, such as court-administered schools and prisons, affirmative action, busing, and the like, which even activists deplore. H. J. Abraham, Book Review, 6 Hastings Con. L. Q. 467, 469, 480 (1979); Louis Lusky, Book Review, id. 403, 424.

30. Perry 269. Perry grants that "The historical record Berger examines does in fact establish that the Framers decided against giving the judiciary any part of a certain sort of veto, a negative to be used like the Presidential veto, *on any ground whatsoever.*" Id. Judicial invalidation on extraconstitutional grounds can and does proceed "on any ground whatsoever."

31. Id. 264.

exercise such review."[32] In short, "to say that the Framers did not intend the judiciary to undertake a noninterpretive function is not necessarily to say that the Framers intended the judiciary not to undertake such a function."[33] The short answer might be that of Chief Justice Marshall: the words of the Constitution are not to be "extended to objects *not . . . contemplated* by its framers."[34] What was "not intended" was "not contemplated," and hence was not authorized. Perry recognizes that a claimed authorization of noninterpretive review would "have been a remarkable delegation for politicians to grant to an institution like the Supreme Court, given their commitment to policymaking . . . by those accountable, unlike the Court, to the electorate."[34a] By implication, no such delegation was made; it follows, the power being withheld, that "the Framers intended the judiciary *not* to exercise such review." Otherwise the courts could make that "remarkable

32. Id. 269. Perry's difference with me seems to be merely semantical, for he adds, "By the same token, if the Framers did not contemplate noninterpretive review thus circumscribed—and certainly *they did not contemplate* anything like the noninterpretive review exercised by the modern Supreme Court—*it cannot be said that the Framers intended* that the judiciary exercise such review." The justification for that practice must be sought elsewhere." Perry 269 n. 34. It "must be sought elsewhere" because it is not to be found in the Constitution (see also id. 275), and that is the core of my position, for which the Framers' rejection of judicial participation in the veto furnishes only one item of positive evidence.

In Hammer v. Dagenhart, 247 U.S. 251, 280 (1918), Justice Holmes wrote, the "Court always had disavowed the right to intrude its judgment upon questions of policy or morals." Dissenting opinion in which Brandeis, McKenna, Clarke, JJ., concurred.

33. Perry 269.

34. Ogden v. Saunders, 25 U.S. (12 Wheat.) 213, 332 (1827), dissenting opinion. Justice Douglas opined that "when the Court used substantive due process to determine the wisdom or reasonableness of legislation, it was indeed transforming itself into the Council of Revision which was rejected by the Constitutional Convention." Flast v. Cohen, 392 U.S. 83, 107 (1968). "The courts are without authority to declare such policy. With the wisdom of the policy adopted . . . the courts are both incompetent and unauthorized to deal." Nebbia v. New York, 291 U.S. 502, 537.

34a. Perry 266.

delegation" to themselves. Then too, the burden is on one who claims power to show where it "is enumerated in the Constitution."[35] Perry observes that "the principle of *electorally accountable policymaking* is axiomatic; it is judicial review, not that principle, that requires justification."[36] The corollary, as Perry himself noted, is that there is no need to prove that power was withheld before evidence is introduced to show it was granted, no need to prove the negative before the affirmative is demonstrated.[37]

Perry's distinction between judicial participation in an "all-purpose veto" and a declaration of invalidity under a "circumscribed noninterpretive review" is puzzling. Both extinguish the statute; in the one case it is stillborn, in the other it is declared invalid after enactment. What is "circumscribed" about an invalidation that all but permanently bars the way, whereas a veto may be overridden or overcome by a fresh legislative attempt? If there is no "peculiar" judicial qualification for policymaking before enactment, it is not miraculously conceived when judges sit in judgment on the statute. The Framers' opposition to judicial participation in the veto was based, said Corwin, on the principle that "the power of *making* ought to be kept distinct from that of *expounding* the laws."[38] The sweep of that principle is not limited by the happenstance that it was *applied* to judicial participation in the veto.

The absence of that "remarkable delegation" need not, however, be left to conjecture. It is foreclosed by the historical evidence, in summary, of (1) the Founders' belief in a fixed Constitution of unchanging meaning, alterable only by the people, not the courts; (2) the inferior place of the judiciary in the federal scheme, deriving from the suspicion of the innovative judicial review[39] by judges theretofore regarded with "aversion";[40] (3) the Founders' "profound distrust" of judicial discretion; (4) their at-

35. Supra text accompanying note 1.
36. Perry 262–263.
37. Id. 286 n. 103.
38. Corwin, supra note 21 at 42.
39. For the vigorous reaction to early State court judicial review, see Berger, *Congress v. Court* 38–42.
40. Infra Chapter 6, text accompanying note 98.

tachment to the separation of powers and insistence that courts should not engage in policymaking but act only as interpreters, not makers, of the law. Hamilton, foremost advocate of judicial review, iterated that there "is no liberty, if the power of judging be not separated from the legislative and executive powers."[41] That he did not mean to authorize the judiciary to take over legislative functions is demonstrated by his statement that courts may not "on the pretense of a repugnancy ... substitute their own pleasure to the constitutional intentions of the legislature."[42] Justice James Iredell, himself a powerful proponent of judicial review, put the matter unequivocally: within their constitutional boundaries legislatures are not controllable by the courts.[43] And Hamilton assured the Ratifiers that judges could be impeached for "deliberate usurpations on the authority of the legislature."[44] As these excerpts indicate, the Founders viewed the courts not with awe but with apprehension. The foregoing materials, to my mind, undermine Perry's conclusion that *"no historical materials suggest that any group of Framers ever constitutionalized any theory of the proper scope of judicial review, whether narrow, like interpretivism, or broad."*[45] *Lawmaking*, at any rate, *was* considered outside "the proper scope of judicial review."

What then is the proper role of the Court? It is not wrapped in mystery. Fearful of the greedy expansiveness of power, the Founders sought to confine their delegates to the power conferred. To insure that their delegates would not "overleap" those bounds,[46] the courts were designed to *police* those boundaries.[47] No reference

41. Federalist No. 78 at 504.
42. Id. at 507.
43. Fully quoted infra text accompanying note 48.
44. Federalist No. 81 at 526–527.
45. Perry 300, italics in the original.
46. For the Founders' preoccupation with "overleaping" see Berger, *Congress v. Court* 13–16. Such remarks were addressed to legislative usurpation; judicial review was a debatable and unseasoned innovation.
47. James Wilson said it is necessary that Congress be "kept within prescribed bounds, by the interposition of the judicial department." 2 Elliot 445. The courts, said Oliver Ellsworth, were a "check" if Congress should

to judicial review beyond that policing function is to be found in the records of the several conventions; there is not the slightest intimation that the courts might supersede the legislature's exercise of power *within* its boundaries. Justice Iredell, a Founder whose defense of judicial review anticipated Hamilton, drew the line clearly. Referring to constitutional limitations on legislative power, he declared:

> Beyond these limitations ... their acts are void because they are not warranted by the authority given. But *within* them ... the legislatures only exercise a discretion expressly confided to them by the constitution ... It is a discretion *no more controllable* ... by a court ... than a judicial determination is by them.[48]

Hamilton, it will be recalled, considered that judicial encroachment on the legislative prerogative would be an impeachable offense. Two distinguished jurists, James Bradley Thayer and Judge Learned Hand, shared Iredell's view;[49] the contrary view can avouch no evidence in the historical records. Professor Perry himself sums up: "There is no plausible textual or historical justification for constitutional policymaking by the judiciary—no way to avoid the conclusion that non-interpretive review ... cannot be justified by reference either to the text or to the intention of the Framers of the Constitution." Continuing, he states, "The justification for the practice, if there is one, must be functional: if non-interpretive review serves a crucial governmental function that no other practice realistically can be expected to serve, and if it serves

---

"overleap their limits," "make a law which the Constitution does not authorize." Id. 196. For additional citations, see Berger *G/J* 304–305. Charles Black stressed that it is "a prime postulate that the government [the courts included] is not to travel outside its allocated sphere." C. L. Black, *The People and the Court* 41 (1960).

48. Ware v. Hylton, 3 U.S. (3 Dall.) 199, 266 (1796).

49. Learned Hand, *The Bill of Rights* 66, 31 (1958); J. B. Thayer, "The Origin and Scope of the American Doctrine of Constitutional Law," 7 Harv. L. Rev. 129, 135 (1893).

the function in a manner that somehow accommodates the principle of electorally accountable policymaking, then that function constitutes the justification for noninterpretive review."[50] Simply put, judicial power must be drawn from outside the Constitution on the plea of necessity. Pending Perry's explanation of his accommodation with "electorally accountable policymaking," comment necessarily must be inadequate. Nevertheless, account should be taken of a few threshold obstacles, not least the declaration in *Ex parte Quirin* that "courts possess no power not derived from the Constitution."[51] Confessedly, as we have seen, noninterpretive review cannot draw on the text and the original understanding of the Constitution.

Who but the Court would decide in a given situation that it must perform this "useful governmental function," thereby conferring power on itself?[52] Thus the theory posits that the Court can enlarge its own powers, contrary to Hamilton's assurance that "An agent cannot new model his own commission."[53] If, for example, the Court were to create "entitlements" for the impoverished because the legislature cannot, or refuses, to do so, it would obliterate the line drawn by the separation of powers—"the judiciary shall never exercise the legislative power."[54] And in the case

---

50. Perry 275. Perry's "function" theory recalls the "interpolation" theory of Judge Learned Hand. Hand was "unwilling to rest on the historical evidence" for judicial review and preferred to "interpolate" a power of judicial review in order to "keep the States, Congress and the President within their prescribed powers," a "practical condition upon [the] successful operation" of the Constitution. Berger, supra note 46 at 219. But where Hand sought to preserve the separation of powers Perry would obliterate it.

51. 317 U.S. 1, 25 (1942).

52. Lord Chief Justice Denman cautioned, "The practice of a ruling power in the State is but a feeble proof of its legality." Stockdale v. Hansard, 112 E. R. 1112, 1171 (Q. B. 1839).

53. "Letters of Camillus," 6 Alexander Hamilton, *Works,* ed. H. C. Lodge 166 (1904).

54. If a constitutional power of the legislature may not be "abdicated," United States v. Morton Salt Co., 338 U.S. 632, 647 (1950), still less can it be taken over by the Court. Charles Pinckney, one of the Framers, said in

of State legislation it would breach the federalism basic to our constitutional system. The fact that such an additional power might be advantageous cannot justify the judicial amendment;[55] that power is exclusively reserved to the people by Article V. Madison stated: "Had the power of making treaties, for example, been omitted, however necessary it might have been, the defect could only have been lamented, or supplied by an amendment to the Constitution."[56] The Court was not designed to be a "Mr. Fixit."[57] It remains to be said that there are judicial acknowledgments that policymaking is for the legislature, not the Court,[58] but generally in dissent from the other Justices' embodiment of *their* predilections, conveniently forgotten when the Justices' own goals are at issue.[59]

the House of Representatives in 1798 that their object was "that the powers of the Government should be distributed among the different departments, and that they ought not to be assigned or relinquished." 3 Farrand 376. "The judicial power . . . can no more be shared with the Executive Branch than . . . Congress [can] share with the judiciary the power to override a Presidential veto." United States v. Nixon, 418 U.S. 683, 704 (1974). See supra note 18.

55. Washington's caution needs to be remembered: "let there be no change by usurpation; for though this, in one instance, may be an instrument of good, it is the customary weapon by which free governments are destroyed." 35 George Washington, *Writings,* ed. J. C. Fitzpatrick 228–229 (1940). Addressing the substitution "of the individual sense of justice," Cardozo wrote, "That might result in a benevolent despotism if the judges were benevolent men. It would put an end to the reign of law." Benjamin Cardozo, *The Nature of the Judicial Process* 136 (1921).

56. 2 Annals of Congress 1900–1901 (February 2, 1791). United States v. Worrall, 2 U.S. (2 Dall.) 384, 395 (C. C. D. Pa., 1798), per Justice Chase: "judges cannot remedy political imperfections, nor supply any legislative omission."

57. Chief Justice Marshall declared, "The Constitution . . . was not intended to furnish the corrective for every abuse of power which may be committed by the state governments." Providence Bank v. Billings, 29 U.S. (4 Pet.) 514, 563 (1830).

58. Infra text accompanying notes 125–131, and Chapter 6, text accompanying notes 48–54.

59. "The responsibility of this Court, however, is to construe and enforce the Constitution and laws of the land as they are and not to legislate

When the Court's assumption of visitorial power over *State* legislatures is in question, as is the case with death penalties, there is
still other controverting evidence. The State, successor to the Col-
ony, was trusted, the federal newcomer was not;[60] there was a
deep-rooted devotion to local autonomy. Hamilton adverted to
the "strong and uniform attachment" exhibited by members of
the Continental Congress "to the interests of their own States,"
which "have too often been preferred to the welfare of the
Union."[61] Midway in the Convention, Washington wrote: "independent sovereignty is so ardently contended for . . . the local
views of each State . . . will not yield to a more enlarged view of
politicks."[62] James Wilson grasped the "dread that the boasted
state sovereignties will, under this system, be disrobed of part of
their power."[63] Hamilton assured the Ratifiers in the New York
Convention that the States "will ever" have "ascendancy over the
national government."[64] The State jealousy that surfaced in the
debate over *express* grants is utterly incompatible with unlimited
Supreme Court hegemony under color of values drawn from outside the Constitution. It was to "State governments," Oliver Ellsworth said in the Convention, that "he turned his eyes . . . for the
preservation of his interests,"[65] and this was strikingly confirmed

---

social policy on the basis of our personal inclinations." Evans v. Abney, 396
U.S. 435, 447 (1970). Consider Justice Douglas' statement in Griswold v.
Connecticut, 381 U.S. 479, 482 (1965), the contraceptive case: "We do not
sit as a super-legislature to determine the wisdom, need, and propriety of
laws that touch . . . social conditions. This law, however, operated immediately on an intimate relation of husband and wife." Where does he derive
authority to sit as a "super-legislature" in cases involving the "intimate relation of husband and wife?"

60. See Berger, *Congress v. Court* 31–33 (1969).
61. 2 Elliot 266.
62. 3 Farrand 51. George Read said, "Too much attachment is betrayed
to the State Governments." 1 Farrand 136.
63. 2 Elliot 443.
64. 2 Elliot 239.
65. 1 Farrand 492.

by the First Congress' grant to State courts of exclusive jurisdiction of "cases arising under this Constitution."

Because many, like William Grayson of Virginia, felt that "State courts were the principal defense of the states," their "only defensive armor,"[66] the stubborn insistence on State court arbitrament persisted and was expressed in the Judiciary Act of 1789. "Arising under" jurisdiction was first conferred by Congress on the inferior federal courts by the Civil Rights Act of 1866 and extended in the next decade because the Reconstruction Congresses distrusted Southern readiness to do justice to the freedmen.[67] The appellate jurisdiction of the Supreme Court was portrayed by Iredell in modest colors, as a way "of securing the administration of justice *uniformly* in the several States. There might be otherwise, as many different adjudications on the same subject as there are States."[68] The point was earlier made by Hamilton: "Thirteen independent courts of final jurisdiction over the same causes, arising under the same laws, is a hydra in government, from which nothing but contradiction and confusion can proceed."[69] The fact that it was thought necessary to justify the role of the Court in such limited terms showed that it never was envisioned as an engine that could reshape State laws by resorting to values drawn outside the Constitution. Had the Founders sniffed such possible judicial hegemony, it would have wrecked adoption of the Constitution; hence Hamilton's reassurances that the "judiciary is next to nothing," that judges would be impeached for "deliberate usurpation on the authority of the legislature."

It is time to consider the impact of the Fourteenth Amendment. Like their 1789 forebears, the framers of 1866 were devoted to State sovereignty.[70] The Fourteenth Amendment represents a

66. 3 Elliot 563; see Berger, supra note 60 at 263.
67. Berger *G/J* 224–225.
68. 4 Elliot 147.
69. Federalist No. 80 at 516; and see id. No. 22 at 139.
70. For State sovereignty; (1) 1787, supra text accompanying notes 60–67; (2) 1866, supra Chapter 2, text accompanying notes 72–73. See also Berger *G/J* 60–64.

limited departure from the principle for the purpose of thwarting efforts of the recalcitrant South to return the freed slaves to serfdom. To protect them against "damnable violence," "fiendish oppression," the framers, quoting Chancellor Kent's paraphrase of Blackstone, sought to assure blacks "absolute rights ... the right to personal security, the right of personal liberty, and the right to enjoy and acquire property."[71] William Lawrence emphasized, "It is a mockery to say that a citizen may have a right to live, and yet to deny him the right to make a contract to secure the privileges and rewards of labor."[72] Accordingly, the Civil Rights Act of 1866 prohibited racial discrimination with respect of the right to own property, to contract, to have access to the courts, and to have the "equal benefit of all laws and proceedings for the *security of person and property,"*[73] said by Lawrence to be the "necessary incidents of these absolute rights."[74] Justice Bradley summed up in the *Civil Rights Cases* that the 1866 Act sought to secure

> Those fundamental rights which are the essence of civil freedom, namely the same right to make and enforce contracts, to sue ... to inherit, purchase ... property, as is enjoyed by white citizens. [C]ongress did not assume ... to adjust what may be called the social rights of men ... but *only* to declare and vindicate these fundamental rights.[75]

71. Berger *G/J* 25–27, 21. Referring to the "malignant" Black Codes, Burton C. Cook of Illinois said, "Vagrant laws have been passed; laws which, under the pretense of selling men as vagrants, are calculated and intended to reduce them to slavery again; laws which provide for selling these men into slavery in punishment of crimes of the slightest magnitude." *Congressional Globe* at 1123. In the 39th Congress, Senator William M. Stewart explained, "This section [§1] is simply to remove the disabilities existing by laws tending to reduce the negro to a system of peonage. It strikes at that, nothing else ... That is the whole scope of the law." *Congressional Globe* 1785.

72. *Globe* 1833.

73. Quoted more fully in Berger *G/J* 24.

74. *Globe* 1833.

75. 109 U.S. 3, 22 (1883). Explaining the Civil Rights Act, Samuel Shellabarger of Ohio said, "whatever rights *as to each of these enumerated* civil (not political) matters the State may confer upon one race ... shall be

The Act and §1 of the Amendment were deemed by the framers to be "identical,"[76] the purpose of the latter being to remove doubts as to the constitutionality of the Act and to protect it from repeal. From this there was no dissent in the debates.

The evidence that the enumerated rights of the Civil Rights Act were picked up by the *"privileges or immunities"* clause is too copious for adequate summary. Initially those enumerated rights had been preceded by the general terms "civil rights and immunities," but these were deleted to "obviate" a construction going beyond the specific enumerated rights.[77] The words were drawn

---

held by all races in equality." *Globe* 1293. Alexander Bickel concluded that "the Senate Moderates, led by Trumbull and Fessenden, who espoused this [civil rights] formula, assigned a limited and well-defined meaning to it," namely, "the right to contract" and the like, "also a right to equal protection in the literal sense of benefitting equally from the laws *for the security of person and property.*" Bickel, "The Original Understanding and the Segregation Decision," 69 Harv. L. Rev. 1, 56 (1955). James Wilson, said Bickel, "presented the Civil Rights Bill to the House as a measure of limited and definite objectives. In this he followed the lead of the majority in the Senate . . . And the line he laid down was followed by others who spoke for the bill in the House." Id. 17.

76. As Charles Fairman observed, "over and over again in this debate [on the Amendment] the correspondence between Section One of the Amendment and the Civil Rights Act is noted. The provisions of the one are treated as though they were essentially identical with those of the other." Fairman, "Does the Fourteenth Amendment Incorporate the Bill of Rights?" 2 Stan. L. Rev. 5, 44 (1949). For confirmatory citations, see Berger *G/J* 22–23. I found no contradictory remarks. Harry Flack, a devotee of a broad construction of the Amendment, wrote, "nearly all said it was but an incorporation of the Civil Rights Bill . . . there was no controversy as to its meaning." Flack, *The Adoption of the Fourteenth Amendment* 81 (1908).

77. This was the explanation made by James Wilson, Chairman of the House Judiciary Committee. *Globe* 1361.

This history was encapsulated by Justice Stewart in Georgia v. Rachel, 384 U.S. 780, 791 (1966): "The legislative history of the 1866 Act clearly indicates that Congress intended to protect a limited category of rights . . . The Senate bill did contain a general provision forbidding "discrimination in the civil rights or immunities" preceding the specific enumeration of rights . . . Objections were raised in the legislative debates to the breadth of

from the "privileges and immunities" of Article IV—themselves taken over from the Article IV "privileges and immunities" of the Articles of Confederation—which gave out-of-state migrants the right to own realty and similar rights of "trade and commerce," and were so construed by a couple of early State cases.[78] Thus, by 1866 "privileges and immunities" were words of art,[79] and Article IV was frequently cited by the framers.[80] Justice Bradley declared in 1870, "the civil rights bill was enacted at the same session, and but shortly after the presentation of the Fourteenth Amendment and . . . [it] was in pari materia . . . the first section of the bill

---

the rights of social equality that might be encompassed by a prohibition so general . . . An amendment was accepted [in the House] striking the phrase from the bill."

78. Raoul Berger, "Incorporation of the Bill of Rights in the Fourteenth Amendment: A Nine-Lived Cat," 42 Ohio State. L. J. 435, 439 (1981). "Trade and commerce" appeared in the antecedent Article IV of the Articles of Confederation, and the successor Article IV was so construed by Campbell v. Morris, 3 H. & McH. 535 (Md. 1797), as well as by Abbot v. Bayley, 6 Pick. 89 (Mass. 1827). Article IV threw around privileges and immunities "no security for the citizen of the State in which they were claimed or exercised. Nor did it profess to control the power of the state governments over their own citizens. Its sole purpose was to prevent discrimination against out of state citizens with respect to rights granted to its own citizens. Slaughter-House Cases, 16 Wall. 36, 77," Blake v. McClung, 172 U.S. 239, 252 (1898). Senator Lyman Trumbull, chairman of the Senate Judiciary Committee, purposed to extend this protection to the State's *resident* Negroes. Berger *G/J* 41.

79. Justice Harlan stated: "We should not assume that Congress . . . used the words 'advocate' and 'teach' in their ordinary dictionary meaning when they had already been construed as words of art carrying a special and limited connotation." Yates v. United States, 354 U.S. 298, 319 (1957). Chief Justice White declared in United States v. Wheeler, 254 U.S. 281, 294 (1920): "the Constitution plainly intended to preserve and enforce the limitation as to discrimination imposed by Article IV of the Articles of Confederation . . . the text of Article IV, §2 of the Constitution makes manifest that it was drawn with reference to the corresponding clause of the Articles of Confederation and was intended to perpetuate its limitations."

80. Berger *G/J* 29, 30, 38–39, 41.

covers the same ground as the Fourteenth Amendment."[81] Speaking for the four dissenters in the *Slaughter-House Cases,* Justice Field asked, "What then are the privileges and immunities which are secured against abridgment by the States?" and answered, "In the first section of the Civil Rights Act Congress has given its interpretation of these terms ... the right 'to make and enforce contracts [etc]'."[82] Although the majority of the Court took an even narrower view of the "privileges or immunities" clause, it found that it went no further than the antecedent clause of Article IV.[83] These contemporaneous constructions, faithful to the legislative history, carry greater weight than recent rationalizations of the Justices' predilections.

In addition to proof of what the framers meant to provide there is unmistakable evidence of what they meant to *exclude,* for example, suffrage, the right, Senator Charles Sumner maintained, without which all others were empty.[84] Because the Court's "one person, one vote" doctrine so plainly overturns that exclusion and strikingly exemplifies the Court's willful revision of the Constitution, I may be indulged for setting out a few confirmatory facts. Justice Brennan, himself a perfervid activist, observed that "17 or 19" Northern States had rejected black suffrage between 1865 and 1868.[85] Consequently, Roscoe Conkling stated it would be "futile to ask three-quarters of the States to do ... the very thing most of them have already refused to do."[86] Another member of the Joint Committee, Senator Jacob Howard, made a similar statement.[87]

81. Live-Stock Dealers' & Butchers' Ass'n. v. Crescent City Live-Stock Landing & Slaughter-House Co., 15 F. Cas. 649, 655 (C. C. D. La. 1870) (No. 8,408). Where terms have been given a meaning in a prior act that is in pari materia, that meaning will be given to the terms in a later act. Reiche v. Smythe, 80 U.S. (13 Wall.) 162, 165 (1871).

82. 83 U.S. (16 Wall.) 36, 96 (1872).

83. Id. at 75.

84. *Congressional Globe* 1008 (40th Cong., 3d Sess.) (1869).

85. Oregon v. Mitchell, 400 U.S. 112, 256 (1970), dissenting in part.

86. *Globe* 358.

87. Id. 2766: "three-fourths of the States of this Union could not be induced to vote to grant the right of suffrage."

The chairman of the Committee, Senator William Fessenden, said of a suffrage proposal that "there is not the slightest probability that it will be adopted by the States."[88] The unanimous Report of the Joint Committee doubted that "the States would consent to surrender a power they had exercised, and to which they were attached," and therefore thought it best to "leave the whole question with the people of each State."[89] That such was the vastly preponderant opinion is confirmed by a remarkable fact. During the pendency of ratification, radical opposition to the readmission of Tennessee because its constitution excluded Negro suffrage was voted down in the House 125 to 12. Senator Sumner's parallel proposal was rejected 34 to 4.[90] Hence the Fifteenth Amendment was later adopted, as its framers stated, to fill the gap left by the failure of the Fourteenth to provide for Negro suffrage.[91] Summing up, former Solicitor General Robert Bork stated: "The principle of one man, one vote ... runs counter to the text of the fourteenth amendment, the history surrounding its adoption and ratification and the political practice of Americans from Colonial times up to the day the Court invented the new formula."[92] Chief

88. Id. 704.

89. Report of the Joint Committee on Reconstruction xiii (39th Cong., 1st Sess.; 1866), quoted more fully in Berger *G/J* 84, and reprinted in Alfred Avins, *The Reconstruction Amendments' Debates* 94 (1967). For additional citations see Berger *G/J* 58–60.

90. For details, see Berger *G/J* 56, 59–60, 79.

91. For citations, see Raoul Berger, "The Fourteenth Amendment: Light From the Fifteenth," 74 Nw. U. L. Rev. 311, 321–323 (1979).

92. R. J. Bork, "Neutral Principles and Some First Amendment Problems," 47 Ind. L. J. 1, 18 (1971). "The ultimate justification for the *Reynolds* ruling is hard if not impossible to set forth in constitutionally legitimate terms. It rests, rather, on the view that the courts are authorized to step in when injustices exist and other institutions fail to act. This is a dangerous—and I think illegitimate—prescription for judicial action." Gerald Gunther, "Some Reflections on the Judicial Role: Distinctions, Roots and Prospects," 1979 Wash. U. L. Q. 817, 825.

Justice Harlan truly affirmed that this doctrine flew "in the face of irrefutable and still unanswered history to the contrary." Griswold v. Connecticut, 381 U.S. 479, 501 (1965), concurring. Activist Louis Lusky wrote that

Justice Warren's flourish—"legislators represent people, not trees"[93]—merely illustrates his inveterate substitution of rhetoric for historical fact.

Although Professor Perry differs with my view that the Court cannot derive power outside the Constitution, he concurs that by "privileges or immunities" the framers "meant only to protect against state action discriminating on the basis of race, a narrow category of 'fundamental' rights: those pertaining to the physical security of one's person, freedom of movement, and capacity to make contracts (including contracts to work), and to acquire, hold or transfer chattels and land—life, liberty, and property in the original sense."[94] A Reconstruction historian who helped the NAACP chart the course of the desegregation case, Alfred Kelly, conceded a decade later that "the commitment to traditional state-federal relations [State sovereignty] meant that the radical Negro reform program *could be only a very limited one."*[95] Professor Ely, however, regards the "privileges or immunities" clause as "quite inscrutable."[96] By the Supreme Court's test the terms had become "words of art"[97] and were so understood by the framers. History rebuts Ely's conclusion that the clause "was a delegation

---

Harlan's demonstration is "irrefutable and unrefuted." Louis Lusky, Book Review 6 Hastings Con. L. Q. 403, 406 (1979). See also Nathaniel Nathanson, Book Review, 56 Tex. L. Rev. 579, 581 (1978); Henry J. Abraham, Book Review, 6 Hastings Con. L. Q. 467–468 (1979); Wallace Mendelson, Book Review, id. 437, 453.

93. Reynolds v. Sims, 377 U.S. 353, 362 (1964). Bickel remarked, "the Court is not the place for the heedless break with the past . . . or for action supported by nothing but rhetoric, sentiment, anger or prejudice." Bickel 87.

94. Perry 273.

95. Kelly, "Comment on Harold M. Hyman's Paper," in H. M. Hyman, ed., *New Frontiers of the American Reconstruction* 40 (1966). Eric Foner referred to the blacks' speedy discovery of "the limits of the Northern commitment to black rights." *New York Times,* Nov. 1, 1981, Book Rev. Sec. 7, 20.

96. J. H. Ely, *Democracy and Distrust* 98 (1981).

97. Supra note 79.

to future constitutional decision-makers [the judiciary] to protect certain rights that the [Constitution] neither lists, or at least not exhaustively, nor even in any specific way gives directions for finding." So wide-open an "invitation"[98] would render meaningless the framers' interminable debate about what rights to confer,

98. Supra note 96 at 28. Ely considers that the framers of the Fourteenth Amendment issued an "open and across-the-board invitation to import into the constitutional decision process considerations that will not be found in the amendment nor even . . . elsewhere in the Constitution." J. H. Ely, "Constitutional Interpretivism: Its Allure and Impossibility" 53 Ind. L. J. 399, 415 (1978). This is a variant of Bickel's "open-ended" theory, advanced as a tentative hypothesis. Bickel recognized that the 39th Congress would not go beyond the Civil Rights Act, that the Republicans drew back from a "formulation dangerously vulnerable to attacks pandering to the *prejudice of the people,"* and speculated that the framers employed language that would permit "future advances." Bickel, supra note 75 at 60–61. In short, the framers concealed the future objectives they dared not reveal lest the whole enterprise be imperiled. For such speculation there is no evidence whatever. In fact, the framers shared the prejudices of their constituents. For citations, see Berger *G/J* 13, 105, and Berger, supra note 91 at 312–313. Henry P. Monaghan, "Professor Jones and the Constitution," 4 Vt. L. Rev. 87, 91 (1979): "no satisfactory evidence exists to show that the judicial development of a *lex non scripta* reflects the purpose of either the draftsmen or ratifiers of the eighteenth century Constitution or of the Civil War Amendments."

John Burleigh considers that the open-endedness "rhetoric is, of course, sand in the eyes." Burleigh, "The Supreme Court vs. the Constitution," in *The Public Interest* (Winter 1977) 151, 152. Perry wrote that Berger "devastated the notion that the framers of the fourteenth amendment . . . intended it to be 'open-ended.' " Michael Perry, Book Review, 78 Colum. L. Rev. 685, 695 (1978). Upon subsequent reexamination, he observed, "It should give the theorists of the open-ended Constitution pause, moreover, that not even the most activist courts have ever grounded their claims for legitimacy in arguments along these lines." Perry 274 n. 52. Bickel himself later wrote, "The Framers of the Fourteenth Amendment explicitly rejected the option of an open-ended grant of power to Congress to meddle with conditions within the States, so as to render them equal in accordance with Congress' own notions. Rather, federal power, legislative as well as judicial, was to be limited by the terms of the Amendment." Bickel 48. "Open-ended" terms would relieve of all limits. For rejection of such notions by Madison, see supra Chapter 4, note 69.

culminating in the few rights enumerated in the "identical" Civil Rights Act.[99] A limited purpose is not expanded by "inscrutable" words. Given that the framers distrusted the courts and specifically confided enforcement by §5 to Congress, not the courts, the notion that the framers gave a blank check to the judiciary is fantastic.

"Due process of law" is exempted from inscrutability by Ely. He repudiates the Court's fabrication of substantive due process, as the Court itself has done,[100] considers that it is procedural and contains no "invitation to substantive oversight."[101] History, we have seen, forecloses a contrary view. Charles P. Curtis considered that the procedural meaning of due process had been "chiselled" into the common law,[102] as Hamilton made plain on the eve of the Convention.[103] Nothing daunted by the history of due process, Justice Douglas referred to the "vagaries of due process."[104]

Not less remarkable is Justice Frankfurter's passage from distrust of the clause to embracing it as a vehicle of judicial freewheeling. Douglas and Frankfurter, commonly regarded as at opposite ends of the judicial spectrum, shared the irresistible impulse to manipulate constitutional terms of fixed meaning in the service of *their* predilections, an impulse likewise exemplified by the Court's death penalty decisions. Let Frankfurter speak. During Franklin Roosevelt's Court-Packing Plan, Frankfurter, then a professor, wrote: "The central fact . . . is that a few blind men impervious to rational, disinterested argument have written their narrow prejudices into the Fundamental Law of the land—for 30 years."[105] He had been "in favor of repealing the due process clause of the Fourteenth Amendment because of its use in invali-

99. See Madison, supra Chapter 4, note 69.

100. See infra text accompanying notes 125–126.

101. Ely, supra note 96 at 18, 15–18.

102. Supra Chapter 4, text accompanying note 74.

103. Supra Chapter 2, text accompanying note 43.

104. Supra Chapter 1, text accompanying note 15; Chapter 4, text accompanying notes 65–70.

105. H. N. Hirsch, *The Enigma of Felix Frankfurter* 122 (1981).

dating progressive social legislation."[106] In 1925 he wrote that the contents of the clause "are derived from the disposition of the Justices,"[107] elaborating in 1926: "through its steady expansion of the meaningless meaning of the 'due process' clause of the Fourteenth Amendment, the Supreme Court is putting constitutional compulsion behind the private judgment of its members upon disputed and difficult questions of social policy."[108] Complementing this may be posed his statement as Justice Frankfurter that "a term gains technical content" by "the deposit of history"; "[n]o changes or chances can alter the content of the verbal symbol of 'jury.' "[109] By the same token, "due process" and "cruel and unusual punishments" were employed by the Framers because they had a fixed, known meaning and were therefore unalterable. In the case of "due process," "the deposit of history" had crystallized in Hamilton's sharply etched 1787 statement, "incisively chiselled into the law."

Notwithstanding, as Justice, Frankfurter invoked "the consensus of society's opinion which, for purposes of due process, is the standard enjoined by the Constitution,"[110] invoking a "judgment that reflects deep, even inarticulate, feelings of our society."[111] Further, a judge should "have antennae registering feeling and judgment beyond logical, let alone quantitative proof,"[112]

106. Id. 135n.

107. Bickel 25.

108. Quoted in Philip B. Kurland, *Politics, the Constitution and the Warren Court* xiv (1970).

109. Rochin v. California, 342 U.S. 165, 169–170 (1952).

110. Louisiana ex rel. Francis v. Resweber, 329 U.S. 459, 471 (1947), concurring opinion.

111. Haley v. Ohio, 332 U.S. 596, 603 (1948), concurring opinion.

112. Felix Frankfurter, *Of Law and Men,* ed. Philip Elman 39 (1956). Experience has shown, wrote Lusky, "that the Justices are not endowed with divine insight into the needs of a society." Louis Lusky, *By What Right* 107 (1975). Ely observes, "Lenin used to claim this god-like gift of divination of the people's 'real' interests." J. H. Ely, "Foreword: On Discovering Fundamental Values," 92 Harv. L. Rev. 5, 51 n. 198 (1978). Justice Frankfurter wrote, "As history amply proves, the judiciary is prone to

resembling not a little the forked stick that a dowser uses for the discovery of water. Yet he stated in *Dennis v. United States,* "Courts are not representative bodies. They are not designed to be a good reflex of a democratic society."[113] Nevertheless, he embraced "the inescapable judicial task in giving substantive content, legally enforced, to the Due Process Clause, and it is a task ultimately committed to this Court."[114] This "inescapable" task of substituting the Court's own "content" for the unalterable "deposit of history" was "committed," Justice Black observed, to the Court by the Court.[115]

Frankfurter had more than a little capacity for self-delusion. In the desegregation case he had asked, "What justifies us in saying that what was equal in 1868 is not equal now?"[116] and formulated his own answer in a file memorandum, presumably meant to justify him in the eyes of posterity:

> the equality of laws enshrined in a constitution which was "made for an undefined and expanding future" . . . is not a fixed formula defined with finality at a particular time. It does not reflect, as a congealed summary, the social arrangements and beliefs of a particular epoch . . . The effect of changes in men's feel-

---

misconceive the public good by confounding private notions with constitutional requirements." A.F. of L. v. American Sash & Door Co., 335 U.S. 538, 556 (1949), concurring opinion.

113. Dennis v. United States, 341 U.S. 494, 517 (1951), concurring opinion.

114. Sweezy v. New Hampshire, 354 U.S. 234, 267 (1957), concurring opinion.

115. Supra Chapter 4, text accompanying note 75. "There are times," said Justice Frankfurter, "when I sit in this chair and wonder whether that isn't too great a power to give to any nine men, no matter how wise, how well disciplined, how disinterested. It covers the whole gamut of political, social, and economic activities." Felix Frankfurter, *Of Law and Life and Other Things that Matter* 129 (1965). If he ever sought to locate in the history of the Constitution where this power was "given" it has escaped my attention.

116. Richard Kluger, *Simple Justice* 601 (1976).

ing for what is right and just is equally relevant in determining whether a discrimination denied the equal protection of the laws.[117]

He was closer to the mark when he later declared, "Legal doctrines . . . derive meaning and content from the *circumstances that gave rise to them,* and from the purposes they were designed to serve. To these they are *bound* as a live tree to its roots."[118] The framers were well aware that Article V provided the means to avoid "congealment," as before long was evidenced by adoption of the Fifteenth Amendment to fill the black suffrage gap in the Fourteenth. The real issue, therefore, was not whether the Constitution must be "congealed," but who was to make the change, the people or the Justices. His perception of the change in "men's feelings" runs aground on the Court's rejection of Justice Jackson's plea to tell the people that the Court was "declaring new law

117. Id. at 685. For the meaning "equal protection" had for the framers, see infra Appendix A. Madison rejected the notion that those who advocated restricted grants permitted the employment of words that rendered the restrictions fruitless. Quoted supra Chapter 4, note 69. Then, too, as Justice Frankfurter declared in Youngstown Sheet & Tube Co. v. Sawyer, 343 U.S. 579, 609 (1952), "It is quite impossible, however, when Congress did specifically address itself to a problem . . . to find secreted in the interstices of legislation the very grant of power which Congress consciously withheld," concurring opinion. Nevertheless, he found in the "interstices" of equal protection the very school desegregation that the framers had "consciously" excluded. Also illustrative of Frankfurter's capacity for self-delusion are his remarks about "ordered liberty"—the concept the Court fashioned out of no cloth at all. Supra Chapter 2, text accompanying notes 27–40. This concept, he wrote, "was not frozen as of . . . 1868. While the language of the Constitution does not change, the changing circumstances of a progressive society for which it was designed, yield new and fuller import to its meaning." Sweezy v. New Hampshire, 354 U.S. 234, 266 (1957). Of course "the concept of ordered liberty . . . was not frozen" as of 1868; it had not even been conceived. For the difference between applying a principle to "changing circumstances" and changing the principle itself, see supra Chapter 4, text accompanying notes 59–60. Frankfurter's "new and fuller import" is a transparent assertion of a right to judicial discard of the original meaning: judicial revision of the constitutional text.

118. Reid v. Covert, 354 U.S. 1, 50 (1957), concurring opinion.

for a new day."[119] Frankfurter well knew that disclosure courted disaster, that an amendment to express *his* feelings was unprocurable.[120] Moreover, the framers did not use words to defeat their purposes.[121] His influential pressure for the desegregation decision[122] is the less understandable in light of his subsequent condemnation of the Court's "malapportionment" decision, equally excluded from the Fourteenth Amendment, as a "massive repudiation of the experience of our whole past."[123]

It is not my purpose merely to descant on judicial inconsistency,[124] but to emphasize that the most "restrained" of Justices also was given to identifying his predilections with constitutional mandates. We are therefore entitled to look behind every decision contrary to majoritarian wishes in order to be satisfied that the Constitution, rather than the Justices, bars the way. That emphatically is not the case with the "cruel and unusual punishments" clause, which the Court once again uses as a vehicle to impose its own morals on the people.

The summary of due process herein set forth is by no means heterodox. The Court itself has abjured its past sins, referring to "our abandonment of the use of the 'vague contours' [?] of the Due Process Clause to nullify laws which a majority believe to be

119. Kluger, supra note 116 at 681–689; see Berger *G/J* 130–131.

120. At the end of the oral argument Justice Jackson said, "I suppose that realistically the reason this case is here is that action couldn't be obtained from Congress." Bickel 7.

121. See Madison, supra Chapter 4, note 69.

122. Berger *G/J* 128–129. Bickel, who as Frankfurter's law clerk played an influential role, id., wrote, "when the entire history of that [desegregation) case is known, we may find that he was a moving force in its decision." Bickel 33.

123. Baker v. Carr, 369 U.S. 186, 267 (1962), dissenting opinion.

124. Frankfurter's disciple, Alexander Bickel, charitably explained that Frankfurter "never achieved a rigorous general accord between judicial supremacy and democratic theory." Bickel 34. Such an accord would reconcile the irreconcilable. Bickel 112, himself observes that "Analytically supreme [judicial] autonomy is not easily reconciled with any theory of political democracy." I would suggest that Frankfurter preached self-restraint to his fellows, but slipped from grace where his own predilections were involved, as in the desegregation case.

economically unwise ... We refuse to sit as a superlegislature to
weigh the wisdom of legislation."[125] In 1970 it recalled the "era
when the Court thought that the Fourteenth Amendment gave it
power to strike down state laws 'because they may be unwise, im-
provident, or out of harmony with a particular school of thought'
... That era has long ago passed into history."[126] "We have re-
turned," it said, "to the *original constitutional principle that courts do
not substitute their social and economic beliefs for the judgment of the
legislative bodies* who are elected to pass laws."[127] These statements
are not altogether accurate. At the same time that it engaged in
this overdue renunciation of usurped power in the economic
sphere the Court expanded the application of substantive due process to libertarian categories.[128] But as Judge Learned Hand observed, "There is no constitutional basis for asserting a larger
measure of judicial supervision over" liberty than property;[129] in
the due process clause they are on a par. For the Founders property, in fact, was "the basic liberty, because until a man was secure
in his property ... life and liberty could mean little."[130] This his-

125. Ferguson v. Skrupa, 372 U.S. 726, 731 (1963)
126. Dandridge v. Williams, 397 U.S. 471, 485 (1970).
127. Ferguson v. Skrupa, 372 U.S. at 730.
128. Berger *G/J* 266–281.
129. Learned Hand, *The Bill of Rights* 50–51 (1958).
130. 1 Page Smith, *John Adams* 272 (1962). "Equality in the enjoyment
of property rights was regarded by the framers of [the Fourteenth]
Amendment as an essential pre-condition to the realization of other basic
rights and liberties which the Amendment was intended to guarantee." "In
fact, a fundamental interdependence exists between the personal right to
liberty and the personal right in property. Neither could have meaning
without the other." Lynch v. Household Finance Corp., 405 U.S. 538, 544,
552 (1972). Activists have been constrained to concede, as does Dean
Harry Wellington, "that the language of the Constitution does not justify
'a different scope of review ... of legislation restricting personal or civil as
distinguished from economic liberties'; ... And the notion that 'personal
liberties are more important, and in that sense more fundamental, than economic liberties' is simply elitist." Paul Brest, "The Fundamental Rights
Controversy: The Essential Contradictions of Normative Scholarship," 90
Yale L. J. 1063, 1085 (1981).

tory was related to the "cruel and unusual punishments" clause by
Justice White in *Robinson v. California:*

> If this case involved economic regulation, the present Court's al-
> lergy to substantive due process would surely prevent the Court
> from imposing its own philosophical predilections upon state
> legislatures and Congress. I fail to see why the Court deems it
> more appropriate to write into the Constitution its own abstract
> notions of how best to handle the narcotics problem, for it ob-
> viously cannot match either the States or Congress in expert un-
> derstanding.[131]

The Court itself declared, "the dichotomy between personal liberties and property rights is a false one."[132] Its substitution of its
"social and economic beliefs for the judgment of legislative
bodies" is no more excusable under the "cruel and unusual punishments" clause than under due process.

The vogue of the "liberty" to which Justice Harlan pinned his
faith is traceable to the noxious "liberty of contract" doctrine.
Blackstone had explained "liberty" as consisting "in the power of
locomotion, of . . . moving one's person to whatever place one's
inclination may direct,"[133] a definition read to the House by James
F. Wilson, chairman of the House Judiciary Committee.[134] Slaves
had been riveted to their plantations, forbidden to go about, and
that was perpetuated in the Black Codes;[135] so a prime aim of the
framers, in the words of Senator Trumbull, was to secure the
"great fundamental . . . right to go and come at pleasure."[136] This

131. 370 U.S. 660, 689 (1962), dissenting opinion.
132. Lynch v. Household Finance Corp., 405 U.S. 538, 552 (1972).
133. 1 Blackstone 138.
134. *Globe* 1118.
135. Citing the prewar Slave Code of Mississippi, which prohibited,
among other things, travel from one county to another, Senator Trumbull
proposed to "destroy all these discriminations." *Globe* 474. The Opelusa
Ordinance, a Black Code, promulgated even closer restrictions—curfew,
etc. Id. 516.
136. Id. 475.

was what "liberty" meant to the framers, apart from freedom to contract, own property, and go to court, for which express provision was made.

In mounting enthusiasm for capitalistic free enterprise, the Court, in *Allgeyer v. Louisiana* (1897)[137] struck down as violative of the Fourteenth Amendment's due process a State statute making it a misdemeanor for a resident to contract for insurance by mail with a New York company not licensed to do business in Louisiana. "The liberty mentioned in that amendment," it stated, "means not only the right to be free from the mere physical restraint of his person," but included the right, shortly stated, to "enter into all contracts."[138] The issue, however, was whether the States had surrendered their right to *regulate* contracts.[139] The framers meant to endow blacks with the same rights as whites. They studiously refrained from interference with the States' right to withhold rights from *both* blacks and whites. They struck at *discrimination* with respect to contracts; there is not a hint that they meant to curtail nondiscriminatory regulation of contracts. To the contrary, the States were left free, absent racial discrimination, to grant or withhold rights.[140]

The erosion of State sovereignty by resort to the freshly minted "liberty of contract" reached its finest hour in *Lochner v. New*

137. 165 U.S. 578 (1897).

138. Id. at 589.

139. Justice Holmes told how the "unpretentious assertion of the liberty to follow the ordinary callings" flowered "into the dogma Liberty of Contract." Adkins v. Children's Hospital, 261 U.S. 525, 568 (1923), dissenting. As Thomas Gerety observes of the impairment of contracts clause, "the Constitution hardly suggests an absolute privilege to contract on conditions or terms entirely of one's making." Gerety, "Doing Without Privacy," 42 Ohio St. L. J. 143, 161 (1981).

140. See Trumbull, supra text accompanying note 136, and Chapter 2, text accompanying notes 57–59. In Barbier v. Connolly, 113 U.S. 27, 31 (1885), Justice Field declared, "Neither the [14th] amendment . . . nor any other amendment, was designed to interfere with the power of the state, sometimes termed its police power, to prescribe regulations, to promote health . . . education . . . good order of the people."

York.[141] There the Court invalidated a statue that limited working hours in a bakery to 10 hours daily and 60 hours weekly, branding it with grim sophistry an interference with a baker's right to work longer hours.[142] Preserve us from such protectors! Justices Brandeis and Holmes were inspired to employ this disreputable doctrine for the protection of free speech. "Holmes was against extending the Fourteenth Amendment, Brandeis reported. But that meant, Brandeis said, that 'you are going to cut down freedom through striking down regulation of property, but not give protection' " to "fundamental rights."[143] This report is confirmed by Holmes's dissent in *Gitlow v. New York,*[144] stating that free speech—which only three years earlier the Court held the States were under no constitutional obligation to confer—[145] "must be taken to be included in the Fourteenth Amendment *in view of the scope that had been given* to the word 'liberty.' "[146] Thus, illegitimacy was sanctified for a benign purpose. With the demise of "liberty of contract" in the field of property, one might suppose that the branch would fall with the tree. But, no, constitutional logic gave way before judicial good intentions.

Brandeis sought to defend the extension on the ground that those "who won our independence" believed that free speech "should be a fundamental principle of the American Government."[147] Another revered figure, Justice Cardozo, declared that free speech is "the matrix, the indispensable condition, of nearly

141. 198 U.S. 45 (1905). Now that judicial enterprise has shifted from the economic to the libertarian field, Justice Holmes's dissent should be required reading.

142. By "liberty of contract," Corwin wrote, was meant "the freedom of employers to drive hard bargains with those seeking employment." Corwin, supra note 21 at 79–80.

143. Bickel 27.

144. 268 U.S. 652 (1925).

145. Prudential Ins. Co. v. Cheek, 259 U.S. 530, 538 (1922); Holmes and Brandeis joined in this decision.

146. 268 U.S. at 672.

147. Whitney v. California, 274 U.S. 357, 373, 375 (1927), concurring opinion.

every other form of freedom."[148] But the fact remains that when the American people had the opportunity to express themselves on the issue with respect to the Bill of Rights, the First Congress voted down interference with State control of free speech and religion.[149] The exclusion was not remedied by "incorporation" of the Bill of Rights in the Fourteenth Amendment, as is demonstrated by an amendment proposed by James G. Blaine, a framer, in 1875 in a Congress which included twenty-three other members of the 39th Congress. Prior thereto he had written a letter published in the *New York Times* indicating that the Fourteenth Amendment did not forbid States from establishing official churches or maintaining sectarian schools. Consequently, he proposed that "No State shall make any law respecting an establishment of religion or prohibiting the free exercise thereof."

> Not one of the several Representatives and Senators who spoke on the proposal even suggested that its provisions were implicit in the amendment ratified just seven years earlier . . . Remarks of Randolph, Kernan, White, Bogy, Eaton and Morton give confirmation to the belief that none of the legislators in 1875 thought the Fourteenth Amendment incorporated the religious provisions of the First.[150]

No more did it incorporate the companion free speech provision. So for a second time the representatives of the people chose to leave these matters to State control.

148. Palko v. Connecticut, 302 U.S. 319, 327 (1937).
149. Supra Chapter 2, text accompanying notes 13–16.
150. F. W. O'Brien, *Justice Reed and the First Amendment* 116 (1958). In the same year, 1875, Chief Justice Waite declared that the First Amendment right to assemble "was not intended to limit the powers of the State government . . . but to operate upon the National government alone . . . for their protection in its enjoyment, therefore, the people must look to the States. The power for that purpose was originally placed there, and it *has never been surrendered to the* United States." United States v. Cruikshank, 92 U.S. 542, 552 (1875). The italicized phrase is the more significant because the Court discussed the Fourteenth Amendment (id. at 554–555) without intimating that it effected any change with respect to the First Amendment.

There remains *"equal protection of the laws."* The "indeterminate," "vague and ambiguous" nature of those words,[151] their in-
applicability to jury sentencing,[152] were earlier noticed. Powers reserved to the States by the Tenth Amendment are not to be diminished under cover of vague language. That Amendment raises
a presumption that control over matters of local concern, declared
by Madison to be "inviolable," and reserved to the States,[153] can
be overcome only by clear language manifesting the States' intention to surrender this or the other local matter to federal control,
as they have done by one amendment after another extending the
right of suffrage. Such an intention, Justice Miller held on the
heels of the Fourteenth Amendment, must be expressed in language "which expresses such a purpose too clearly to permit of
doubt."[154] Senator Frederick Frelinghuysen, one of the framers,
said in a subsequent Reconstruction Congress, "The fourteenth
amendment must . . . not be used to make the General Government imperial . . . It must be read . . . together with the tenth
amendment."[155] The Court's disregard of the Tenth's reser-

151. See supra Chapter 3, note 123.
152. See supra Chapter 3, text accompanying notes 117–132. For the
narrow scope equal protection had for the framers, see infra, Appendix A.
153. Supra Chapter 2, text accompanying notes 80–82. Justice Stone observed that the Tenth "amendment states but a truism that all is retained
which has not been surrendered." It was merely "declaratory" of the existing relationship between State and federal governments; its purpose was
"to allay fears that the new federal government might seek to exercise
power not granted, and that the states might not be able to exercise fully
their reserved powers." United States v. Darby, 312 U.S. 100, 124 (1941).
154. Slaughter-House Cases, 83 U.S. (16 Wall.) 36, 78 (1872). Justice
Brennan, Polsby remarks, found the meaning of the Eighth Amendment
"obscure and elusive," Daniel Polsby, "The Death of Capital Punishment?
Furman v. Georgia," 1972 S. Ct. Rev. 1, 16. Chief Justice Burger found its
language "uncertain," surrounded by a "haze," "enigmatic." Furman
375–376.
155. *Congressional Globe* (42d Cong., 1st Sess.) 501 (1871). Consequently, he did not deem it "expedient for the General Government to assume a general municipal jurisdiction over crimes in the States." Id. Senator Trumbull likewise rejected a federal "right to pass a general criminal
code for the States." Id. at 579. For additional citations, see Berger, supra
note 91 at 325.

vation of power to the States would transform our federal government of limited powers to an illimitable judicial empire, a prospect that even the "invitation" theorist finds "frightening" and "scary."[156] It cannot be that the power of the Court alone among the branches knows no limits, or that the Court alone can define its own limits. If power is boundless, Jefferson wrote, "then we have no Constitution."[157]

The history of the Fourteenth Amendment makes plain that the States did not intend to turn over supervision of their criminal justice system to the Supreme Court.[158] "It was never intended," Justice Black stated, "to destroy the States' power to govern themselves."[159] "It has not," said Justice Cardozo, "displaced the procedure of ages,"[160] among it the long-established right of the people to enact death penalties and to leave the final say in sentencing to the jury. The intrusion of the Court into this domain, it needs to be said bluntly, is only one of many lawless curtailments of the people's right to govern themselves.[161] That it re-

156. Ely observed that "read for what it says the Ninth Amendment seems open-textured enough to support almost anything one might wish to argue, and that thought can get pretty scary." J. H. Ely, *Democracy and Distrust* 34 (1980). The "invitation apparently extended by the 'privileges or immunities' clause is frightening." Ely, "Constitutional Interpretivism: Its Allure and Impossibility," 53 Ind. L. J. 399, 425 (1978).

157. 8 Thomas Jefferson, *Writings,* ed P. L. Ford 247 (1897).

158. Supra note 155, and Chapter 2, text accompanying note 79.

159. Oregon v. Mitchell, 400 U.S. 112, 126 (1970), dissenting in part. He added, "it cannot be successfully argued that the Fourteenth Amendment was intended to strip the States of their power, carefully preserved in the original Constitution, to govern themselves." Id. 127. See also Barbier v. Connolly, supra note 140.

160. Snyder v. Massachusetts, 291 U.S. 97, 111 (1934). Brest considers that "The text and history of the [equal protection] clause are vague and ambiguous and cannot, in any event, infuse the antidiscrimination principle with moral force or justify its extension to novel circumstances and new beneficiaries." Brest, "Foreword: In Defense of the Antidiscrimination Principle," 90 Harv. L. Rev. 1, 5 (1976).

161. Its intrusion into desegregation and suffrage has earlier been noted. The Court's invalidation of State residence requirements for recipients of

flects high moral purpose only serves to recall Crane Brinton's comment on Robespierre: "If Frenchmen would not be free and virtuous voluntarily, then he would force them to be free and cram virtue down their throats."[162] Americans, however, like that wisest of jurists, Judge Learned Hand, do not want to be ruled by nine "Platonic Guardians."[163]

---

welfare represents another overthrow on the flimsiest grounds of a centuries-old practice. See Raoul Berger, "Residence Requirements for Welfare and Voting: A Post-Mortem," 42 Ohio St. L. J. 853 (1981).

162. Crane Brinton, John Christopher, and Robert Wolff, *A History of Civilization* 115 (1955). From "their experience under the Protectorate, Englishmen learned . . . [that] the claims of self-appointed saints to know by divine inspiration what the good life should be and to have the right to impose their notions on the ungodly could be as great a threat as the divine right of kings." Sydney Smith, *Selected Writings,* ed. W. H. Auden, Introduction xvi (1956). So, too, Augustus, wrote Will Durant, tried "to make people good as well as happy; it was an imposition that Rome never forgave him. Moral reform is the most difficult and delicate branch of statesmanship; few rulers have dared to attempt it." Will Durant, *Caesar and Christ* 221 (1944).

163. Learned Hand, *The Bill of Rights* 88 (1958). In 1923, after the Court overturned the Minimum Wage Law by a vote of 5 to 3, Frankfurter wrote Judge Learned Hand, "My own mind has about found lodgment where yours has, namely, that the possible gain wasn't worth the cost of having five men without any reasonable probability that they are qualified for the task, determine the course of social policy for the states and the nation." H. N. Hirsch, *The Enigma of Felix Frankfurter* 132 (1981). After commending several "liberal" decisions by the pre-1937 Court, Frankfurter wrote, "In rejoicing . . . we must not forget what a heavy price has to be paid for these occasional services to liberalism." "The cost," he concluded, "was on the whole greater than the gains." Bickel 25. See also Dean Charles Clark, infra Chapter 8, text accompanying note 19.

6

The Cases*

ACADEMICIANS uneasily have criticized the Court's shoddy craftsman-
ship.[1] That is not nearly as important as
its arbitrary substitution of antihistorical premises for the will of
the Framers. The cases surveyed in this chapter are replete with
transparent rationalizations of judicial predilections and bare-

* Justice Blackmun stated truly in Furman that "The several concurring
opinions acknowledge, as they must, that until today capital punishment
was accepted and assumed as not unconstitutional *per se* under the Eighth
Amendment or the Fourteenth Amendment. This is either the flat or im-
plied holding of a unanimous Court in *Wilkerson v. Utah,* 99 U.S. 130,
134–135, in 1878; of a unanimous Court in *In re Kemmler,* 136 U.S. 436,
447, in 1890; of the Court in *Weems v. United States,* 217 U.S. 349, in 1910;
of all the members of the Court in *Louisiana ex rel. Francis v. Resweber,* 329
U.S. 459, 463–464, 471–472, in 1947; of Mr. Chief Justice Warren, speaking for himself and three others (Justices Black, Douglas, and Whittaker)
in *Trop v. Dulles,* 356 U.S. 86, 99, in 1958; and of Mr. Justice Black in
McGautha v. California, 402 U.S. 183, 226, decided only last term on May 3,
1971."

1. For citations see Berger *G/J* 343, 344, 347 n. 44.

faced manipulation of the constitutional text. Let the reader judge.

Weems v. United States[2] is the abolitionist magic fountain, the primal source from which all blessings flow. Defendant, a United States official in the Philippines, made two false entries amounting to 616 pesos. He was sentenced under the Spanish penal code to fifteen years, a fine of 4,000 pesetas, hard and painful labor, to carry a chain at the ankle hanging from the wrist, followed by perpetual surveillance, loss of voting rights, and disqualification from public office. The Philippine Bill of Rights contained a "cruel and unusual punishments" clause. After adverting to Patrick Henry's remarks about torture, the Court speculated, "surely they [the Framers] intended more than to register a fear of the forms of abuse that went out of practice with the Stuarts . . . We cannot think that the possibility of a coercive cruelty being exercised through other forms of punishment was overlooked."[3] Yet there were forms of "coercive cruelty" repulsive to our modern sensibilities which the Founders plainly did not bar. Branding and mutilation were established punishments.[4] The Judiciary Act of 1789 recognized "whipping, not exceeding thirty stripes";[5] whipping was by the first Crimes Act of April 30, 1790, "part of the punishment of stealing or falsifying records."[6] Justice Field's dissent in

2. 217 U.S. 349 (1910). For appeals to Weems, see Furman 242, 264, 265, 266, 267, 271, 275, 325, 331, 332, 343. Justice Thurgood Marshall said: "Weems is a landmark case because it represents the first time that the Court invalidated a penalty prescribed by the legislature for a particular offense." Furman 325.

3. 217 U.S. at 372. A breach of the Tenth Amendment cannot be justified by speculation as to the Framers' motives in drafting the Eighth Amendment. Sidney Hook emphasizes that "the evidence for probabilities must include more than abstract possibilities." Hook, *Philosophy and Public Policy* 122 (1980).

4. Infra text accompanying notes 27–28, note 29; supra Chapter 3, text accompanying note 80.

5. Section 9, 1 Stat. 73 ff.

6. Chapter 9, 1 Stat. 112 ff. Justice Brennan's reference to "the discontinuance of flogging as a constitutionally permissible punishment, Jackson v. Bishop, 404 F. 2d 571 (8th Cir. 1968)," Furman 287–288, takes no ac-

O'Neil v. Vermont, another abolitionist text, declared that "The State has the power to inflict personal chastisement, by directing whipping for petty offenses—repulsive as such punishment is."[7] *Weems'* speculation runs head on into Chief Justice Marshall's canon that an intention to depart from an established practice requires unequivocal statement.[8]

Throughout *Weems* is characterized by specious reasoning. Its appeal to "new *conditions*" for "wider application" of a principle, it has been noted, cannot justify the substitution of the Court's new *principle* for that of the Framers'.[9] Similarly, its "resistance to narrow constructions of the *grants* of power to the National government"[10] overlooks that the Bill of Rights was a *restriction* on the delegated powers.[11] The Court's argument would overturn Congress' enactment of death penalties under *its* grant of powers; applied to the States, the Court's rejection of a "narrow construction" would curtail the Tenth Amendment's reservation of undelegated power. A "narrow construction" is essential[12] to avoid constitutional doubts raised by invasion of such reserved powers. In a powerful dissent joined by Justice Holmes, Justice Edward White stated,

> That in England it was nowhere deemed that any theory of *proportional punishment* was suggested by the bill of rights or that a protest was thereby intended against the severity of punishments, speaking generally, is demonstrated by the practice which prevailed in England as to punishing crime

---

count of these statutes or of the fact that flogging was discontinued *by statute,* not by the courts. It is part of his grand assumption that the Court is empowered to bring the Constitution in tune with the times.

7. 144 U.S. 323, 340 (1892). For citations to Field, see Furman 249, 277 n. 21, 279, 323.

8. Supra Chapter 2, text accompanying note 53; see also supra Chapter 2, note 61.

9. Supra Chapter 4, text accompanying notes 59–60.

10. 144 U.S. at 374.

11. Supra Chapter 2, text accompanying note 82.

12. See Henkin, supra Chapter 3, text accompanying note 94.

from the time of the bill of rights to the time of the American Revolution.[13]

As we have seen, thefts above the value of a few shillings were capital crimes.[14] Such facts contradict *Weems'* conclusion that "it is a precept of justice that punishment for crime should be graduated and proportioned to the offense."[15] The common law knew no such precept. In shutting its eyes to the history which illuminates the meaning of the "cruel and unusual punishments" clause, the Court betrayed that it was merely "making an essentially moral judgment."[16] Whatever the merits of *Weems'* proportionality argument, it cannot be invoked for abolition of the death penalty because that was excepted from its holding by its tacit approval of *Wilkerson v. Utah:* "The court pointed out that death was an usual punishment for murder . . . It was hence concluded that it was not forbidden by the Constitution of the United States as cruel or unusual."[17]

13. 217 U.S. at 393. Blackstone concluded that "there cannot be any regular or determinate method of rating the quantity of punishments for crimes, by any one uniform rule; but they must be referred to the will and discretion of the legislative power." 4 Blackstone 14–15. Justice Holmes remained of this view in Badders v. United States, 240 U.S. 391, 393 (1916), where seven counts of mail fraud for the deposit of seven letters, resulted in a fine of $1,000 on each count, and five years imprisonment on each, to run concurrently. He summarily rejected the argument that if the statute "makes the deposit of each letter a separate offense subject to such punishment as it received in this case it imposes cruel and unusual punishment and excessive fines." In Rummel v. Estelle, 445 U.S. 263, 274 (1980), the Court held that "the length of the sentence actually imposed is purely a matter of legislative prerogative" (a noncapital case).

14. Supra Chapter 3, text accompanying note 28.

15. 217 U.S. at 366–367. For Justice Brennan, the "Court in *Weems* decisively rejected the 'historical' interpretation of the Clause." Furman 266. But the "historical" interpretation is not subject to changing fashions, for, as Justice Story stated, the common law "definitions are necessarily included, as much as if they stood in the text of the Constitution." Supra Chapter 4, note 19.

16. Furman 394, Burger, C.J.

17. 217 U.S. at 369–370. This was noted by Justice Brennan, Furman 276 n. 19, and by Justice Blackmun, supra starred note. Justice White

Fifty years after *Weems* came *Trop v. Dulles,*[18] a no less aberrational 5 to 4 decision. Under an act deriving from a Civil War statute, a court-martial held that a native American, guilty of wartime desertion, lost his citizenship. *Trop* is altogether without relevance to death penalties, for Chief Justice Warren stated:

> At the outset, let us put to one side the death penalty as an index of the constitutional limit on punishment. Whatever the arguments may be against corporal punishment, both on moral grounds and in terms of the accomplishing the purposes of punishment—and they are forceful—the death penalty has been employed throughout our history, and, in a day when it is still widely accepted, it cannot be said to violate the constitutional concept of cruelty.[19]

Justice Powell observed "It is anomalous that the standard . . . 'evolving standards of decency that mark the progress of a maturing society' should be derived from an opinion that so unqualifiedly rejects their arguments."[20] It is more than "anomalous"—it is perverse to cite an opinion for what it expressly *excepts.*

------

stated, "it may not be doubted, and indeed is not questioned by any one, that the cruel punishments against which the bill of rights provided were the atrocious, sanguinary inhuman punishments which had been inflicted in the past." 217 U.S. at 390, dissenting opinion.

18. 356 U.S. 86 (1958).

19. Id. at 99. Justice Brennan, dwelling on the words *"in a day* when it is still *widely accepted"* considers that "This statement, of course, left open the future constitutionality of the punishment." Furman 285 n. 33 (emphasis in the original). "Of course" grandly assumes that when something is no longer "widely accepted" the meaning of the Constitution changes, bother the need for amendment. But see Hamilton, infra, text accompanying note 47.

Labeling Warren's threshold exception of death penalties from the holding "purely dictum," Justice Marshall said, *"Trop v. Dulles* is merely 15 years old now, and 15 years change many minds about many things." Furman 329–330 n. 37. The subsequent "stampede" to enact new death penalty statutes on the heels of Furman, infra text accompanying note 60, demonstrates that it was the minds *of the Justices* that changed, not of the people.

20. Furman 425.

Warren put aside the issue whether the loss of citizenship for desertion was "excessive," given that "wartime desertion is punishable by death." Instead he asked "whether this penalty subjects the individual to a fate forbidden by the principles of civilized treatment guaranteed by the Eighth Amendment.' "[21] He reasoned that the penalty resulted in "the total destruction of the individual's status in organized society . . . [I]t destroys for the individual the political existence that was for centuries in the development [as does the death penalty] . . . He may be subject to banishment, a fate universally decried by civilized people."[22] All this merely reflects *his* twentieth-century predilections; if we look to the presuppositions of the Framers, their oracle of the common law, Blackstone, recounts that "exile and banishment" were staples of punishment.[23] During the Revolutionary War a number of States banished Loyalists.[24] Warren soars above such mundane considerations and, reaching back to Magna Carta, concludes that "The basic concept underlying the Eighth Amendment is nothing less than the dignity of man."[25] This is judicial fantasy at its finest. As Daniel Polsby noted, "All punishment affronts human dignity."[26] Blackstone wrote that some punishments "fix a *lasting stigma* on the offender, by slitting the nostrils or branding on the

---

21. 356 U.S. at 99. "[A]s late as 1865 a law was enacted by Congress which prescribed as a punishment for a crime the disqualification to enjoy rights of citizenship. Rev. Stat. §§1996, 1997, 1998." Weems v. United States, 217 U.S. 349, 400 (1910), Justice Edward White dissenting.

22. 356 U.S. at 101–102.

23. 4 Blackstone 377.

24. For citations, see Raoul Berger, "Bills of Attainder: A Study of Amendment by the Court," 63 Cornell L. Rev. 355, 378 n. 155, 379 (1978).

25. 356 U.S. at 100. Warren had been anticipated by, of all men, Justice Frankfurter in Louisiana ex rel. Francis v. Resweber, 329 U.S. 459, 468 (1947): the Fourteenth Amendment meant "to withdraw from the States the right to act in ways that are offensive to a decent respect for the dignity of man." The framers' exclusion of suffrage, mixed schools, and jury service alone stamps this as "instant history."

26. Daniel Polsby, "The Death of Capital Punishment? Furman v. Georgia," 1972 S. Ct. Rev. 1, 19.

hand or cheek"; other punishments "consist principally in their *ignominy* ... such as whipping ... the pillory, the stocks, and ducking stool."[27] Lord Camden, who had been Chief Justice of the Court of Common Pleas, referred in the course of the 1791 debate on Fox's Libel Act to the punishment that might "be inflicted ... whether it was fine, imprisonment, loss of ears, whipping or *any other disgrace.*"[28] Such punishments were common in colonial and early State law,[29] and they reduce Warren's "basic concept ... the dignity of man" to empty rhetoric.

Here, as in *Brown v. Board of Education,* to borrow from Philip Kurland, Warren "abandoned the search for the framers' intent ... and chose instead to write a Constitution for our times."[30]

27. 4 Blackstone 377.

28. Quoted by Justice Gray in Sparf and Hansen v. United States, 156 U.S. 51, 136 (1895), dissenting opinion.

29. In the colonies, among the "demeaning, degrading ... 'engines of punishment' " were "the stocks, bilboes, pillory, brank, ducking stools." These "exposed to the free gibes and constant mockery of the whole community." Branding and mutilation were common. Alice M. Earle, *Curious Punishments in Bygone Days* 3, 318 (1969). The "whipping post was promptly set up, and the whip set to work in all the American colonies." Id. 72. In New England, Quakers "had been stripped naked, whipped, pilloried, stocked ... branded and maimed." Id. 139. In 1771 a counterfeiter in Newport was sentenced to the pillory, "to have both ears cropped, to be branded on both cheeks." Id. 147, 148. A Massachusetts law of 1791 provided that highway robbers should be burned on the forehead or hand." Richard Perry, *Sources of Our Liberties* 237 (1978). See also H. E. Barnes, *The Repression of Crime* 45 (1969). As late as 1823 Nathan Dane noted that "Punishments clearly infamous, are death, gallows, pillory, branding, whipping." 2 Dane Ab. 569, 570, quoted in Ex parte Wilson, 114 U.S. 417, 428 (1885). The "punishments of whipping and standing in the pillory were abolished [in the federal domain] by the act of February 28, 1839, ch. 36, §5, 5 Stat. 322." Id. 114 U.S. at 417. Incontrovertibly, branding and ear-cropping, "which are commonplace at the time of the adoption of the Constitution, passed from the penal scene without judicial intervention because they became basically offensive to the people and the legislature responded to this sentiment." Burger, C.J., Furman 384.

30. Philip Kurland, "Brown v. Board of Education Was the Beginning," 1979 Wash. U. L. Q. 309, 313. On other occasions "the Warren

Throughout he identified his own revulsion with constitutional
imperatives, papering over the absence of solid constitutional
footing with eloquence.[31] Nevertheless, "human dignity" has become the abolitionist slogan. Justice Brennan converts this shib-
boleth into an axiom: "death stands condemned as fatally offensive to human dignity," and "therefore 'cruel and unusual,' " so
that "the States may no longer inflict it as a punishment for
crimes."[32] Neither "Chief Justice Warren in *Trop* nor Justice

---

Court has purported to discover in the history of the Fourteenth Amendment . . . and of other constitutional provisions, the crutch that wasn't
there." Bickel 47. Justice Frankfurter referred to Warren's work as "dishon-
est nonsense." H. N. Hirsch, *The Enigma of Felix Frankfurter* 190 (1981).
Let it suffice to label his "dignity of man" doctrine as arrant nonsense. One
who regards him as a "hero," John Hart Ely, wrote of Warren's reading
"equal protection" into the Fifth Amendment in Bolling v. Sharpe, 347
U.S. 497 (1954), on the ground that "if the Constitution prohibits the
states from maintaining racially segregated public schools it would be unthinkable that the same Constitution would impose a lesser duty on the
Federal Government," that "This is gibberish both syntactically and historically." Ely, *Democracy and Distrust* 32 (1980). What else can be said of locating in the Constitution of 1787 what was first (allegedly) expressed in
1866? Of a similar "reading," Bickel wrote, "In Jones v. Mayer Co., 392
U.S. 409 (1968) the Court appears to have had no feeling for the truth of
history, but only to read it through the gloss of the Court's own purpose.
It allowed itself to believe impossible things." Bickel 98. For elaborate
proof of this charge, see 6 Charles Fairman, *History of the Supreme Court of
the United States* 1207–1259 (1971). For similar wishful thinking by the
Justices, see supra, Powell, Chapter 3, text accompanying note 54; Douglas,
Chapter 3, text accompanying note 64; Marshall, Chapter 3, text accompanying note 73.
    31. Chief Justice Vaughan observed in Bushell's Case, 124 E. R. 1006,
1010 (1671), "We must take of this vail and colour of words which make a
show of being something, and in truth are nothing."
    32. Furman 305. See also Stewart, Powell, and Stevens, J. J., Gregg v.
Georgia, 428 U.S. 153, 173 (1976). For Justice Marshall, "the question is
. . . whether capital punishment is 'a punishment no longer consistent with
our own self-respect' and, therefore violative of the Eighth Amendment,"
ignoring that Lord Chancellor Gardiner addressed the quoted remark to

Brennan in *Furman* offered any analytical support for the dignity concept."[33] Justice Douglas rejected "canons of decency" when the judgment of his fellows did not jibe with his own "gut reaction" because judgment would then turn on "the idiosyncrasies of the judges."[34]

Trop does not merely stand history on its head, it is incompatible with a case decided at the very same term, *Perez v. Brownell*,[35] where a citizen was expatriated for voting in a Mexican election. Justice Brennan uneasily sought to account for Warren's differentiation:

> It is, concededly, paradoxical to justify as constitutional the expatriation of the citizen who has committed no crime by voting in a Mexican political election, yet finds unconstitutional a stat-

---

Parliament; it was not an interpretation of the "cruel and unusual punishments" clause.

Although Justice Brennan rejects the view that the "Due Process Clause vests judges with a roving commission to impose their own notions of wise social policy upon the States," McGautha 255 n. 4, he is utterly oblivious of the fact that this is exactly what he is doing by his reading of the "cruel and unusual punishments" clause. For history shows beyond peradventure that it applied only to "barbarous" punishments and had no "human dignity" component nor doctrine of "excessive" or disproportionate punishment.

33. Malcolm Wheeler, "Toward a Theory of Limited Punishment II: The Eighth Amendment After *Furman v. Georgia,"* 25 Stan. L. Q. 62, 67 (1972).

34. Rochin v. California, 342 U.S. 165, 179 (1952). Dissenting from the majority's condemnation of use of a stomach pump to obtain evidence of narcotic traffic, Justice Douglas, noting that the outlawed practice "would be admissible in the majority of states where the question has been raised," refused to hold that it violates the " 'decencies of civilized conduct' when formulated by responsible courts with judges as sensitive as we are." Id. 177–178. How much more is this true with respect to death penalties, which had been accepted practice for 181 years before Douglas labeled those who disagreed with him "sadists," demonstrating that he was truly guided by his "gut reactions," not by enduring principles.

35. 356 U.S. 44 (1958).

ute which provides for the expatriation of a soldier guilty of the
very serious crime of desertion in time of war. The loss of citizenship may have as ominous significance for the individual in
the one case as in the other.[36]

Noting that *Perez* sustained a sanction against the disturbance of
our foreign relations, "voting by an American citizen in political
elections of other nations," Brennan likewise recognized Congress' power to deal with the problem of desertion, "an act plainly
destructive of the Nation's ability to wage war effectively."[37] He
resolved the dilemma by deciding that expatriation is not "reasonably calculated to achieve this legitimate end," citing *Mc-
Culloch v. Maryland*—it was not "reasonably calculated to effect
any of the objects entrusted to the government."[38] But halting
desertion *was* "calculated to effect" an object entrusted to Congress, the task of "waging war effectively" under its power to
declare war and maintain armies. Inquiry as to whether it was
"reasonably" calculated to do so can draw no comfort from
Marshall, for he refused to "undertake here to inquire into the
degree of its necessity" for exercising the power, explicitly disclaiming "all pretensions to such power."[39] That was for the legislature.

Then there is Warren's contempt for the demands of logic.
Wartime desertion, as Justice Frankfurter pointed out, has been a
capital offense "from the first year of Independence," 1776, and he
mordantly asked, "Is constitutional dialectic so empty of reason

36. Trop v. Dulles, 356 U.S. at 105.
37. Id. 106, 107.
38. Id. 114.
39. McCulloch v. Maryland, 17 U.S. (4 Wheat.) 315, 423 (1819). He
expressly recognized "the right of the legislature to exercise its best judgment in the selection of measures to carry into execution the constitutional
powers of the government." Id. at 421. He contented himself with jurisdiction over "objects not entrusted to the government," id. at 423, that is,
beyond drawn boundaries leaving, as did Iredell before him, supra Chapter
5, text accompanying note 48, matters within the "authority given" to the
discretion of Congress.

that it can be seriously urged that the loss of citizenship is a fate worse than death?"[40] Demonstrably, Justice Brennan commented, "expatriation is not 'a fate worse than death' ... Although death, like expatriation, destroys the individual's 'political existence' and his 'status in organized society,' it does more, for unlike expatriation, death also destroys '[h]is very existence. There is, too, at least the possibility that the expatriate will, in the future regain the right to have rights.' Death forecloses even that possibility."[41] Warren's reasoning would have it that the part is greater than the whole. His *Trop* opinion, which mustered only a plurality of four, joined by the troubled Brennan, and balanced by four dissenters, exhibits another dismal triumph of result-oriented jurisprudence over constitutionalism.

JUDICIAL DIVINATION OF THE PEOPLE'S WILL

The keystone of the abolitionist argument, in Chief Justice Warren's words, is that the Eighth Amendment "must draw its meaning from the evolving standards of decency that mark the progress of a maturing society."[42] Presumably he had in mind resort to Frankfurter's "antennae" to register "the consensus of society's opinion,"[43] a euphemism for judicial soothsaying. What, asks Dean Terrance Sandalow, are courts "to look for?" If values "change over time, by what standards are courts to determine whether a particular step in the evolutionary process is or is not permissible?"[44] No explanation of the "instant evolu-

40. 356 U.S. at 125, dissenting opinion joined by Burton, Clark, and Harlan, JJ.

41. Furman 289–290.

42. Trop v. Dulles, 356 U.S. at 101. Warren illustrates Justice Holmes's observation: "nothing but confusion of thought can result from assuming that the rights of man in a moral sense are equally rights in the sense of the constitution and the law." O. W. Holmes, *Collected Legal Papers* 171–172 (1920).

43. Supra Chapter 5, text accompanying note 112.

44. Terrance Sandalow, "Judicial Protection of Minorities," 75 Mich. L. Rev. 1162, 1181 (1977). Chief Justice Burger observed, "it is the legisla-

tion"[45] that took place in the 14 months between *McGautha* and *Furman* was proffered by the Court; it is explicable only, I suggest, by the accession of new votes. However fine-tuned the judicial antennae, in the end, John Hart Ely has convincingly shown, a divorce between a judge's personal values and the social "consensus" that he divines is delusory. What he is "really ... discovering ... are his own values"; and judges are by no means "best equipped to make moral judgments."[46] This search for a social "consensus"—double talk for amending the Constitution without consulting the people—collides with Hamilton's assurance in the midst of his defense of judicial review in *Federalist* No. 78:

> Until the people have, by some solemn and authoritative act, annulled or changed the established form, it is binding upon themselves collectively, as well as individually; and no presumption, or *even knowledge of their sentiments,* can warrant their representatives in a departure from it, prior to such an act.[47]

Simply put, amendment is confined to the people under Article V.

From the beginning the Founders rejected judicial participation in legislative policymaking, believing that judges have no "peculiar" competence in that field,[48] reflected in Justice Frankfurter's statement that the courts are "not designed to be a good reflex of a democratic society."[49] The Court itself declared, per Justice

---

ture, not the Court, which responds to public opinion and immediately reflects the society's standards of decency." Furman 383; see also infra, text accompanying note 50.

45. Furman 382. Chief Justice Burger alluded to "the swift changes in positions of some Members of this Court in the short space of five years." Coker v. Georgia, 433 U.S. 584, 614 (1977).

46. J. H. Ely, "Foreword: On Discovering Fundamental Values," 92 Harv. L. Rev. 5, 16 (1978). See also supra Chapter 5, text accompanying notes 111–115.

47. Federalist at 509.

48. Supra Chapter 5, text accompanying notes 22–28.

49. Dennis v. United States, 341 U.S. 494, 517 (1951), concurring opinion.

Holmes, that adoption of a statute "expressed a deep-seated conviction on the part of the People concerned as to what that policy
required."[50] And it repeated, per Justice Cardozo, that the statutes
of a state "are the authentic forms through which the sense of
justice of the People . . . expresses itself in law,"[51] paraphrased by
Justice Powell, "In a democracy the first indicator of the public's
attitude must always be found in the legislative judgments of the
people's chosen representatives."[52] Chief Justice Burger, therefore,
merely echoed orthodox tradition in saying that "in a democratic
society legislators, not courts, are constituted to respond to the
will and consequently the moral values of the people."[53] The
point was underscored by Justice Powell: "It is too easy to pro-
pound our subjective standards of wise policy under the rubric of
more or less universally held standards of decency."[54] The judge,

50. Otis v. Parker, 187 U.S. 606, 609 (1903).

51. Snyder v. Massachusetts, 291 U.S. 97, 122 (1934).

52. Furman 436–437. Powell also stated, "The assessment of popular
opinion is essentially a legislative, not a judicial function." id. 443. Bickel
concluded that the Court "is too remote from conditions . . . It is not accessible to all the varied interests that are in play in any decision of great
consequence . . . it is, in a vast, complex, changeable society, a most unsuitable instrument for the formulation of policy." Bickel 175.
One would not gather from Justice Brennan's pronouncement, "Legal
authorization, *of course,* does not establish acceptance," Furman 279, that
there exists weighty authority to the contrary. This is not much different
from Justice Marshall's formulation, "abolition is not dependent on a successful grass roots movement in a particular jurisdiction [for example, the
California Amendment overruling the California court's abolition of the
death penalty] but is demanded by the Eighth Amendment." Furman 342.

53. Furman 383. Justice Blackmun considers that authority to deal with
capital punishment lies with the legislative branches and "should not be
taken over by the judiciary in the modern guise of an Eighth Amendment
issue." Furman 410. Justice Frankfurter, dissenting in Trop v. Dulles, 356
U.S. at 120, stated, "it is not the business of this Court to pronounce policy."

54. Furman 431. Writing in 1974, Bedau found that "Out of a total of
fifty-two civil jurisdictions . . . only five—Alaska, Hawaii, Maine, Minne-
sota, and Wisconsin—had totally abolished capital punishment for all
crimes." Bedau 81. "With the possible exception of Oregon . . . the six

Judge Learned Hand believed, "has no right to divination of public opinion which runs counter to its last formal expression."[55]

Notwithstanding such expressions, the Court shook the foun-
dations of the death penalty in *Furman,* largely relying on what
may be described as tea-leaf readings of public sentiment. So Justice Brennan appealed to the "increasingly rare" infliction of the
penalty, the history of "successive restrictions,"[56] not, it bears
reemphasis, by courts but by legislatures.[57] From such facts Brennan concluded that "its rejection by contemporary society is virtually total,"[58] taking no account of State referenda between 1964
and 1970 rejecting abolition and, to say the least, divided public
sentiment on the subject.[59] The "backlash" was stunning and immediate—"a virtual stampede of State reenactments" by 35
States.[60] Justices Stewart, Powell, and Stevens handsomely acknowledged that that event had "undercut" the assumption on
which *Furman* rested: "it is now evident that a large proportion of

---

states that abolished the death penalty in this country in the past decade
probably did so without the support of a majority of the public." Bedau 65.

55. Learned Hand, *The Spirit of Liberty* 14 (1952); The Chinese Exclusion Case, 130 U.S. 581, 600 (1889): "the last expression of the sovereign
must control."

56. Furman 299. Ely remarks, "Justices Brennan and Marshall based
their votes largely on the claim that capital punishment was out of accord
with current community values. Such claims always have a good chance of
being nonsense and this one was, as the post-Furman spate of reenactments
tragically testified." J. H. Ely, *Democracy and Distrust* 173 (1980).

57. Bedau wrote in 1974: "No death sentence had ever been voided as a
violation of due process, equal protection, or on any other ground." Bedau
81. Compare supra Chapter 3, note 52.

58. Furman 305.

59. Bedau 64–65. Legislatures, said Bedau, 41, "yield to the collective
wish for vengeance." "In the only statewide referendum occurring since
Furman . . . the people of California adopted a constitutional amendment
that authorized capital punishment, in effect negating a prior ruling by the
Supreme Court of California . . . that the death penalty violated the Constitution." Gregg v. California, 428 U.S. 153, 181 (1976). Earlier and similar referenda are noted id. n. 25.

60. J. H. Ely, *Democracy and Distrust* 65 (1980).

American society continues to regard [the death penalty] as an appropriate and necessary criminal sanction."[61] Justice Marshall insisted, however, that "the American people [*if*], *fully informed* as to the purposes of the death penalty and its liabilities, would in my view reject it as morally unacceptable." If, he continued, "the constitutionality turns, as I have urged, on the opinion of an *informed* citizenry, then even the enactment of new death statutes cannot be viewed as conclusive."[62] Thus, statutes must yield to Marshall's speculations as to what the people would do if informed of data Marshall deems decisive. What price blind adherence to a theory? The philosopher Sidney Hook decries those "who know what the basic human needs *should* be, who know not only what these needs are but what they require *better* than those who have them or should have them." "It is arrogant," he adds, to assume that "some self-selected elite can better determine what the best interests of other citizens are than those citizens themselves."[63]

Although the *Gregg* plurality—Justices Stewart, Powell, and Stevens—quote Chief Justice Burger's statement that legislatures, not courts, must respond to the will and moral values of the people, and recognize that the "specification of punishment" is "peculiarly" a question "of legislative policy," they conclude that "the Eighth Amendment demands more than that a challenged punishment be acceptable to contemporary society. The Court also must ask whether it comports with the basic concept of hu-

61. Gregg v. Georgia, 428 U.S. 153, 179 (1976).

62. Id. 232, dissenting opinion.

63. Sidney Hook, *Philosophy and Public Policy* 28, 29 (1980). Noel Annan, Vice Chancellor of the University of London, rejects the theory that governments "can identify what people would *really* want were they enlightened . . . and understand fully what was needed to promote a good, just and satisfying society. For if it is true that this can be satisfied then surely the state is justified in ignoring what ordinary people say they desire or detest." Introduction to Isaiah Berlin, *Personal Impressions* xvii (1981). J. H. Ely, *Democracy and Distrust* 68 (1981): "the theory that the legislature does not truly speak for the people's values, but the Court does, is ludicrous."

man dignity at the core of the amendment."[64] Whence does it draw this "basic concept"? From "the evolving standards of decency that mark the progress of a maturing society," that is, "cruel and unusual punishments" may "acquire meaning as public opinion becomes enlightened by a humane justice."[65] Thus, the desires of "contemporary society" must yield to a "basic concept" that is drawn from "public opinion"—a pretty example of circular reasoning. Such is the "human dignity" that is contravened by the degrading punishments extant at the adoption of the Constitution, which were abandoned by *legislatures* in response to "public opinion." Even Justice Field, though revolted by such punishments, recognized that they are constitutional.

McGAUTHA AND FURMAN

To deal comprehensively with all the arguments of *McGautha v. California* and *Furman v. Georgia* would vastly expand the bulk of this study: the one covers 129 pages, the other 232. In great part the arguments for death penalty curtailment rely on what Justice Stewart described as "inconclusive empirical evidence"[66]— statistics, criminological, and social science studies which are disputed—to show that death penalties fail to deter and the like.[67]

64. Supra note 61 at 175–176, 182.

65. Id. 173, 171. Justice Blackmun, dissenting, complained that the plurality focused "not on the essence of the death penalty itself but primarily upon the procedures employed by the State to single out persons to suffer the penalty of death." 428 U.S. at 227. It is death that "is degrading to human dignity," id. 229, the springboard of the Court's repudiation of the past. No one has claimed that the "procedures," that is, discretionary sentencing, were "degrading."

66. Furman 307.

67. Id. 454–455. Justice Blackmun noted, "as the concurring opinions observe, the statistics prove little, if anything." Furman 406. Underlining that the abolitionist case "rests primarily on factual claims, the truth of which cannot be tested by conventional judicial processes," Chief Justice Burger concludes that evaluation is best performed by the legislature "with

These are questions of policy which were left to Congress and the States. At best they are arguments as to what the Constitution *ought* to be were the Justices empowered to rewrite it; they have no relevance to the Constitution framed by the Founders, as Justice Douglas tacitly admitted in saying that the majority "has history on its side." He recognized that "Once it was a capital offense to steal from the person something 'above the value of a shilling,'" but triumphantly asks, "Who today would say it was not cruel and unusual punishment . . . to impose the death sentence on a man who stole a loaf of bread."[68] Douglas failed to perceive that "punishments such as branding and the cutting off of ears, which were commonplace at the time of the adoption of the Constitution, passed from the penal scene without judicial intervention because they became basically offensive to the people and the legislatures responded to this sentiment."[69] At issue is not whether a man may be hanged for stealing a loaf of bread, but whether the Court is authorized to take that decision away from the legislature and the people.

In *McGautha* the issue was whether the absolute discretion of

---

the familiar and effective tools available to them as they are not to us." Id. 405. Justice Marshall acknowledges that there is a "paucity of useful data," on the issue of deterrence. Furman 347. The four dissenters declare that "The five opinions in support of the judgments . . . make sweeping factual assertions, unsupported by empirical data concerning the manner of imposition and effectiveness of capital punishment." Furman 405. Chief Justice Burger cites to "responsible legal thinkers of widely varying persuasions [who] have debated the sociological and philosophical aspects of the retribution question for generations, neither side being able to convince the other." Id. 394-395. Such a division of opinion on the basic facts affords a poor foundation for a startling repudiation of the historical past.

68. McGautha 241, 242.

69. Burger, C. J., Furman 384. Referring to the "world-wide trend toward limiting the use of capital punishment, Chief Justice Burger shows that "the change has generally come about through legislative action, often on a trial basis." Id. 404. As Justice Blackmun observed in Furman 413, "the elected representatives of the people" are "far more conscious of the temper of the times, of the maturing of society, and of the contemporary demands for man's dignity, than we who sit cloistered on this Court."

the jury to decide whether the defendant should live or die, without standards to guide that discretion, violated the due process clause of the Fourteenth Amendment. The Court, per Justice Harlan, held there was no violation, Justices Douglas, Brennan, and Marshall dissenting. Fourteen months later, by a plurality of three (joined by Justices Brennan and Marshall, who maintained that death penalties were unconstitutional per se), the Court held in *Furman* that standards were required by the "cruel and unusual punishments" clause,[70] leading Justice Blackmun to exclaim against "the suddenness of the Court's perception of progress in the human attitude" since *McGautha*.[71] This abrupt about-face exemplifies the very "government by whim" against which Justice Brennan inveighed in *McGautha* on the ground that ours is a "government of laws, not of men."[72] Activists know better: because the subsequent *Gregg v. Georgia* did not go far enough for him, Bedau complained that "Hidden beneath the veneer of constitutional argument is that the Court has proved itself arbitrary and discriminatory in its defense of the death penalty,"[73] an abolitionist's confession that what counts is effectuation of his predilections, not the "veneer of constitutional argument."

Furman toppled the settled law that whether to impose or withhold the death penalty lies within the jury's discretion.[74]

70. The core complaint, articulated by Justice Douglas, was that "no standards govern the selection of the penalty." Furman 253, as the subsequent Gregg v. Georgia, 428 U.S. 153 (1976), makes clear.

71. The four dissenters in Furman stated, "Before recognizing such an instant evolution in the law, it seems fair to ask what factors have changed that capital punishment should now be 'cruel' in the constitutional sense as it had not been in the past. It is apparent that there has been no change of constitutional significance in the nature of the punishment itself." Furman 382. The per curiam opinion in Furman, 239–240, stated, "The Court holds that the imposition and carrying out of the death penalty in these cases constitutes cruel and unusual punishment in violation of the Eighth and Fourteenth Amendments."

72. McGautha 250.

73. Bedau 118.

74. Id. 24. Justice Powell fairly summarized the primary reasons assigned by the majority for their repudiation of the historical practice: "Mr. Justice

Writing for a plurality of four in 1978, Chief Justice Burger correctly stated that "The Court had never intimated prior to *Furman* that discretion in sentencing offended the Constitution."[75] To the contrary, in 1899 the Court, per Justice Horace Gray, upheld an Act of Congress which provided for the jury's choice between imprisonment and death and declared, "The Act does not itself prescribe, *nor authorize the court* to prescribe, any rule defining or circumscribing the exercise of this right, but commits the whole matter of its exercise to the judgment and consciences of the jury."[76] The Ninth Circuit Court of Appeals stated in 1931 that "The discretion of the jury is unlimited and unrestricted."[77] As late as 1966, in *Giaccio v. Pennsylvania*[78]—a case Justice Brennan

---

Douglas concludes that capital punishment is incompatible with notions of 'equal protection' that he finds to be 'implicit' in the Eighth Amendment . . . Mr. Justice Brennan bases his judgment primarily on the thesis that the penalty 'does not comport with human dignity' . . . Mr. Justice Stewart concludes that the penalty is applied in a 'wanton' and 'freakish' manner . . . For Mr. Justice White it is the 'infrequency' with which the penalty is imposed that renders its use unconstitutional . . . Mr. Justice Marshall finds that capital punishment is an impermissible form of punishment because it is 'morally unacceptable' and 'excessive.' " Furman 415. In a thoughtful study Daniel Polsby concludes that "in terms of reasoned judgments, the majority Justices in *Furman* did not have one of their finest hours." Polsby, supra note 26 at 40.

75. Lockett v. Ohio, 438 U.S. 586, 598 (1978). For the history of jury discretion, see McGautha 196–200.

76. Winston v. United States, 172 U.S. 303, 313 (1899). The most tenderhearted of judges, Chief Judge Cardozo, wrote that he had "no objection to giving [the jury] this dispensing power" in choosing between degrees of murder. Benjamin N. Cardozo, *Law and Literature* 70, 100 (1931). In 1910 Justice Edward White observed that "the legislation of all the States . . . exemplifies the exertion of legislative power to define and punish crime according to the legislative conception of the necessities of the situation . . . without suggestion of judicial power to control the legislative discretion." Weems v. United States, 217 U.S. 349, 402 (1910), dissenting opinion, joined by Justice Holmes. His copious citations to State cases are contained id. 407 n.

77. Smith v. United States, 47 F. 2d 518, 520 (9th Cir. 1931).

78. 382 U.S. 399 (1966).

cited to show that in the "absence of any standards sufficient to enable defendants to protect themselves against the arbitrary and discriminating imposition of costs," a state law was invalid[79]—the Court took pains to declare:

> we intend to cast no doubt whatever on the constitutionality of the settled practice of many States to leave to juries finding defendants guilty of a crime the power to fix punishment within legally prescribed limits.[80]

In 1977 Justices Stevens, Stewart, and Powell noted that in *Williams v. New York* (1949), the Court "assumed," per Justice Black, that "a trial judge had complete discretion to impose any sentence within the limits prescribed by the legislature." But in the intervening years there have been two constitutional developments: (1) "five Members of the Court have now expressly recognized that death is a different kind of punishment from any other"; and (2) "it is now clear that the sentencing process . . . must satisfy the requirements of due process."[81] In short, the established sentencing discretion, considered to be inherent in the jury's function, has been overcome by the Court's freshly fashioned judicial constructs.

It needs immediately to be emphasized that the "cruel and unusual punishments" clause was concerned solely with the *nature* of the punishment—barbarous, torturous—not with the *process* whereby the sentence was handed down.[82] Until *Furman* over-

79. McGautha 262.

80. 382 U.S. at 405 n. 8. As in the case of Trop v. Dulles, supra text accompanying notes 18–19, it matters not a whit to Brennan that jury discretion was specifically excepted from the reach of Giaccio.

81. Gardner v. Florida, 430 U.S. 349, 357 (1977). Polsby remarked, "Why Justices Stewart and White found the due process arguments unconvincing in *McGautha* but persuasive in *Furman* is an unusual riddle." Polsby, supra note 26 at 26.

82. The point was made by Chief Justice Burger, Furman 399, and Justice Rehnquist, Gardner v. Florida, 430 U.S. 349, 371 (1977). Speaking on behalf of the Court in Powell v. Texas, 392 U.S. 514, 531 (1968), Justice

turned the established sentencing discretion, it was recognized as "settled" that juries had untrammeled sentencing discretion. And since jury discretion was the established practice in 1789 and before, it "cannot be deemed inconsistent with due process of law."[83]

Justice Brennan drew on far-fetched twentieth-century analogies, for example, the doctrine that a statute is "void for vagueness."[84] What murderer can be misled by a statute which warns that murder is punishable and leaves it to the jury to choose between death and imprisonment? Brennan also invoked the requirement that administrative bodies must make findings and supply reasons so that critics may "compare one case with another";[85] and he called upon juries to "explain why they had reached that decision, and the facts upon which it is based," citing the practice in *civil* cases.[86] He desired the "accumulation of a

---

Marshall said, "The primary purpose of a [cruel and unusual] clause has always been considered, and properly so, to be directed at the method and kind of punishment imposed."

83. Owenbey v. Morgan, 256 U.S. 94, 111 (1921). The "cruel and unusual" clause is even less relevant to jury discretion. Chief Justice Burger points out that "The decisive grievance of the [majority] opinions—not translated into Eighth Amendment terms—is that the present system of discretionary sentencing in capital cases has failed to produce evenhanded justice . . . that the selection process has followed no rational pattern. This claim of arbitrariness . . . manifestly fails to establish that the death penalty is a 'cruel and unusual punishment.' " Furman 398–399.

"It would be difficult to conceive a better security than this right to [trial by jury] affords against any arbitrary violence on the part of the crown." William Forsyth, *History of Trial by Jury* 426 (1852). In Gregg v. Georgia, 428 U.S. at 203, the plurality—Justices Stewart, Powell, and Stevens—stated that "the proportionality requirement is intended to prevent caprice in the decision to inflict the penalty." There was no doctrine of proportionality at common law, and to this extent the plurality's drive to obviate jury "arbitrariness" can draw no support from the Eighth Amendment.

84. McGautha 257.

85. Id. 274.

86. Id. 286.

body of precedent," forgetting, as he himself noted, that "capital sentencing juries are drawn essentially at random and called upon to decide one case and one case only"[87]—unlikely soil on which to grow a "body of precedent."

Brennan's requirements[88] run counter to the basic theory of trial by jury. In his 1791 Philadelphia Lectures, Justice James Wilson, second only to Madison as an architect of the Constitution, counted it a prime virtue of the jury system that "changed as they constantly are, their errors and mistakes can never grow into a dangerous system. The native uprightness of their sentiments will not be bent under the *weight of precedent* and authority."[89] Having regard to the purposes served by jury trial, Thomas Cooley, Chief Justice of the Michigan Supreme Court and renowned commentator on constitutional law, observed, "the jury must be left to weigh the evidence ... by their own tests. They cannot properly be furnished for this purpose with balances that leave them no discretion."[90] "The purpose of establishing trial by jury," Justice Horace Gray remarked, "was not to obtain general rules of law for future use, but to secure impartial justice between the government and the accused in each case as it arose."[91] Justice Brennan quotes Lord Camden: discretion is "the law of tyrants: It is different in different men ... It is always unknown; and depends upon the constitution, temper, passion.—In the best it is often caprice; In the worst it is every vice, folly and passion to which human nature is liable."[92] But he overlooks that *Camden spoke of judges:* "The discretion of a judge is the law of tyrants." The *dis-*

87. Id. 297, 295.

88. Brennan also draws upon a case overturning a State procedure for determining voting qualifications because it imposed "no definite and objective standards upon registrars of voters for the administration of the interpretation test." McGautha 267. All of his tests are drawn from twentieth-century decisions totally unrelated to jury practice.

89. 2 James Wilson, *Works,* ed. R. G. McCloskey 541 (1967).

90. People v. Garbutt, 17 Mich. 9, 27–28 (1868).

91. Sparf and Hansen v. United States, 156 U.S. 51, 174–175 (1895), dissenting opinion.

92. McGautha 285.

cretion of juries, however, was prized by the common law as a shield
against judges. In "many of the States the arbitrary temper of the
colonial judges, holding office directly from the Crown, had made
the independence of the jury . . . of much popular importance."[93]
And, as Justice Horace Gray commented, "it is a matter of common observation, that judges and lawyers . . . are sometimes
too much influenced by technical rules; that those judges
who are wholly or chiefly occupied in the administration of
criminal justice are apt, not only to grow severe in their sentences, but to decide questions of law too unfavorably to the
accused."[94]

The Founders' view of the relative roles of courts and juries was
antipodal to that of Justice Brennan. The jury was their darling,
the age-old buckler against judicial and executive oppression, the
central pillar of the society they sought to erect; whereas judicial
review, unmentioned in the Constitution—in contrast to the
twice-mentioned trial by jury[95]—was a suspect innovation which
on several occasions led to violent protests and movements in the
fledgling States[96] for removal of judges. Of this the Framers were
aware, so that Hamilton was constrained to assure the jealous
Ratifiers that of the three departments the judiciary "is next to
nothing."[97] In fact, the colonial experience resulted in an "aversion" to judges, so that Justice James Wilson, a leading Framer,
counseled in 1791 that it was time to view them more recep-

93. Supra note 91 at 89.
94. Id. at 174. In Duncan v. Louisiana, 391 U.S. 145, 156 (1968), the
Court stated per Justice White: "an inestimable safeguard against . . . the
compliant, biased or eccentric judge . . . the jury trial provisions . . . reflect
. . . a reluctance to entrust plenary powers over the life and liberty of the
citizen to one judge or to a group of judges. Fears of unchecked power
found expression in the criminal law in this insistence upon community
participation in the determination of guilt or innocence." William Forsyth,
History of Trial by Jury 445 (1852): "The jury acts as a constant check
upon, and corrective of, that narrow subtlety to which professional lawyers
are so prone."
95. Article III, §2(3); Sixth Amendment.
96. Berger, *Congress v. Court* 38–42.
97. Federalist No. 78 at 504.

tively.[98] Writing about juries, Blackstone, whose influence can be traced into the very terms of a number of State Constitutions and utterances of the Founders, stated: "the liberties of England cannot but subsist so long as this *palladium* remains sacred and inviolate."[99] The North Carolina Constitution of 1776 provided that "the ancient mode of trial by jury ... ought to remain sacred and inviolable."[100] Massachusetts, New Hampshire, Pennsylvania, and Vermont provided that it "shall be held sacred,"[101] Georgia, South Carolina, and New York, that it was "inviolate forever."[102] In the Virginia Ratification Convention the Wythe Committee recommended an amendment: that "the ancient trial by jury is one of the greatest securities to the rights of the people, and is to remain sacred and inviolable."[103] George Mason in Virginia termed it "This great palladium of national safety," and in North Carolina James Iredell referred to it as "that noble palladium of liberty."[104] No such apostrophes to judicial review are found in the constitutional records. No element of judicial proceedings aroused such anxious inquiry as did preservation of trial by jury in the "ancient mode." In our own day Lord Justice Devlin wrote, "trial by jury is more than an instrument of justice and more than one wheel of the constitution: it is the lamp that shows freedom lives."[105]

98. The judiciary "were derived from a different and foreign source ... they were directed to foreign purposes. Need we be surprised, that they were objects of aversion and distrust ... But it is high time that we chastise our prejudices." 1 James Wilson, *Works,* ed. R. G. McCloskey 292–293 (1967).

99. 4 Blackstone 350.

100. Article XIV, 2 Poore 1410.

101. Massachusetts (1780), Article XV Declaration of Rights, 1 Poore 959; New Hampshire (1784), Article 20, 2 Poore 1282; Pennsylvania (1776), Article XI, 2 Poore 1542; Vermont (1777), Chapter I, Section XIII, 2 Poore 1860.

102. Georgia (1777) Article LXI, 1 Poore 382; South Carolina (1790), Article XI, Section 6, 2 Poore 1633; New York (1777), Article XLI, 2 Poore 1339.

103. 3 Elliot 658.

104. Mason, id. 528; Iredell, 4 Elliot 148.

105. Sir Patrick Devlin, *Trial by Jury* 164 (1956).

The attachment of the Founders to the "ancient *mode* of trial by jury" was sharply articulated in the Declaration of Rights adopted by the Continental Congress in 1774, where it was resolved that

> the respective Colonies are entitled to the common law of England, and more especially to the great and inestimable privilege of being tried by their peers of the vicinage, *according to the course of that law.*[106]

Kalven and Zeisel wrote, "The right to trial by jury . . . has generally been taken to mean the right as it stood at common law at the adoption of the Constitution."[107] A striking illustration that the "course of that law" was well-understood and prized by the Ratifiers is found in the Virginia Ratification Convention: when the delegates anxiously inquired whether the right to challenge jurors was secured, they were repeatedly assured by John Marshall, Edmund Randolph, and Edmund Pendleton, the venerable mentor of its highest court, that "trial by jury" embraced all its attributes.[108] The jury's sentencing discretion in a criminal trial was just such an attribute, and therefore *constitutionally immune* from judicial curtailment.

In a decision of the New York Court of Appeals, quoted by the Supreme Court, Judge Selden referred to "the unquestionable power of juries to find general verdicts,"[109] that is, guilty or not guilty. At its option, the jury might render a special verdict—a special finding—in a criminal case, but it could not be compelled

---

106. 1 *Journal of the Continental Congress* 69 (1904). See 1777 Georgia Constitution, Article XLIII, 2 Poore 382.

107. Harry Kalven and Hans Zeisel, *The American Jury* 15 (1966). The Supreme Court said of "trial by jury," "That it means trial by jury as understood and applied at common law, and includes all the essential elements as they were recognized in this country and England when the Constitution was adopted, is not open to question." Patton v. United States, 281 U.S. 276, 288 (1930).

108. 3 Elliot 463, 546, 549, 559.

109. Sparf and Hansen v. United States, 156 U.S. 51, 83 (1895).

to do so.[110] Judge Selden also stated that "the law has provided no means, in criminal cases of reviewing their decisions, whether of law or fact, or of ascertaining the grounds upon which their verdicts are based."[111] Anciently jurors were punished for a wrong verdict by the process of attaint.[112] But *Bushell's Case* made plain that "no attaint lay in a criminal case,"[113] as Hamilton noticed.[114] Lord Bacon said that wherever an attaint did not lie, the "judgment of the jury, commonly called verdict, was considered as a kind of gospel."[115] It was the jury, a 1676 New Jersey statute provided, "in whom only, the judgment resides, and not otherwise."[116] Speaking for the Massachusetts court, Chief Justice Lemuel Shaw stated that the verdict "stands conclusive and unquestionable, in point both of law and fact," for there "is no judicial power by which ... that verdict can be ... inquired into."[117] Lord Somers wrote in 1681 that "from their verdict there

110. Id. 115, 129, Justice Gray dissenting. During the course of the debate on the Fox Libel Bill in 1791, Lord Camden observed that a special verdict expressed a desire for help in the law: "But this was only in cases of extraordinary difficulty, and even here the judge should interpose nothing but his advice; if he attempted to control them, there was an end to trial by jury. Indeed, there was no legal power to control them." 29 Parlty. Hist. of England (1817).

111. Id. 83. Kalven and Zeisel, supra note 107 at 2, wrote, "The law permits [jury] to ... report their final judgment without giving reasons for it." Similarly, "no federal constitutional objection would have been possible if the judge here had sentenced appellant to death ... giving no reason at all." United States v. Rosenberg, 195 F. 2d 583, 609 (2d Cir. 1952).

112. 156 U.S. at 116, Justice Gray dissenting.

113. 124 E. R. 1006, 1011 (1671).

114. Quoted in Sparf and Hansen v. United States, 156 U.S. at 148, Justice Gray dissenting.

115. Id. 117.

116. Id. 151.

117. Quoted id. 80. Compare with this the views of the plurality—Justices Stewart, Powell, and Stevens—in Gregg v. Georgia, 428 U.S. at 195: "Where the sentencing authority is required to specify the factors it relied upon in reaching its decision, the further safeguard of meaningful appellate review is available to insure that death sentences are not imposed capriciously or in a freakish manner."

lies no appeal."[118] This was also the American law as summarized
by the Supreme Court in 1894 in *McKane v. Durston:*

> A review by an appellate court of the final judgment in a crimi-
> nal case, however grave the offense of which the accused is con-
> victed, was not at common law and is not now a necessary ele-
> ment of due process of law. It is wholly within the discretion of
> the State to allow or not to allow such review ... the right of
> appeal may be accorded by the State upon such terms as it deems
> proper.[119]

Even when a right to review is afforded by statute, the Court,
rightly stated Justice Horace Gray, "cannot supersede or impair
the lawful power of the jury under the Constitution."[120] History
therefore confirms the Court's judgment in *McGautha:* "we find it
quite impossible to say that committing to the untrammeled discretion of the jury the power to pronounce life or death in capital
cases is offensive to anything in the Constitution."[121]

The plurality in *Gregg v. Georgia* mistakenly inferred from the
judicial practice of giving instructions to the jury about what law
to apply to "the merits" that "guidance" must be furnished to the
jury respecting what factors are "relevant to the *sentencing* decision." "It would be virtually unthinkable," they stated, "to follow
any other course in a legal system that has traditionally operated
by following prior precedents and fixed rules of law."[122] Yet the
plurality did not find it "unthinkable" to overturn jury discretion
and hobble death penalties in the teeth of long-standing "prior
precedents and fixed rules of law." Here, as Justice Holmes observed, "a page of history is worth a volume of logic."[123] For centuries, including 181 years of the American experience, it was not

118. Quoted id. 123, Justice Gray dissenting.
119. 153 U.S. 684, 687 (1894).
120. Sparf and Hansen v. United States, 156 U.S. at 176, Justice Gray
dissenting.
121. McGautha 207.
122. Gregg v. Georgia, 428 U.S. 153, 192 (1976).
123. New York Trust Co. v. Eisner, 256 U.S. 345, 349 (1921).

only "thinkable" but the practice to allow juries free rein without regard to creating a system of "precedent" or "fixed rules." The jury is a unique institution with its own quite different tradition. In contrast to the long-established practice of giving instructions as to the law governing the verdict, "precedent" controverts "guidance" to the jury in sentencing. Speaking for Chief Justice Burger and Justices White, Rehnquist, and himself, Justice Powell correctly referred to the "fundamental difference" between "determinations of guilt and sentencing." "Underlying the question of guilt or innocence," he said, "is an objective truth: the defendant, in fact, did or did not commit the acts constituting the crime charged," whereas "the sentencer's function is not to discover a fact, but to mete out just deserts *as he sees them.*"[124] History, it bears reemphasis, establishes that discretion in sentencing withinstatutoryprescriptionshasbeentheinviolablejurydomain.

THE "STANDARDS" FIASCO

Justice Harlan foresaw that the promulgation of standards to govern jury sentencing was a vain endeavor:

> such criteria do not purport to provide more than the most minimal control over the sentencing authority's exercise of discretion. They do not purport to give an exhaustive list of the relevant considerations or the way in which they may be affected by the presence or absence of other circumstances ... And, of course, they provide no protection against the jury determined to decide on whimsy or caprice ... and they bear witness to the intractable nature of the problem of "standards" ... The infinite variety of cases and facets to each case would make general standards either meaningless "boiler-plate" or a statement of the obvious that no jury would need.[125]

124. Bullington v. Missouri, 101 S. Ct. 1852, 1863–1864 (1981).
125. McGautha 207–208; see also Bedau, infra text accompanying note 130. Herbert Wechsler, Reporter for the Model Penal Code, consid-

Responding to the discretion entailed in balancing "aggravating" against "mitigating" circumstances, Justices Stewart, Powell, and Stevens stated: "they require no more line drawing than is commonly required of a fact finder . . . For example, juries have traditionally evaluated the validity of defenses such as insanity."[126] It is not easy to conceive of wider discretion than is afforded the jury by the confused subject of legal insanity,[127] an illustration of the plurality's failure to grasp the inescapable discretion that resides in "standards." Justices Brennan and Marshall, who maintained in *McGautha* that sentencing *was* "capable of rational treatment,"[128] and who subsequently tipped the scales in *Furman* in favor of standards, confessed error in 1980 in light of the post-*Furman* experience: "the Court was substantially correct in concluding that the task of selecting in some objective way those persons who should be doomed to die is one that remains beyond the capacities of the criminal justice system," that "the enterprise on which the Court embarked in *Gregg v. Georgia* . . . increasingly appears to be doomed to failure," that the "task of eliminating arbitrariness in the infliction of capital punishment is proving to be one which our criminal justice system—and perhaps any criminal justice system—is unable to perform."[129]

---

ered that "No draftsman can really trust his capacity to enumerate all the possible mitigations that might be perceived, or indeed even all the aggravations." Quoted in Bedau 26.

126. Profitt v. Florida, 428 U.S. 242, 257 (1976).

127. Leland v. Oregon, 343 U.S. 790, 801 (1952): "This whole problem [of legal insanity] has evoked wide disagreement among those who have studied it."

128. McGautha 280, 249.

129. Godfrey v. Georgia, 446 U.S. 420, 442, 434, 440 (1980). Justice White read the majority to endorse the argument that government "is incompetent to administer" the death penalty, id. 456, dissenting opinion. Upon the basis of a study of 30 years of sentencing in Arizona, George E. Dix concluded that "it may be impossible to develop useful appellate guidelines for civil sentencing." Dix, "Appellate Review of the Decision to Impose Death," 68 Geo. L. J. 97, 98 (1979).

That view had been anticipated by prominent abolitionists. Bedau perceived that a list of standards left the jury at large, because "there is nothing to prevent juries from weighing these relevant factors in a different way every time." He concluded: "it is beyond human capability to draw up a statute that will provide the death penalty for only the worst of murders, that will be imposed without procedural unfairness, and that will yield effective deterrence."[130] Charles Black observed that the post-*Furman* state statutes "do not effectively restrict the discretion of juries by real standards. They never will."[131] By the testimony of the abolitionists themselves the Court's insistence on State enactment of standards has been an exercise in futility. The cure, Justices Brennan and Marshall maintain, as they did from the beginning, is that "the death penalty must be abandoned altogether."[132] Given that

130. Bedau 27, 98.

131. Quoted id. 100. Ely comments on Gregg: "even if the jury does find the presence of one or more aggravating circumstances, it is empowered to spare the defendant's life if it finds them outweighed by mitigating circumstances (not enumerated) 'which, in fairness and mercy, may be considered as extenuating or reducing the degree' of moral culpability or appropriate punishment. 'In this way the jury's discretion is channelled,' Justice Stewart wrote for the plurality. 'No longer can a jury wantonly and freakishly impose the death sentence; it is always circumscribed by the legislative guidelines.' In less serious circumstances this would be amusing." Ely observes, "I'm sure we could do a better job of channelling jury discretion than the legislatures whose 'systems' the Court upheld in 1976 had done, but I'm also sure we couldn't do a very good one. So long as the jury is entrusted with the job of deciding whether the defendant acted with 'malice aforethought' (which typically makes a killing murder rather than manslaughter) and 'premeditation' (which makes it first degree)—and it is difficult to imagine a decision compelling the elimination of those time-honored terms from the definition—there will inevitably be a substantial amount of play in the joints." J. H. Ely, *Democracy and Distrust* 175 (1980).

Bedau concluded that "the post-Furman death statutes achieved little or no change from the pre-Furman statutes, with their unbridled discretion and arbitrary and discriminatory impact." Bedau 116.

132. Godfrey v. Georgia, 446 U.S. at 442. Justices generally " 'bow to the authority' of an earlier case despite their 'original and continuing belief

by a vote of 7 to 2 the Court justly upheld the constitutionality of death penalties, it would be more appropriate if the plurality, whose insistence on standards prevailed only with the aid of the two Justices whose unremitting aim is to discredit death penalties, would acknowledge that their efforts are fruitless.[133] In fact, as will appear, the plurality has rendered insistence on standards meaningless.

MANDATORY SENTENCING

Justice White, one of the original *Furman* plurality, charged in 1978 that "The Court has now completed its about-face since *Furman v. Georgia*,"[134] a course described by Justice Rehnquist as "from pillar to post."[135] These were utterances in a case, *Lockett v. Ohio*, arising under a mandatory death penalty, and to appreciate its ironies it should be viewed in historical perspective. At the adoption of the Bill of Rights, "the States uniformly followed the common law practice" of mandatory death sentences.[136] That, on

---

that the decision was constitutionally wrong.' " Justice Rehnquist dissenting in Lockett v. Ohio, 438 U.S. 586, 628 (1978). See also Justice Powell in Coker v. Georgia, 433 U.S. 584, 602 n. 1 (1977), dissenting in part. Brennan's and Marshall's reiteration in case after case that death penalties are unconstitutional marks them as stubborn crusaders.

In justice to Brennan and Marshall, it should be noted that Anthony G. Amsterdam, "the principal architect of legal efforts to abolish capital punishment," thinks of "the present Supreme Court lineup" as consisting of "two horsemen and seven mules," "exempt[ing] from his criticism" Brennan and Marshall, who are "dissenting in virtually isolated splendor," as contrasted with "the *atrocious* opinions which Justice Rehnquist is capable of writing." *New York Times,* Dec. 10, 1981, B-1, B-2.

133. "If the death penalty is constitutional, then it is also constitutional to give the decision as to when to inflict it to the jury to decide according to its own untutored judgment." Polsby, supra note 26 at 5.

134. Lockett v. Ohio, 438 U.S. 586, 622 (1978), dissenting in part.

135. Id. at 629, dissenting in part.

136. Woodson v. North Carolina, 428 U.S. 280, 289 (1976).

principles earlier discussed, insulates mandatory sentencing from judicial curtailment, although legislatures of course are free to abandon it, as in fact they did. Over the years juries reacted unfavorably to the harshness of mandatory death sentences, resulting in "jury nullification" where juries believed death penalties "inappropriate."[137] Various legislative devices to curb such action proved unsatisfactory, so finally legislatures "adopted the method of forthrightly granting juries the discretion which they had been exercising in fact."[138] A prime factor was that the jury, as the Justices have repeatedly recognized, maintains a "link without which the determination of punishment could hardly reflect 'the evolving standards of decency that mark the progress of a maturing society.' "[139] At times no doubt the jury allows "feelings of compassion for the prisoner, or repugnance to the punishment which the law awards" to overpower "their sense of duty. They usurp in such cases the prerogative of mercy."[140] It is just such compassion that produced acquittals under harsh mandatory statutes. In consequence, as said by Kalvin and Zeisel, the "jury has long been regarded as a bulwark of protection for the criminal defendant."[141]

Confused by the mixed signals broadcast by the five majority opinions in *Furman*,[142] ten States, as Justice Blackmun foresaw, removed the element of discretion altogether and once more made death penalties mandatory.[143] Bedau had opined that "Legislatures

137. Justice Marshall, Furman 339; McGautha 198 et seq.

138. McGautha 199.

139. Witherspoon v. Illinois, 391 U.S. 510, 519 n. 15 (1968), per Justice Stewart.

140. William Forsyth, *History of Trial by Jury* 430 (1852).

141. Kalven and Zeisel, supra note 107 at 58. The jury, they concluded, represents "an impressive way of building discretion, equity and flexibility into a legal system." Id. at 498.

142. "Predictably the variety of opinions supporting the judgment in *Furman* engendered confusion as to what was required in order to impose the death penalty in accord with the Eighth Amendment." Lockett v. Ohio, 438 U.S. 586, 599 (1978). "The signals from this Court have not, however, been easy to decipher." Id. 602.

143. Furman 413.

could obviate the entire problem of sentencing standards in capital cases by restoring mandatory capital punishment. No question of jury discretion in sentencing would then arise."[144] He little allowed for doctrinaire judicial logic. Such enactments, Justices Stewart, Powell, and Stevens declared, merely "reflect attempts by the States to retain the death sentence in a form consistent with [the plurality's view of] the Constitution, rather than a renewed societal acceptance of mandatory death sentencing."[145] Thus, the plurality elevated society's alleged aversion of yesteryear over the legislature's more recent formal expression of society's desires, which the Court, by Justice Cardozo, considered to express the will of the people.[146] It was open to the ten States to abandon death penalties; instead they elected mandatory sentencing as they thought the Court demanded. It may have been reluctant, but nonetheless it represents an election, a "renewed societal acceptance of mandatory death sentencing." Certainly the decisions of a badly split Court do not better reflect "societal" values.

Mandatory penalties, the plurality considered, "simply papered over the problem of the unguided and unchecked jury discretion" because juries can refuse in many cases to convict.[147] As an example of ill-considered mercy, the same three Justices criticized an instruction in first-degree murder cases permitting the jury to consider second-degree murder or manslaughter, "even if there is not a scintilla of evidence to support the lesser verdicts. [I]t plainly *invites* jurors to disregard their oaths and choose a verdict for a lesser offense whenever they feel the death penalty is inappropriate. There is an element of capriciousness."[148] But merciful ac-

144. Bedau 25.

145. Woodson v. North Carolina, 428 U.S. 280, 298 (1976).

146. Supra text accompanying note 51; see also id. at note 55.

147. Woodson v. North Carolina, 428 U.S. at 302.

148. Roberts v. Louisiana, 428 U.S. 325, 335 (1976). The same three Justices stated in Gregg v. Georgia, 428 U.S. 153, 182 (1976), that "the reluctance of juries in many cases to impose the [death] sentence may well reflect the humane feeling that this most irrevocable of sanctions should be reserved for a small number of extreme cases."

quittals were thought to be one of the glories of trial by jury.[149]
Even the skilled lawyers who sought in *McGautha* to overturn
death penalties acknowledged that "jury sentencing discretion . . .
was introduced as a mechanism for mercy."[150] Mercy is an act of
compassion, not of reason; it defies reason in the shape of the
"law,"[151] and is still less susceptible to categorization because different juries have higher or lower thresholds of compassion.
Under the guise of protecting the criminal in the name of
"human dignity," the plurality insists on the ultimate indig-
nity—death; it is in fact undermining his chance for survival. The
Texas statute imposing standards met with Justice White's approval because it "does not extend to juries discretionary power to
dispense mercies,"[152] because a penalty that will "not be imposed
freakishly or rarely but will be imposed *with regularity*" will serve
as "a credible deterrent."[153] On the basis of pure speculation respecting deterrence "regularity" is exalted over mercy, the age-old
virtue of jury verdicts.[154] Whatever the content of "cruel and un-

149. Kalven and Zeisel, supra note 107 at 218, 189, considered that "the
jury's sense of justice leads it to policies which differ from official legal policies," "an expression of the community's conscience."

It seems as "inherently plausible that juries, judges . . . conduct themselves with deliberation and caution so as to err on the side of mercy, reserving their ultimate punishment for those whose transgressions are most
clearly established and seem to them most revolting." Polsby, supra note 26
at 20.

150. McGautha 203.

151. Dean Wigmore wrote, The "judge must apply the law as he finds it
alike for all." The jury, however, "adjusts the general rule of law to the
justice of the particular case." J. H. Wigmore, "A Program for the Trial of
Jury Trial," 12 Jour. Amer. Judic. Soc. 166, 170 (1929).

152. Jurek v. Texas, 428 U.S. 262, 279 (1976).

153. Profitt v. Florida, 428 U.S. 242, 267 (1976). Apparently such reasoning has Justice Brennan's sympathy, for he approved the British view
that "death should be the sentence of the law and not of the tribunal."
McGautha 282.

154. Chief Justice Burger ironically commented on the notion that "capital punishment can be made to satisfy the Eighth Amendment values if its
rate of imposition is somehow multiplied; it seemingly follows that the

usual punishments," only the wildest fantasy can attribute to its framers an intention to curtail the jury's traditional dispensation of mercy.

Representative of the Court's increasingly doctrinaire approach is *Roberts v. Louisiana*,[155] wherein the Court overturned a mandatory death penalty for the murder of a policeman. For this it relied on its freshly minted pronouncement, "the fundamental *respect for humanity* underlying the Eighth Amendment [?] . . . requires consideration of the character and record of the individual offender and circumstances of the particular offense as a constitutionally indispensable part of the process of inflicting the penalty of death."[156] Given the jury's proclivity for mercy, it is reasonable to assume that it would consider "the circumstances" of the murder.[157] As violence in the streets increasingly mounts, policemen who patrol crime-infested areas take their lives in their hands; more and more policemen are killed in the line of duty. Not unreasonably legislators have concluded that policemen require the utmost protection in the shape of mandatory capital punishment for assailants. As Justice White stated,

> Even if the character of the accused *must* be considered under the Eighth Amendment, surely a State is not constitutionally forbidden to provide that the commission of certain crimes conclusively establishes that the criminal's character is such that he deserves death. Moreover, quite apart from the character of a crime, a State should constitutionally be able to conclude that the need to deter some crime and that the likelihood that the death penalty will succeed in deterring those crimes is such that the death penalty may be made mandatory for all who commit them.[158]

---

flexible sentencing system created by legislatures, and carried out by juries and judges, has yielded more mercy than the Eighth Amendment can stand." Furman 398.

155. Roberts v. Louisiana, 431 U.S. 633 (1977).

156. Id. 636.

157. Legislators, Bedau, 106, wrote, "know that their statutory enactments will never be given rigid or literal application."

158. Roberts v. Louisiana, 428 U.S. 325, 358 (1976).

"Respect for humanity" is little furthered by erecting ramparts for those who gun down policemen. And rejection of mandatory sentencing on the ground that it promotes jury discretion is at war with the plurality's insistence upon regard for the "record of the murderer" and the "circumstances" of the crime.

The difficulties in which the Court has entangled the States may be illustrated by *Godfrey v. Georgia*.[159] After *Furman* the Georgia statute was amended to require findings among ten aggravating circumstances. Apparently the only pigeonhole into which the murder could fit was No. 7: the offense "was outrageously and wantonly vile, horrible or inhuman in that it involved torture, depravity of mind, or an aggravated battery to the victim." The murderer told the police that he had committed a "hideous" crime.[160] But the plurality (Justices Stewart, Blackmun, Powell, and Stevens) observed, "a person of ordinary sensibility could fairly characterize almost every murder as 'outrageously or wantonly vile, horrible and inhuman,'" and it held that the murder did not reflect "a consciousness materially more 'depraved' than that of any person guilty of a murder,"[161] thereby suggesting differentiation across the spectrum of depravity and atrociousness. Each atrocity must be carefully weighed at the risk that the Court, looking over the jury's shoulder, will conclude that the murder was not really "wantonly vile, horrible," thus acting in the role, Justice White acidly remarked, "of a finely tuned calibrator of depravity."[162] Chief Justice Burger rightly commented that the Court assumed the responsibility "of determining on a case-by-case basis whether a defendant's conduct is egregious enough to warrant a death sentence,"[163] the very thing

159. 446 U.S. 420 (1980).

160. Id. at 443.

161. Id. at 428, 433.

162. Id. at 456 n. 6, dissenting opinion. "The appellants, however, have all committed atrocious crimes. Given the enormity of their crimes, the task of identifying specific characteristics that society may use to determine whether a particular appellant should be executed is impossible." Dix, supra note 129 at 161.

163. 446 U.S. at 443, dissenting opinion.

Justices Stewart, Powell, and Stevens (and Justice Marshall before
them) had warned against in *Gregg v. Georgia:* "Caution is necessary lest this Court become 'under the aegis of the Cruel and Unusual Punishments Clause the ultimate arbiter of the standards of
criminal responsibility . . . throughout the country.' "[164]

That caution fell on deaf ears, as the progressive intrusion of
the Court into matters of State administration testifies. So, a death
penalty for rape was struck down in *Coker v. Georgia.*[165] The rapist,
in prison for murder and two rapes, escaped and raped a sixteen-
year-old; in addition to being a rapist he was therefore a repeater, a
proven menace to society. Here looking at the murderer's
"record" did not suffice. The plurality concluded that a death sentence "is grossly disproportionate and excessive punishment for
the crime of rape and is therefore forbidden by the Eighth
Amendment as cruel and unusual punishment."[166] The common
law, it will be recalled, knew no doctrine of disproportionate or
excessive punishment. To hang a highwayman for the theft of a
few shillings was vastly more "disproportionate" than to hang a
rapist, yet such was the "disproportion" that prevailed at the
adoption of the Constitution. Lesser crimes than rape—forgery of
public securities, robbery—were visited with death penalties by
the Act of April 30, 1790.[167] Death penalties for rape were a commonplace in the colonies; and the federal Act of 1825 punished
rape with death.[168] For present purposes there is no need for de-

164. 428 U.S. at 176.

165. 433 U.S. 584 (1977).

166. Id. at 592. In Coker v. Georgia, 433 U.S. 584, 597 (1977), the plurality (White, Stewart, Blackmun, and Stevens, JJ.) said, "it is true that in
the vast majority of cases, at least 9 out of 10 juries have not imposed the
death sentence." Kalven and Zeisel, supra note 107 at 253, found that "The
jury convicts of rape in just 3 of 42 cases of simple rape," and that "If
forced to choose in these cases [of aggravated assault] between total acquittal and finding the defendant guilty of rape, the jury will usually
choose acquittal as the lesser evil," hardly a situation that cries out for re-
medial action by the judiciary.

167. Supra Chapter 3, text accompanying note 86.

168. Act of March 3, 1825, c. 65 §4, 4 Stat. 115.

tailed examination of the empirical argument for the legislative right to punish rape with death, a case vigorously made by Chief Justice Burger.[169] It suffices that the Court's overthrow of capital punishment for rape represents another judicial displacement of a settled constitutional practice, a substitution, as Chief Justice Burger charged, of the Court's "policy judgment for that of the state legislature."[170]

The Court came full circle in *Lockett v. Ohio*.[171] Lockett was sentenced to death for aiding and abetting a murder. She had par-

169. 433 U.S. at 611–612. Justice Powell wished to reserve the death penalty for cases of "aggravated rape": "Some victims are so grievously injured physically and psychologically that life *is* beyond repair." 433 U.S. at 603, italics in the original. Chief Justice Burger rightly rejected Powell's "excessively brutal" versus "moderately brutal" test, id. at 412, saying, it is "not irrational—nor constitutionally impermissible—for a legislature to make the penalty more severe than the criminal act it punishes, in the hope it would deter wrongdoing: 'We may not require the legislature to select the least severe penalty . . .' Gregg v. Georgia, 428 U.S. at 175," 433 U.S. at 619. For an acute rejection of the abolitionist argument against the death penalty for rape, see Herbert Packer, "Making the Punishment Fit the Crime," 77 Harv. L. Rev. 1071 (1964).

170. 433 U.S. at 604. In a pretty example of how to play both sides of the street, Justice White, who experienced no difficulty in Furman in ignoring the all but *universal practice* of jury discretion, now emphasized that a majority of the States did not authorize capital punishment for the rape of an adult female. 433 U.S. at 593. As if the Constitution empowered the Court to impose one and the same standard on every State in the Union, thus undertaking the abjured role of "ultimate arbiter of the standards of criminal responsibility." Supra text accompanying note 164. In 1971, just prior to Furman, 16 States and the federal government had death penalties for rape, 433 U.S. at 593. Justice White places great stress on the fact that most reenactments after Furman dropped rape, but, as Chief Justice Burger pointed out, given the uncertain status of death penalties in the wake of Furman, the States might well have sought to narrow conflict with the Court. 433 U.S. at 614.

Usurpation grows by what it feeds on. In Bullington v. Missouri, 101 S. Ct. 1852 (1981), the Court, by a vote of 5 to 4, overturned the established rule that double jeopardy applies only to conviction, not to sentencing.

171. 438 U.S. 586 (1978).

ticipated in planning the robbery, procured the fatal gun as a pre-
caution, guided the principal actor, Parker, to the pawnshop, and
sat in the car with engine running while Parker killed the pawn-
broker. The plurality found it unnecessary to consider Justice
White's argument that a death penalty for aiding and abetting
was disproportionate to the crime.[172] Instead it sharpened its earlier pronouncement: the "Eighth and Fourteenth Amendments
require" that the jury must "not be precluded from considering,
as a mitigating factor, any aspect of the defendant's character or
record and *any of the circumstances* of the offense that the defendant
proffers."[173] It is hard to differ with Justice Rehnquist's judgment

172. Id. at 624–625, 635. Justice Rehnquist correctly observed that
"centuries of common-law doctrine establishing the felony-murder doctrine, dealing with the relationship between aiders and abettors and princi-
pals, would have to be rejected to adopt this view." 438 U.S. 635. As the
law stood in the eighteenth century, "a principal in the second degree was a
person 'who is present, aiding, and abetting the act to be done . . .' as when
one commits a robbery or murder, another keeps watch on guard at some
convenient distance.' " 1 Leon Radzinowicz, *History of the English Criminal
Law* 67 (1948). For a federal statute declaratory of the doctrine see United
States v. Mills, 32 U.S. (7 Pet.) 138, 141 (1833); for recognition of the
English common law, see Morei v. United States, 127 F. 2d 827, 830–831
(6th Cir. 1942). Under 18 U.S.C. §2, the "aider and abettor statute," "the
acts of the actual perpetrator become the acts of the aide and the latter can
be charged with having done the act itself." United States v. J. R. Watkins
Co., 127 F. Supp. 97, 101 (D. Minn. 1954). One who operates the get-
away-car assures the perpetrator that he may escape unscathed. Without
such assurance there would often be a failure of nerve. As Colin Clark, a
convicted murderer in Louisiana, said, "Even though I didn't pull the trig-
ger and had nothing to do with the stabbing, Mr. Schmidt would be alive
today if I hadn't planned the job." *New York Times,* Oct. 22, 1981, A-18.
For some of the difficulties that attend a requirement of "intent" to kill
from the accomplice, see opinion of Justice Blackmun, 438 U.S. at
614–615.

173. 438 U.S. at 604, italics in the original. Ely remarked that "the U-
turn was completed, when in *Lockett v. Ohio* the Court seemed to opt for
maximum discretion by holding it unconstitutional to exclude from the
consideration of the jury anything that might plausibly be thought to bear
on whether the defendant should be executed. Opponents of capital pun-

that the Court's direction to consider any "mitigating circumstances" will "not guide sentencing discretion but will totally un-
leash it."[174] It opens wide the floodgates of discretion that the
Court's demand for "standards" was meant to limit.

What, too, of "the gross disparities in [general] sentencing . . .
for every 'hanging judge' who imposes excessively severe sentences, there are several whose illusions or softness cause them to
err in the opposite direction," so that, Bedau tells us, "a shock-
ingly large number of criminals go unpunished." "All criminal
justice," he considers, "is riddled with inequalities"; "nowhere
else in the law [noncapital cases] are such statutory sentencing
standards available to the criminal trial jury."[175] Why not? In the
Constitution a deprivation of liberty stands on a par with the deprivation of life. Against this, John Hart Ely argues that death is
irreversible and therefore requires that we be "supremely scrupulous," insisting on "the utmost procedural regularity in the imposition of the death penalty."[176] If by this he refers to "standards," he himself stressed that their formulation is an intractable
task.[177] And "even if we *could* succeed in channeling the jury,
there are, as Charles Black has demonstrated, opportunities for
discretionary selection all along the process—from the pre-trial
decision [by the prosecutor] of what charge to bring to the post-
trial decision [of the Executive] on clemency."[178] This "vast reser-

---

ishment can find some solace in this game of hide-and-seek, since in operation it has meant the reversal of a good many death sentences imposed
under systems modelled on what the Court had previously seemed to indicate what it wanted"; J. H. Ely, *Democracy and Distrust* 174 (1980).

174. 438 U.S. at 631, dissenting in part. How can the plurality's insistence that "an individualized decision is essential in capital cases," based
upon consideration of "any aspect of a defendant's character or record and
any of the circumstances of the defense that the defendant proffers," id. at
605, be reconciled with sentencing pursuant to "standards"?

175. Bedau 112, 8, 27.

176. J. H. Ely, *Democracy and Distrust* 176–177n. (1980).

177. Id. at 174–175.

178. Id. 175.

voir of discretion"[179] was untouched by *Furman* and its progeny.
If all discretion is baneful, as Charles Black insists, a logical jurisprudence requires that these too be rationalized, a Sisyphean task.
All this on the basis of an indefensible reading of "cruel and unusual punishments" that plainly transmogrifies the meaning the
words had for the Framers.

The foregoing compressed summary of the clashing views expressed in the several decisions barely scratches the surface of the
voluminous plurality, concurring, and dissenting opinions in each
case which, as the Justices acknowledge, have engendered confusion and, to say the least, cast doubt on the capacity of a badly divided Court to divine society's "evolving sense of decency." The
Court has created a minefield through which the perplexed legislators tread at their peril. Bedau exulted that *Gregg* "opened up for
defense lawyers" a "virgin field of argument . . . new possibilities
that with imaginative and resourceful litigation may avoid and
nullify many death sentences." There is "new hope in cases where
the defendant's guilt is beyond doubt"![180] Little wonder that running the consequent judicial gauntlet has stalled almost all executions for years.[181]

179. Bedau 105.
180. Id. 116. Goldberg and Dershowitz, supra Chapter 2, note 46 at
1818, counsel that the Court should "continue to chip away at [capital
punishment] by enforcing strict procedural safeguards in capital cases."
181. Justice Marshall noted that "while hundreds have been placed on
death row in the years since *Gregg* [1976], only three persons have been
executed." Godfrey v. Georgia, 446 U.S. 420, 439 (1980), concurring
opinion. *New York Times,* June 14, 1981, A-28, reported that "in the 35
States that have enacted new death penalty statutes to meet the constitutional requirements laid down by the Court, the death row population has
reached an all-time high of more than 780 convicted murderers." In Coleman v. Balkcom, *New York Times,* April 2, 1981, D-23, Justice Rehnquist
charged that the Court has "made it virtually impossible for states to enforce with reasonable promptness their constitutionally valid capital punishment statutes," that "the existence of the death penalty in this country
is virtually an illusion" due to "endlessly drawn-out legal proceedings."
Supra Chapter 1, note 20.

7

Congressional Contraction of Judicial Jurisdiction*

WHAT can be done to restore control of their institutions, death penalties included, to the people? Activists may urge that the exclusive remedy is by amendment. But that would come with ill grace from those who defend judicial revision of the Constitution on the ground that the amendment process is too "cumbersome."[1] If it is too cumbersome to seek popu-

* In part this chapter draws on my "Congressional Contraction of Federal Jurisdiction," 1980 Wis. L. Rev. 801.

1. Eugene Rostow considers that "Given the possibility of constitutional amendment, there is nothing undemocratic in having responsible and independent judges act as important constitutional mediators." Rostow, "The Democratic Character of Judicial Review," 66 Harv. L. Rev. 193, 197 (1952). "Constitutional mediation" hardly describes the Court's overturn of State control of death penalties against the will of the people.

153

lar consent to constitutional alteration, it is too cumbersome to
require that the people reverse judicial usurpation by amendment.[2] A less exacting remedy is the congressional withdrawal of
jurisdiction from the federal courts. A number of such bills dealing with school prayer and the like, sponsored by Senator Jesse
Helms and his coterie, including the Reverend Jerry Falwell of the
Moral Majority, have been roundly denounced by former Solicitor
General Archibald Cox as "radical and unprincipled attacks being
made in Congress on our Constitution and our Supreme Court."[3]
If by "unprincipled" is meant in contravention of constitutional
principles, I am constrained to dissent, notwithstanding that the
Helms-Falwell causes are as unsympathetic to me as to Professor
Cox.[4]

That the withdrawal proposals are not "radical" is evidenced by
Herbert Wechsler's 1965 statement, reflecting a long line of

Paul Brest declares that "the formal process of amendment is too cumbersome." Brest, *Processes of Constitutional Decisionmaking: Cases and Materials*
236 (1975). Louis Lusky noted the Court's "assertion of the power to revise the Constitution, bypassing the cumbersome amendment procedure
prescribed by article V." Lusky, Book Review 6 Hastings Con. L. Q. 403,
406 (1979). McDougal and Lans phrased the matter more blandly: because
"the process of amendment is politically difficult, other modes of change
have emerged." Myres McDougal and Asher Lans, "Treaties and Congressional-Executive or Presidential Agreements-Interchangeable Instruments
of National Policy," 54 Yale L. J. 181, 293 (1945). Stanley Kutler, Book
Review, 6 Hastings Con. L. Q. 511, 525 (1979), likewise condones judicial
alteration because "the path for amendment . . . is often blocked by inertia
or irresponsibility."

2. Randall Bridwell observed that the "cumbersome" argument cuts
both ways: it is an "equally good argument against unrestrained judicial
rule-making at the constitutional level because we will be hard pressed to
gain relief from their decision." Bridwell, "The Federal Judiciary: America's
Recently Liberated Minority," 30 S.C. L. Rev. 467, 472 n. 12 (1979).

3. *New York Times,* Oct. 11, 1981, p. E-1.

4. Back in 1942 I wrote that I liked it no better to have the Court read
my predilections into the Constitution than to have the Four Horsemen
embody theirs. Raoul Berger, "Constructive Contempt—A Post-Mortem,"
9 U. Chi. L. Rev. 602 (1942).

cases,[5] that "Congress has the power by enactment of a statute to strike at what it deems judicial excess by delimitations of the jurisdiction of the lower courts and of the Supreme Court's appellate jurisdiction." And he dismissed the notion that cases having a "constitutional dimension" must be exempted from the congressional power, saying it is "antithetical to the plan of the Constitution for the courts—which was quite simply that the Congress would decide from time to time how far the federal institution should be used within the limits of the federal powers."[6] Indeed, Charles Black considers Congress' power over the jurisdiction of the federal judiciary "the rock on which rests the legitimacy of the judicial work in a democracy," adding that "those people are very badly mistaken who think they *strengthen* the position of the Court by arguing that its jurisdiction is outside congressional control," a view shared by Michael Perry.[7] To evaluate the Cox charge we must first inquire whether the Court itself has been acting "unconstitutionally" (as it demonstrably has with respect to death penalties), and second, if it has, whether power to withdraw the jurisdiction was lodged, as Wechsler declared, in Congress.

5. Henry Hart wrote, "The reports are full of what may be thought injudiciously unqualified statements of the power of Congress to regulate the jurisdiction of the federal courts." Hart, "The Power of Congress to Limit the Jurisdiction of the Federal Courts: An Exercise in Dialectic," 66 Harv. L. Rev. 1362 (1953). See infra text accompanying notes 20–24.

6. Herbert Wechsler, "The Courts and the Constitution," 65 Colum. L. Rev. 1001, 1005 (1965).

7. C. L. Black, "The Presidency and Congress," 32 Wash. & Lee L. Rev. 841, 846, 847 (1975), italics in the original; Michael J. Perry, "Noninterpretive Review in Human Rights Cases: A Functional Justification," 56 N.Y.U. L. Rev. 278, 331–334 (1981). Perry considers that "congressional power over the jurisdiction of the federal judiciary, including the appellate jurisdiction of the Supreme Court, is not disputed." Id. 332.

Unconstitutional Action by the Court

The assertion that the Court has acted "unconstitutionally"[8] may seem so startling to those under the spell of the Court's mystique, as to warrant a few introductory remarks. Justice John Marshall Harlan charged the Court with the "exercise of the amending power,"[9] a power exclusively reserved to the people through the machinery of Article V. Philip Kurland of the University of Chicago wrote that "the most immediate constitutional crisis of our present time [is] the usurpation by the judiciary of general government powers on the pretext that its authority derives from the Fourteenth Amendment."[10] Turning to specifics, former Solicitor General Robert Bork wrote about a reapportionment decision that "The principle of one man, one vote . . . runs counter to the text of the fourteenth amendment, the history surrounding its adoption and ratification and the political practice of Americans from Colonial times up to the day the Court invented the new formula."[11] Gerald Gunther of Stanford University likewise commented: "The ultimate justification for the *Reynolds* ruling is hard, if not impossible, to set forth in constitutionally legitimate terms. It rests, rather, on the view that the courts are authorized to step in when injustices exist and other institutions fail to act. That is a dangerous—and I think illegitimate—prescription for judicial action."[12] My own extensive study led me to

8. In Erie v. Tompkins, 304 U.S. 64, 79 (1938), the Court, per Justice Brandeis, branded the doctrine of Swift v. Tyson, 41 U.S. (16 Pet.) 1 (1842), as "an unconstitutional assumption of power by courts of the United States which no lapse of time should make us hesitate to correct."

9. Reynolds v. Sims, 377 U.S. 533, 591 (1964), dissenting opinion.

10. Letter to Harvard University Press, August 15, 1977. Professor Cox wrote that "the Warren Court behaved even more like a Council of Wise Men and less like a Court than the *laissez faire* Justices." Archibald Cox, *The Role of the Supreme Court in American Government* 50 (1976).

11. Robert J. Bork, "Neutral Principles and Some First Amendment Problems," 47 Ind. L. J. 1, 18 (1971).

12. Gerald Gunther, "Some Reflections on the Judicial Role: Distinctions, Roots and Prospects," 1979 Wash. U. L. Q. 817, 825 (1979).

Ward Elliott reports that Anthony Lewis (who was a leader in the drive conclude that the framers of the Fourteenth Amendment intentionally *excluded* suffrage from the scope of the Amendment,[13] and that Justice Harlan correctly stated that the proof is "irrefutable and unanswered."[14] In these circumstances, Harlan justly stated that "When the Court disregards the express intent and understanding of the Framers, it has invaded the realm of the political process to which the amending power was committed, and it has violated the constitutional structure which it is its highest duty to protect."[15]

Another instance of the Court's unconstitutional exercise of power is its invalidation of prayer in the schools under the aegis of the Fourteenth Amendment, the theory being that the Fourteenth incorporated the First Amendment. But (1) Madison's proposal to extend the ban of the First Amendment to the States was rejected by its draftsmen—the First Congress;[16] and (2) the Fourteenth was limited to "security of person and property," as was underscored by the rejection of an amendment—proposed by James Blaine in 1875 in a Congress which included 23 members of the 39th Congress, among them Blaine—to extend the religion provisions of the First Amendment to the States.[17] This evidences that a considerable body of the framers considered that the Fourteenth Amendment did not extend to matters of religion. Thus the American people, acting through their representatives, twice turned down proposals to deprive the States of control over matters of religion. An effort to restore State control over school

---

that led to the "reapportionment" decision) asked Solicitor General Archibald Cox (who had filed a brief amicus for reapportionment in Reynolds v. Sims) when the Court announced its decision, "How does it feel to be present at the second American Constitutional Convention? Cox retained enough of his old perspectives to answer, 'It feels awful.' " Ward Elliott, *The Rise of a Guardian Democracy* 370 (1974).

13. Supra Chapter 5, text accompanying notes 84–92.

14. Supra Chapter 2, text accompanying notes 67–69.

15. Oregon v. Mitchell, 400 U.S. 112, 202–203 (1970), dissenting in part.

16. Supra Chapter 2, text accompanying notes 13–16.

17. Supra Chapter 5, text accompanying note 150.

prayer may grate on modern sensibilities, my own included, but it hardly deserves to be branded as "unprincipled."

In short, the Court has engaged in rewriting the Constitution, exercising a power not granted to it, identifying its own predilections with constitutional imperatives.[18] It is no justification that it acted from benign motives for, as Washington warned, "let there be no change by usurpation; for though this, in one instance, may be the instrument of good, it is the customary weapon by which free governments are destroyed."[19]

LIMITING UNCONSTITUTIONAL EXERCISE OF JURISDICTION

Is withdrawal of jurisdiction where the Court has exercised ungranted power unconstitutional? Very early in our history the Court held in *Cary v. Curtis* that,

18. For the Court's grafting of a right to support at the terminus upon a "right to travel," which the Justices have considerable difficulty in locating in the Constitution, see Raoul Berger, "Residence Requirements for Welfare and Voting," 42 Ohio St. L. J. 853 (1981).

Ely wrote of Roe v. Wade, the abortion case, "The Court continues to disavow the philosophy of Lochner [v. New York], yet as Justice Stewart's concurrence admits, it is impossible candidly to regard *Roe* as the product of anything else. That alone should be enough to damn it." J. H. Ely, "The Wages of Crying Wolf: A Comment on Roe v. Wade," 82 Yale L. J. 920, 939–940 (1973). Of Lochner, Ely remarked that "the Court had simply manufactured a constitutional right out of whole cloth and used it to superimpose its own view of social policy on those of the legislature." Id. at 937. For a scorching analysis of the decision in the "contraceptive" case, Griswold v. Connecticut, 381 U.S. 479 (1965), per Justice Douglas, see Max Isenbergh, "Thoughts on William O. Douglas' *The Court Years:* A Confession and Avoidance," 30 Am. U. L. Rev. 415, 417–421 (1981).

19. 35 George Washington, *Writings,* ed. J. C. Fitzpatrick 228–229 (1940). The "substitution in every instance of the individual sense of justice," Cardozo wrote, "might result in a benevolent despotism if the judges were benevolent men. It would put an end to the reign of law." B. N. Cardozo, *The Nature of the Judicial Process* 136 (1921). Justice Holmes considered that it is not the function of judges "to renovate the law. That is not their province." Oliver Wendell Holmes, Jr., *Collected Legal Papers* 239 (1920).

the judicial power of the United States, although it has its origin in the Constitution, is . . . dependent for its distribution . . . entirely upon the action of Congress, who possess the sole power . . . of investing [the inferior courts] with jurisdiction . . . and of withholding jurisdiction from them in the exact degree and character which to Congress may seem proper for the public good. To deny this position would be to elevate the judicial over the legislative branch of the government, and to give to the former powers limited by its own discretion merely.[20]

"Not until 1875," wrote Charles Alan Wright, "was there a general grant of federal question jurisdiction; such cases could only be brought in the State courts."[21] What Congress delegates it can withdraw; there is no rule that delegation must be in perpetuity.

The appellate jurisdiction of the Supreme Court, Article III provides, shall be subject to such "exceptions and . . . such regulations as Congress shall make." Chief Justice Marshall declared that although these powers "are given by the Constitution," they "are limited and regulated by the judicial act [of 1789] and by such others as have been passed on the subject."[22] Henry Hart, no friend of these views, wrote: "in perhaps the most spectacular of historic examples [Ex parte McCardle], a unanimous Supreme Court recognized the power of Congress to frustrate a determination of the constitutionality of the post-Civil War reconstruction legislation by withdrawing during the very pendency of an appeal, its jurisdiction to review decisions of the federal circuit courts in habeas corpus. '[T]he power to make exceptions to the appellate jurisdiction is given by express words,' Chief Justice Salmon P. Chase said."[23] Citing Marshall in 1881, Chief Justice Waite de-

20. 44 U.S. (2 How.) 236, 245 (1845); see also Lockerty v. Phillips, 319 U.S. 182 (1943). "As a general matter, Congress may restrict the jurisdiction, and remedies available in the lower courts and may similarly restrict state courts in matters of federal concern." Brest, supra note 1 at 1314–1315.

21. Charles Wright, *Federal Courts* 4 (1963).

22. Durousseau v. United States, 10 U.S. (6 Cranch) 307, 314 (1810).

23. Hart, supra note 5 at 1362–1363. Brest, supra note 1 at 1325, wrote, "The Supreme Court confirmed the breadth of congressional power to

clared: "What those [appellate] powers shall be, and to what extent they shall be exercised are, and always have been, proper subjects of legislative control . . . whole classes of cases [may] be kept out of the jurisdiction altogether,"[24] and a fortiori withdrawn.

When I first studied the effect of Article III, my practice of consulting the legislative history led me to examine the records of the several Conventions for light as to the scope of the "exceptions" clause. There I found that the Founders were preoccupied with preventing the Court from revising the findings of a jury.[25] Those, like Paul Brest, who cite this legislative history,[26] reject resort to the even clearer history of the Fourteenth Amendment:

> Many scholars and judges reject Berger's major premise, that constitutional interpretation should depend chiefly on the intent

control its appellate jurisdiction in the dramatic circumstances of Ex parte McCardle, 74 U.S. (7 Wall.) 506." For the motivation, see infra note 65. McCardle was approved in passing in Glidden v. Zdanok, 370 U.S. 530, 567 (1962).

24. The "Francis Wright," 105 U.S. 381, 396 (1881). Earlier the Court declared per Chief Justice Waite, "it has universally been held that our appellate jurisdiction can only be exercised in cases where authority for that purpose is given by Congress. It is equally well settled that if a law conferring jurisdiction is repealed without any reservation as to pending cases, all such cases fall with the law . . . a party to a suit has no vested right to an appeal . . . Such a privilege once granted may be taken away." Railroad Co. v. Grant, 98 U.S. 398, 401 (1878). Justice Frankfurter, who was among the earliest to devote himself to the study of federal jurisdiction, stated, "Congress need not give this Court any appellate power; it may withdraw appellate jurisdiction once conferred and it may do so even while a case is sub judice. Ex parte McCardle." National Mutual Insurance Co. v. Tidewater Transfer Co., 337 U.S. 582, 655 (1949), dissenting on other grounds, Reed J., concurring. Louis Lusky refers to Congress' "undoubted authority to strip away virtually all power of the federal courts to engage in judicial review." Lusky, Book Review 6 Hastings Con. L. Q. 403, 412 (1979). For an attempt to distinguish an array of such cases, see L. G. Ratner, "Congressional Power Over the Appellate Jurisdiction of the Supreme Court," 109 U. Pa. L. Rev. 157, 173–184 (1960). For comment thereon, see Berger, *Congress v. Court* 285 n. 1 (1969).

25. Berger, id. at 286–289.

26. Brest, supra note 1 at 1329.

of those who favored and adopted such a provision ... [W]hatever the framers' expectations may have been, broad constitutional guarantees require the Court to discern, articulate and apply values that are widely and deeply held by our society.[27]

Brest and his fellow activists cannot have it both ways; resort to legislative history must be evenhanded. Were effect given to the history of the Fourteenth Amendment, the motivation for withdrawal of some of the Court's jurisdiction would disappear. Having rejected reliance on "the framers' expectations" in construing the Fourteenth Amendment, having stressed that *"The most important datum bearing on what was intended is the constitutional language itself,"*[28] the activists cannot legitimately complain if Congress chooses to give effect to the "language" of Article III, particularly in order to effectuate "values that are widely and deeply held by our society"—for example, death penalties. Although activists regard the terms of the Amendment as "open-ended" and "inscrutable,"[29] they yet invoke them to override the *unmistakable* intention of the framers. On this precedent, the unambiguous text, "subject to such exceptions and regulations" as Congress shall make, may be given similar effect. Justice Holmes declared that "the power to regulate ... include[s] the power to prohibit. Regulation means prohibition of something."[30]

Then too, the legislative history of Article III differs markedly from that of the Fourteenth Amendment.[31] The framers of the

27. Paul Brest, Book Review, *New York Times,* Dec. 11, 1977, Book Rev. Sec. at 11, 44.

28. J. H. Ely, "Constitutional Interpretivism: Its Allure and Impossibility," 53 Ind. L. J. 399, 418 (1978), emphasis in the original. Ely adds, "the only reliable evidence of what 'the ratifiers' thought they were ratifying is obviously the language of the provision they approved." Id. at 419.

29. Ely, id. at 414–415; J. H. Ely, *Democracy and Distrust* 41, 98 (1980).

30. Hammer v. Dagenhart, 247 U.S. 251, 277 (1918), dissenting opinion.

31. I would not suggest that legislative history is of no moment, for I cling to the age-old canon: "The intention of the lawmaker is the law." Hawaii v. Mankichi, 190 U.S. 197, 212 (1903). But so far as my 1969 study indicated that the legislative history of Article III was conclusive, I have

Amendment left no doubt about the narrowness of their goals by enumerating them and repeatedly rejecting attempts to abolish *all* discriminations; they unmistakably recorded their intention to *exclude*, for example, suffrage from the scope of the Amendment.[32] On the other hand, the Framers' preoccupation with safeguarding jury findings from revision by the court is unaccompanied by overtones of exclusivity. To the contrary, there is convincing evidence that the terms of Article III were not thought to be limited to insulating jury findings. Although Marshall had been among those who assured the Virginia Ratification Convention that the "exception-regulation" clause "may go to cure the mischief apprehended"[33]—that is, judicial review of jury findings of fact[34]— he said at the same time that "These exceptions certainly go as far as the legislature may think proper for the interest and liberty of the people."[35] And he experienced no difficulty as Chief Justice in holding that the appellate powers are "limited and regulated" by the Judiciary Act of 1789. Enactment of that Act by the First Con-

---

come to believe it mistaken. Twelve years of further study of the sources bearing on the *scope,* rather than the *legitimacy,* of judicial review brought many additional facts to my attention that need to be taken into account in evaluating that legislative history.

One far greater than myself did not hesitate to revise his thinking upon further reflection. Referring to his concurrence in the Debs and Schenck cases, Justice Brandeis said, "I had not then thought the issues of freedom of speech out . . . I would have placed the Debs case on the war power, instead of taking Holmes' line of 'clear and present danger' . . . I didn't know enough in the early cases to put it on that ground." Bickel 27–28. If a later insight stands firmly, it is not discredited because it necessitates revision of an earlier view.

32. Supra Chapter 2, text accompanying notes 67–71; Chapter 5, text accompanying notes 70–94.

33. 3 Elliot 560; see also Berger, *Congress v. Court* 286, 288 (1969).

34. Hamilton wrote that "the expressions, 'appellate jurisdiction, both as to law and fact,' do not necessarily imply a reexamination in the Supreme Court of facts decided by juries in the inferior courts." Federalist No. 80 at 532.

35. 3 Elliot 560.

gress, in which sat a goodly number of Framers and Ratifiers and which Charles Warren described as an "almost adjourned session" of the Convention,[36] testifies that they did not consider that their concern with judicial review of findings of facts of which they had firsthand knowledge, precluded them from "regulating" the Court's appellate jurisdiction.[37] That authoritative construction is fortified by the Court's early acknowledgment, per Chief Justice Marshall, of the legitimacy of such regulation.

Then there is the fact stressed by Madison that "in a republican form of government the legislature necessarily predominates."[38] "No one doubted," wrote Gordon Wood, that "the legislature was the most important part of any government,"[39] whereas the

36. Charles Warren, *Congress, the Constitution and the Supreme Court* 99 (1925). Speaking of the Judiciary Act of 1789, Justice Frankfurter commented that "of the Judiciary Committee of eight that reported the bill to the Senate, five members including the chairman, Senator, later to be Chief Justice, Ellsworth, had been delegates to the Constitutional Convention. In the First Congress itself no less than nineteen members, including Madison who contemporaneously introduced the Bill of Rights, had been delegates to the Convention." Green v. United States, 356 U.S. 165, 190 (1958), concurring opinion.

37. After the above was written and delivered to the publisher, there came to my attention M. H. Redish, *Federal Jurisdiction: Tensions in the Allocation of Judicial Power* 20–21 (1980): "Most, if not all, of those who have studied the relevant historical materials agree that concern over the review of facts influenced the adoption of the exceptions clause. There is disagreement, however, as to whether this was the sole concern, for there are relevant statements indicating the desirability of a broader scope for the exceptions clause. Perhaps the greatest obstacle to this very limited view of the scope of the exceptions clause is the appellate jurisdiction authorized by the Judiciary Act passed just after ratification . . . [limiting] appellate jurisdiction to a far greater extent than the 'review-of-questions-of-fact' would allow."

38. Federalist No. 51 at 388.

39. Gordon Wood, *The Creation of the American Republic, 1776–1787* 162 (1969). Justice Brandeis referred to the deep-seated conviction of the English and American people that they "must look to representative assemblies for the protection of their liberties." Myers v. United States, 272 U.S. 52, 294–295 (1926), dissenting opinion, Holmes, J., concurring.

judiciary, James Wilson noted, was an object of aversion and "distrust."[40] Judicial review was an innovation which had roiled the waters in several States,[41] so that Hamilton was constrained to assure the Ratifiers that of the three departments the judiciary "is next to nothing."[42] He assured them that the courts may not "on the pretence of a repugnancy . . . substitute their own pleasure to the constitutional intentions of the legislature," before long rephrased by Justice James Iredell as an absence of judicial power to control legislative discretion within constitutional boundaries.[43] Such assurances would be empty in the absence of a remedy; and the "exceptions-regulations" clause may be regarded as part of the machinery available for correction of judicial encroachment on the paramount legislative domain.

Against this, it may be urged that impeachment is the proper remedy, for Hamilton assured the Ratifiers in Federalist No. 81 that judges would be impeached "for deliberate usurpation on the authority of the legislature,"[44] subversion of the Constitution being the classic ground for impeachment.[45] But it does not fol-

40. 1 James Wilson, *Works,* ed. R. G. McCloskey 292 (1967).

41. Comparatively innocuous exercises of judicial review provoked movements for removal of the offending judges. Berger, *Congress v. Court* 40–42.

42. Federalist No. 78 at 504 n.*.

43. Id. at 507; for Iredell, see supra Chapter 5, text accompanying note 48.

44. Federalist No. 81 at 526–527.

45. Raoul Berger, *Impeachment: The Constitutional Problems* 32–33, 39 (1973). It was precisely because the narrowly defined "treason" no longer reached "attempts to subvert the Constitution" that "high crimes and misdemeanors" was added to the impeachment provision. Id. 86. James Wilson's remarks in the Pennsylvania Ratification Convention are to be distinguished: "What House of Representatives would dare to impeach or Senate to convict, judges for performance of their duty." 2 Elliot 478. This contemplated judicial invalidation of action in excess of jurisdiction, as Iredell's remarks indicate, and as early State court invalidations of statutes in derogation of constitutional requirements illustrate. See Raoul Berger, " 'Law of the Land' Reconsidered," 74 Nw. U. L. Rev. 1, 14–17 (1979). Encroachment on legislative discretion within the jurisdiction—"usurpation," Hamilton termed it—was something else again.

low that impeachment was meant to be the exclusive remedy. The fact is that impeachment was conceived, in Hamilton's words, "as a bridle in the hands of the legislative body upon the executive servants of the government."[46] Concern with impeachment of the Justices was peripheral, and though there was a belated recommendation that the Justices "shall be triable by the Senate," in the upshot the provision for impeachment was inserted in the Executive Article II and referred to the "President, the Vice-President and all civil officers,"[47] leading a commentator to remark that "There is a legitimate textual question whether judges were included in the impeachment provisions of Article II."[48] This is not to cast doubt upon the impeachability of Justices—so matter-of-factly taken for granted by Hamilton—but merely to urge that the ambiguous inclusion of Justices in the Executive impeachment provision should not be interpreted as exclusive of the unequivocal Article III authorization to make exceptions from and to regulate the appellate jurisdiction of the Court.[49] Given that this authority was postulated by the First Congress and has been acknowledged by the Court for 170 years, the Congress is not to

46. Federalist No. 65 at 425.

47. Raoul Berger, *Impeachment: The Constitutional Problems* 146–147 (1973).

48. Martha Ziskind, "Judicial Tenure in the American Constitution: English and American Precedents," 1969 S. Ct. Rev. 135, 151.

49. These circumstances lend special force to Chief Justice Marshall's statement in Trustees of Dartmouth College v. Woodward, 17 U.S. (4 Wheat.) 517, 644 (1819): "It is not enough to say, that this particular case was not in the mind of the Convention, when the act was framed . . . It is necessary to go farther, and to say that, had this particular case been suggested, the language would have been so varied, as to exclude it." Given the Founders' attachment to legislative paramountcy, their distrust of the judiciary, such an exclusion would have been extremely unlikely. Michael Perry considers that "The amendment process designed by past framers is the proper vehicle for future framers to constitutionalize value judgments. The jurisdiction limiting power, on the other hand, is a proper vehicle for electorally accountable policymakers to revise value judgments constitutionalized [?] not by past framers, but by electorally unaccountable judges." Perry, "Noninterpretivist Review in Human Rights Cases: A Functional Justification" 56 N.Y.U. L. Rev. 278, 339 (1981).

be restricted in its choice of remedies for judicial usurpation of power.

Henry Hart considered, however, that "a necessary postulate of constitutional government [is] that a court must always be available to pass on claims of constitutional right to judicial process."[50] Tested by "rights" asserted under the Fourteenth Amendment—the subject of this discussion—that seems to me to involve circular reasoning. First the Court creates new rights, and then it is insisted that it alone may pass on their legitimacy.[51] Paul Brest acknowledges that "Many of what we have come to regard as the irreducible minima of rights are actually supra-constitutional; almost none of the others are entailed by the text or original understanding."[52] In a word, they are judge-made, often in despite of community sentiment.[53] The argument that courts must retain jurisdiction to protect "rights" they created outside the Constitution would insulate judicial usurpation and deprive the people of the right to govern themselves.

Even in terms of the 1787 Constitution, Hart's "rights" theory encounters hard sledding. For the Founders' "individual rights, even the basic civil liberties that we consider so crucial, possessed little of their modern theoretical relevance when set against the will of the people,"[54] as is confirmed by the fact that they found

50. Hart, supra note 5 at 1372; see also infra Appendix B.

51. Commenting on Hart, Perry justly remarks that it seems "self-serving in the extreme to suppose that 'the essential role of the Supreme Court in the Constitutional plan' is anything more than to enforce the value judgments constitutionalized by the Framers." Perry, supra note 49 at 340.

52. Paul Brest, "The Misconceived Quest for the Original Understanding," 60 B.U. L. Rev. 204, 236 (1980). For further discussion, see Raoul Berger, "Paul Brest's Brief for an Imperial Judiciary," 40 Md. L. Rev. 1, 18–22 (1981).

53. For example, see Berger, supra note 18. Louis Jaffe stated, it is overwhelmingly the case that "the 'public conscience' does not support the claim" of constitutional protection for "obscenity," commenting that "the Legislatures, Federal and State, had openly and universally for upwards of 100 years seen fit to condemn obscenity." Jaffe, "The Court Debated—Another View," *New York Times Magazine*, Jan. 5, 1960, in Leonard Levy, *The Supreme Court under Earl Warren* 199, 205 (1972).

54. Wood, supra note 39 at 63.

no expression in the Constitution. As Gordon Wood wrote, "it was conceivable to protect the common liberties of the people against their rulers, but hardly against the people themselves."[55] Like Elbridge Gerry, the Founders relied "on the representatives of the people [not the courts] as the guardians of their Rights and Interests."[56] No extrapolated "postulate" can overcome their expressed aim to make the legislature paramount. The Court itself refused in 1845 to adopt a position in the "jurisdiction" context that would "elevate the judicial over the legislative branch," explaining that would give the judiciary "powers limited by its own discretion merely."[56a]

SECTION 5 OF THE FOURTEENTH AMENDMENT

Whatever may be the limitations of congressional power under Article III, so far as rights are asserted under the Fourteenth Amendment, they are subject to §5 which, as "the last expression of the will of the lawmaker prevails over the earlier one."[57] Section 5 provides, "*Congress* shall have power to enforce . . . the provisions of this article." Giving effect to the negative pregnant, the Court emphasized in *Ex parte Virginia* that this power was given to Congress, not the Courts,[58] as a number of Justices have reemphasized.[59] Judicial enforcement against the will of Congress

55. Id. For a summary of the similar view of W. Kendall and G. Carey, *The Basic Symbols of the American Political Tradition* (1970), see William Gangi, "Judicial Expansionism: An Evaluation of the Ongoing Debate," 8 Ohio. Nor. U. L. Rev. 1, 64 (1981).

56. 1 Farrand 97–98; see also Justice Brandeis, supra note 39.

56a. Supra text accompanying note 20.

57. Schick v. United States, 195 U.S. 65, 68 (1904).

58. 100 U.S. 339, 345 (1879): "It is not said that the judicial power of the general government shall extend to enforcing the prohibitions and protecting the rights and immunities guaranteed . . . It is the power of Congress which has been enlarged . . . *Some legislation is contemplated* to make the amendment fully effective."

59. Citing Ex parte Virginia, Justice Black declared, "the people in §5 of the Fourteenth Amendment designated the governmental tribunal they wanted to provide additional rules to enforce the guarantees of that

would convert "Congress shall" into "the Court shall," usurping a power withheld. Discretion to enforce was left to Congress; §5 does not mandate enforcement; it does not provide that "Congress *shall* enforce," but rather that "Congress *shall have power* to enforce."[60] That the choice was deliberate and meant to be exclusive clearly emerges from the legislative history.

John A. Bingham, a member of the Joint Committee on Reconstruction, who was "principally concerned with the section dealing with civil rights,"[61] proposed to the Committee, of which he was a member, that "The Congress shall have power to make all laws necessary and proper to secure to all persons in every state . . . equal protection in the rights of life, liberty, and property." On the same day, January 12, 1866, Thaddeus Stevens, also a member of the Committee, proposed, "All laws, state or national, shall operate impartially and equally on all persons without regard to race or color." As Charles Fairman observed, "Stevens' proposal

---

Amendment. The branch of the Government they chose was not the Judicial Branch but the Legislative." Harper v. Virginia Bd. of Elections, 383 U.S. 663, 678 (1966), dissenting opinion. Similarly, Justice Brennan, joined by Chief Justice Warren and Justice Douglas, stated: "Congress, not the judiciary, was viewed as the more likely agency to implement fully the guarantees of equality, and thus it could be presumed the primary purpose of the Amendment was to augment the power of Congress, not the judiciary." United States v. Guest, 383 U.S. 745, 783 n. 7 (1966), dissenting in part. But the Justices overlooked the exclusive nature of this grant, that is, judicial action was dependent on prior legislation and a delegation, as the legislative history discloses.

60. Justice Douglas, in Katzenbach v. Morgan, 384 U.S. 641, 647 (1966) (separate opinion), declared that "The manner of enforcement involves discretion; but that discretion is largely entrusted to Congress, not to the courts." "I am unable to believe that in light of the then prevailing concept of representative democracy, the framers . . . of §1 [of the Fourteenth Amendment] intended the *courts* . . . to weave the tapestry of federally protected rights against state government." Henry P. Monaghan, "The Constitution Goes to Harvard," 13 Harv. C. R.–C. L. L. Rev. 117, 129 (1978).

61. 6 Charles Fairman, *History of the Supreme Court of the United States* 1270 (1971).

... would work by its own force: courts would be bound to disregard invidious laws, and questions could be carried to the Supreme Court. Not so with Bingham's: *Congress* would be empowered—yet nothing would result save as it legislated."[62] Bingham's proposal carried the day. "As Bingham saw the march into the future," Fairman remarks, "it was the Congress, rather than the Court, that was to be Valiant-for-Truth."[63] Bingham did not leave us in the dark as to his reasons. In supporting a bill that would require a vote of two-thirds of the full Court to invalidate an Act of Congress, he said, that of late the Court had "dared to descend from its high place in the discussion and decision of purely judicial questions to the *settlement of political questions* which it has *no more right to decide* for the American people than has the Court of St. Petersburg."[64] This theme was likewise sounded in the Senate; "On February 17—the day the Court was overruling his motion to dismiss *McCardle* for want of jurisdiction [as a political matter]—Trumbull introduced S.363," a bill that "would declare that the *Reconstruction Acts were political* in character and that *no court was competent to question* their validity."[65] Fairman comments that "This bill was like the cocking of a gun, audible in the nearby Supreme Court Chamber."[66] Although the bill was not enacted, proponents of such legislation gained their objective by adding to another bill an amendment to "repeal so much of

62. Id. 1271, emphasis in the original.

63. Id. 462.

64. Id.

65. Id. 464. The stakes were high: the fate of Reconstruction hung in the balance. Charles Fairman recounts that "In February and March 1868 it was generally supposed, and on good reason, that if the Court had an opportunity to decide a case involving the Reconstruction Acts it would pronounce the program as a whole unconstitutional." Fairman, supra note 61 at 509. If "Congress had failed to maintain its authority in Reconstruction, if the ten Southern States had been left in the hands of the class that had fought and lost the war—the Fourteenth Amendment would not have been adopted," id. at 512, and "the Negro's civil status would be whatever the ruling class provided, short of 'slavery.'" Id. 498.

66. Id.

the habeas corpus statute of 1869 as gave an appeal to the Supreme Court." Speedily passed by both Houses, this bill triggered the Court's decision in *McCardle*.[67]

In the Senate, Jacob M. Howard explained that "there is no power given in the Constitution to enforce and to carry out any of these guarantees" of the Amendment.[68] Fairman observes that "Omitting, as though not present in his thought, that Section 1 would itself be enforced by the courts,"[69] Howard stated:

> therefore it is necessary, if they are to be effectuated and enforced ... that additional power should be given to Congress to that end. This is done by the fifth section of this Amendment ... Here is a direct affirmative delegation of power to Congress to carry out all the principles of all these guarantees ... I look upon this clause as indispensable for the reason that it thus imposes upon Congress this power and this duty.[70]

Short of an express exclusion, language could hardly be better calculated to underscore the exclusive nature of the grant to Congress, a grant bred by resentment of the Court's intervention in the "settlement of political questions."[71]

The history of the Fifteenth Amendment confirms that the

67. Id. For details, see id. 464 et seq.

68. *Globe* 2766.

69. Fairman, supra note 61 at 1294.

70. Id., *Globe* 2766, 2768. It was "necessary," said Senator Luke Poland, for many years Chief Justice of the Vermont Supreme Court, that Congress "should be invested with the power to enforce this provision ... and compel its observance." *Globe* 2961.

71. For distrust of the Supreme Court in the 39th Congress see Berger *G/J* 222–223. Its persistence is exemplified by statements in subsequent Reconstruction Congresses. Senator James Nye of Nevada stated that Dred Scott "was an outrage upon the Constitution, a defiant outrage upon the rights of the people." *Congressional Globe,* 41st Cong., 2d Sess. 1513 (1870). Senator Jacob Howard said, "It was a partisan, political decision, the purpose of which was to establish by judicial decision ... for all time to come the legality, the rightfulness, and even the piety of slavery." *Congressional Globe,* 41st Cong., 2d Sess. 1543 (1870).

grant to Congress was meant to be exclusive, and to condition judicial enforcement on prior legislative action. Section 2 of the Fifteenth Amendment is the analogue of §5 of the Fourteenth. In the words of Senator Oliver Morton, a framer of the Fourteenth, "the remedy for the violation of the fourteenth and fifteenth amendments *was expressly not left to the courts,*" but was to "be enforced by legislation on the part of Congress."[72] Senator John Sherman stated that *"before* it shall be enforced in the courts some legislation should be passed by Congress."[73] Senator Matthew Carpenter said, "We must legislate and *then commit* the enforcement of our laws to the Federal tribunals."[74] What Congress "commits," it can withdraw. Nowhere was it intimated that the Supreme Court was exempted from this grant of power to Congress. In fact, §5 responded to the enduring distrust its *Dred Scott* decision had engendered.

Finally, does the due process clause require that a remedy must be provided, on the theory that no one may be deprived of a right without trial?[75] The weakness of this theory with respect to judicially created rights under the Fourteenth Amendment has been

72. *Congressional Globe,* 42nd Cong., 2d Sess. 525 (1872).

73. *Congressional Globe,* 41st Cong., 1st Sess. 3568 (1870).

74. *Congressional Globe,* 42nd Cong., 2d Sess. 897 (1872). For additional citations, see Berger, "The Fourteenth Amendment: Light From the Fifteenth," 74 Nw. U. L. Rev. 311, 351, 352 (1979). "As far as the Fourteenth Amendment is concerned, it is true that the (misplaced) anticipation seems to have been that it would receive its most meaningful enforcement by Congress, acting under Section 5, rather than by the courts." J. H. Ely, *Democracy and Distrust* 40 (1980). Recognition of the grant to Congress and its power to delegate §5 jurisdiction is likewise implicit in Archibald Cox's statement, "Under section five of the Fourteenth Amendment Congress has wide power to frame legislation to protect constitutional rights . . . Congress, therefore . . . could articulate minimum protection standards and delegate further particularization and refinements to a legislative court or administrative agency." Cox, "The Effect of the Search for Equality Upon Judicial Institutions," 1979 Wash. U. L. Q. 795, 815–816.

75. Before I studied the history of the Fourteenth Amendment, I thought due process had that effect. Berger, *Congress v. Court* 296 (1969).

noted. Moreover, the due process clause, like the other provisions of §1, is governed by §5. The clause is one of the "provisions" that "Congress shall have power to enforce." Consequently, even the due process clause comes into play only after Congress exercises that "power" and "commits" enforcement of the clause to the courts. To require a judicial trial against the will of Congress would be to take over power granted to Congress alone, thereby depriving §5 of its intended effect. In short, the due process clause is subordinate to §5, for the framers left it in the discretion of Congress whether to provide an enforcement proceeding.[76]

Those who do not share Paul Brest's belief that the Court is not bound by the Constitution, who consider that its revision was confided to the people, not the Court, should welcome the exercise of congressional power to restore the democratic system of self-government. Liberals should be the last to abandon the rule of law because the desires of Demos are antipathetic to their own.[77] They need ever to bear in mind Charles McIlwain's credo: "The two fundamental correlative elements of constitutionalism for which all lovers of liberty must yet fight are the legal limits to arbitrary power and a complete responsibility of government to the governed."[78] No dispensation has exempted the Court from these requirements.

76. There is likewise the rule going back to Pufendorf, that as between conflicting provisions in the same enactment the last in order of arrangement shall prevail, here fortified by the manifest connotation of §5. United States v. Jackson, 143 F. 783, 787 (9th Cir. 1906); In re Richards, 96 F. 935, 939 (7th Cir. 1899); United States v. Updike, 25 F. 2d 746 (D. Neb. 1928).

77. Bickel wrote with respect to the school prayer decisions that, "There has been very little in the way of general assent to these decisions ... throughout the country." Bickel 92.

78. Charles H. McIlwain, *Constitutions: Ancient and Modern* 146 (1947).

8

Conclusion

THE historical evidence demonstrates that the Constitution left the States free to enact death penalties unencumbered by any measure of proportionality. For the time being, the Court, after having been rebuffed by the people, who cling to death penalties, has by a vote of 7 to 2 sustained them, although leaving an escape hatch. Already it has decreed that death penalties for rape are not proportioned to the crime and are therefore unconstitutional, a decision that is without constitutional warrant.

Abolitionist reliance on the "cruel and unusual punishments" clause assumes first that the Constitution endowed the Court with power *ad libitum* to make selected portions of the Bill of Rights applicable to the States. That, it may be confidently asserted, does violence to the intention of the framers and violates the Tenth Amendment's command. Next, abolitionists assume that the Court may substitute its present-day reading of the clause for the meaning it had for the Framers. The Justices do not dispute that in 1787 the clause outlawed only "barbarous" punishments, not death penalties; it did not require that the punishment must fit the crime, for there was no such doctrine at the adoption of the Constitution. To the contrary, there were many death penalties, such as those for forgery or robbery, that to modern eyes are grossly disproportionate to the offense. The clause, therefore, left the measure of punishment, whether it should be more or less, in the legislature's discretion, so long as it was not "barbarous." So too, the Court's insistence that a penalty must not be offensive to "human dignity" is flatly contradicted by the many punishments that had as their object ignominy, shame and disgrace.

The Court's attempt to impose and police "standards" to curb jury discretion in sentencing has even less constitutional footing and already has resulted in a quagmire of contradictions. It is not alone that there was no judicial assertion of such power prior to 1972, but that the Court has invaded the constitutional province of the jury. Early on the Founders expressed their attachment to the common law mode of trial by jury, whereunder juries could not be called upon to explain their verdicts nor were judges empowered to review verdicts. The jury, in fact, was far closer to the hearts of the Founders than was the judiciary; for protection they looked to the jury rather than the judge.

It is not historicism that dictates adherence to the meaning the common law terms they used had for the Framers. Jealously rationing power, circumscribing it at every step, the Framers perforce resorted to familiar terms in order to prick out those limits. If the Court is free to substitute its own meaning for the established common law content of the constitutional terms, it obliterates those limits and revises the Constitution for the imposition of its own predilections on a people who, in the case of death penalties, lost no time in repudiating the Court's reading of prevailing standards of "human decency." In turning its back on the practice that obtained at the adoption of the Constitution and persisted for 181 years thereafter, the Court assumed power to alter and amend the Constitution, a power exclusively reserved to the people themselves, a power usurped by the Court disguised in soothing double-talk.

One can respect the "reverence for life" that led Dr. Albert Schweitzer to shrink from treading on a scorpion, without scorning those who would unhesitatingly crush a tarantula or shoot off the head of a rattler. To insist that "no killer can be looked upon with anything but horror, even when that killer is the state,"[1] is to ignore that the bulk of the Americans do in fact look upon executions of murderers without horror. People like Lord Justice Denning are not to be consigned to outer darkness because they consider that "some crimes are so outrageous that society insists upon adequate punishment, because the wrong-doer deserves it."[2] Quite the contrary. As Justice Stewart said for the *Furman* plurality:

> The instinct for retribution is part of the nature of man, and channeling that instinct in the administration of criminal justice serves an important purpose in promoting the stability of a society governed by law. When people begin to believe that organized society is unwilling or unable to impose upon criminal offenders the punishment they "deserve," then there are sown the seeds of anarchy—of self-help, vigilante justice and lynch law.[3]

1. Henry Schwarzschild, director of the American Civil Liberties Union Capital Punishment Project, said: "Killing human beings is an act so awesome, so destructive, so irremediable that no killer can be looked upon with anything but horror, even when that killer is the state." *New York Times,* June 14, 1981, p. 28.

2. Quoted in Furman 453. Sir James Fitzjames Stephen wrote: "In cases which outrage the moral feeling of the community to a great degree, the feeling of indignation and the desire for revenge which is excited in the minds of decent people is, I think, deserving of legitimate satisfaction." 1 J. F. Stephen, *History of the Criminal Law of England* 478 (1883); see also Goodhart, infra note 3.

3. Furman 308; see also id. 394–395, 452. A. L. Goodhart, *English Law and the Moral Law* 92–93 (1953), wrote: "There seems to be an instinctive feeling in most ordinary men that a person who has done an injury to others should be punished for it . . . without a sense of retribution we may lose

Sadists or no, the majority of the American people who cling to death penalties are not to be frustrated because some regard capital punishment as immoral.[4]

Who are these murderers whose extinction is regarded by abolitionists with such "horror"? Justice Marshall, foremost among the abolitionist Justices, said in *Furman:* "The criminal acts with which we are confronted are ugly, vicious ... Their sheer brutality cannot and should not be minimized."[5] Justice Powell observed that "brutish and revolting murders continue to occur with disquieting frequency."[6] From time to time murderers escape from jail and commit still other murders.[7] Terror stalks

---

our sense of wrong. Retribution in punishment is an expression of the community's disapproval of crime ... A community which is too ready to forgive the wrongdoer may end by condoning the crime." Bedau 117 rightly emphasizes that punishment, "by its very nature, is retributive ... imprisonment for murder, no less than the death penalty is retributive. The question, of course, is whether it is retributive enough." That is a question of policy for the legislature and the people, not removed from them by the "cruel and unusual punishments" clause.

4. Justices Stewart, Powell, and Stevens, the plurality in Gregg v. Georgia, 428 U.S. 153, 183 (1976), stated: "In part, capital punishment is an expression of society's moral outrage at particularly offensive conduct. This function may be unappealing to many, but it is essential in an ordered society that asks its citizens to rely on legal processes rather than self-help to vindicate their wrongs." This shifts the inquiry from whether the Constitution deprived the people of the right to enact death penalties, which they enjoyed in 1787, to an empirical justification which should be addressed to the people when *they* consider whether to abolish death penalties.

5. Furman 315.

6. Id. 444.

7. A spectacular recent example was the shooting of Pope John Paul II by Mehmet Ali Agca, an escapee from a Turkish prison after conviction for murder. *New York Times,* May 8, 1981, A-1. Laron Williams, convicted murderer and escapee from a Memphis prison, was charged with a fresh murder, *New York Times,* May 18, 1981, D-13. Jack Henry Abbott, an imprisoned murderer admitted to another murder after his parole from prison, *New York Times,* Jan. 16, 1982, p. 27. Joseph Bowen, sentenced in 1971 for the murder of a policeman, was convicted in 1975 of the murder

the streets;[8] the streets, Justice Marshall notices, "inspire fear."[9] Referring to the "compassionate" abolitionists, "for whom the victims of crime are only incidental rather than central to the problem of crime prevention," Sidney Hook asks, "At what point do the victims enter the ethical reckoning?"[10]

While abolitionists prefer imprisonment to capital punishment, it is significant that the beneficiaries of their efforts often prefer death to continued imprisonment.[11] It is a notorious fact that prisons have become jungles where murders of fellow inmates are not uncommon, where homosexual assaults are the norm.

----

of a prison warden and his deputy and reportedly "laughed when he heard himself sentenced to two life terms." On October 29, 1981, he led several prison inmates in the taking of 38 hostages. *New York Times,* Oct. 30, 1981, A-1, A-12. These examples turned up in casual reading over a period of a few months. Walter Berns, *For Capital Punishment* 103 (1979), relates that "Henry Jarrette, convicted murderer, escaped from prison, raped and murdered a black girl." Coker v. Georgia involved a convicted murderer and rapist who escaped and committed another rape, supra Chapter 6, text accompanying note 166. Bedau 8 acknowledges that no one can claim "that life imprisonment (which, of course, does not mean 'life' at all) offers complete protection to society."

8. Justice Blackmun, Furman 414.

9. Id. 371.

10. Sidney Hook, *Philosophy and Public Policy* 136 (1980). Louis Jaffe wrote that judges "have been insensitive to the public's need for a sense of security," Jaffe, "Was Brandeis an Activist: The Search for Intermediate Premises," 80 Harv. L. Rev. 986, 1002 (1967). Justice Holmes, who for many years sat on the Supreme Judicial Court of Massachusetts, stated, "at the present time in this country there is more danger that criminals will escape justice than that they will be subjected to tyranny." Kepner v. United States, 195 U.S. 100, 134 (1904), dissenting opinion joined by Justices Edward White and McKenna.

11. Jacques Barzun takes a bleak view of life imprisonment and "would choose death without hesitation." Hugo Bedau, *The Death Penalty in America* 161–162 (1967).

In Lenhard v. Wolff, 443 U.S. 1306 (1979), the defendant disassociated himself from efforts to secure review of a death sentence. E. B. Prettyman, *Death and the Supreme Court* 15 (1961), relates that Everett Green "would rather go to the chair than spend the rest of his life in jail." Gary

Then too, there are the excessive burdens assumed by the Court in painstaking review of hundreds of records, and the detailed exposition of conflicting views for setting aside this or the other conviction, which fill hundreds of pages in the reports. E. Barrett Prettyman, Jr., a one-time clerk to one of the Justices, concluded that the Court devoted "a disproportionately large amount of time" to capital cases; "they receive more attention than any other class of cases coming before the Court."[12] It was not for this— often guilt is beyond peradventure—that the Court was created,[13] but for consideration of the perplexing problems that arise out of the exigencies of our system of government. I would not suggest that these considerations are conclusive, merely that the pragmatic considerations are not all on the side of the abolitionists. Nor is my concern with the merits of death penalties, but with the right of the people to enact them. It need always to be borne in mind that "the criminal law, after all, is primarily a state rather

---

Gilmore preferred execution to serving "more time behind prison bars in Utah." Bedau 121.

A number of such cases were reported in August–September, 1981. Thomas Lee Harp, a convicted slayer, told the Oklahoma court that "he wanted no further appeals." *New York Times,* Sept. 4, 1981, A-6. Colin Clark, convicted in Louisiana, "said he would rather die than face life in prison." *New York Times,* Sept. 8, 1981, B-12.

Garry Wills refers to the penitentiary as the "most disastrous survival of the enlightenment still grasping at a death-like life." Quoted in Berns, supra note 7 at 62. Berns considers "prisons are terrible places" and quotes the American Friends Service Committee: the "horror that is the American prison system." Id. 64, 74.

12. Prettyman, supra note 11 at 305.

13. For the Founders, "individual rights, even the basic civil liberties that we consider so crucial, possessed little of their modern theoretical relevance when set against the will of the people." Gordon Wood, *The Creation of the American Republic, 1776–1787* 63 (1969). He adds, "it was conceivable to protect the common law liberties of the people against their rulers, but hardly against the people themselves." Id. See also William Gangi, "Judicial Expansionism: An Evaluation of the Ongoing Debate," 8 Ohio Nor. U. L. Rev. 1, 64 (1981).

than a federal responsibility,"[14] and that the Court's intrusion into this field is comparatively recent.

Whatever reservations a Justice may have had before he donned the robe as to the wisdom or judiciality of his predecessors, he entertains few doubts that *he* is richly qualified to impose his vision of the good on the nation. Throughout the judicial spectrum lurks the conviction that Big Brother knows best. That common postulate, which goes to the heart of the judicial function, shows how meaningless are assessments of the Justices in terms of "liberal" and "conservative." Justice Douglas disclosed that at the core of the constitutional decisionmaking process lies the "gut" reaction of the Justices, underlining John Stuart Mill's caution that the universal "disposition of mankind . . . to impose their own opinions and inclinations . . . on others . . . is hardly ever kept under restraint by anything but want of power."[15] The Framers in their wisdom withheld such power from the Justices.

Finally, the track record of the Court does not inspire confidence that it is a better judge of what the people should do than the people themselves. Justice, then Solicitor General, Robert H. Jackson, wrote, "time has proved that [the Court's] judgment was wrong on most of the outstanding issues upon which it has chosen to challenge the popular branches."[16] His view was shared

14. Prettyman, supra note 11 at 311. Justice Frankfurter wrote, the Fourteenth Amendment "is not the basis of a uniform code of criminal procedure federally imposed." Wallace Mendelson, ed., *Felix Frankfurter: The Judge* 99 (1964). Justice Holmes, in one of his last dissents, counseled, "we ought to remember the great caution shown by the Constitution in limiting the powers of the States, and should be slow to construe the [due process] clause in the Fourteenth Amendment as committing to the Court, with no guide but the Court's own discretion, the validity of whatever laws the States may pass." Baldwin v. Missouri, 281 U.S. 586, 595 (1930).

15. J. S. Mill, *On Liberty* 28 (1885).

16. R. H. Jackson, *The Struggle for Judicial Supremacy* 37 (1941). For a similar expression by Dean Charles E. Clark, see his Introduction to Edward Corwin, *The Twilight of the Supreme Court* xviii (1934). "Nothing," wrote Alexander Bickel, the foremost constitutional scholar of his generation, "is more evident in the Supreme Court's past than that most of its

by distinguished scholars. The Court would do well to heed the counsel of Justice Holmes: "when the people ... want to do something I can't find anything in the Constitution expressly forbidding them to do, I say, whether I like it or not, 'Goddamit, let 'em do it!' "[17] The "cruel and unusual punishments" clause constitutes no such prohibition. "After all," wrote Dean Charles E. Clark of Yale Law School in October 1934, "is it a sound and practical theory, as well as a robust and vigorous doctrine, suited to an independent people, to hold that control and direction of its future should be committed to an aloof judicial tribunal, however, esteemed?"[18] No such commitment was ever made by the American people. Instead, the death penalty cases represent a blatant perversion of the "cruel and unusual punishments" clause that thwarts their indubitable will.

---

prior major enterprises ... have not worked out." Bickel 176. He averred, "I have come to doubt ... that judicial supremacy can work and is tolerable in broad areas of social policy." Id. at 99. The Court is "too remote from conditions ... It is not accessible to all the varied interests that are in play in any decision of great consequence ... it is, in a vast, complex, changeable society, a most unsuitable instrument for the formulation of policy." Id. at 175. My studies have convinced me that such power was consciously withheld. For an excoriating comment on the socioeconomic record of the pre-1937 Court see H. S. Commager, "Judicial Review and Democracy," 19 Va. Q. Rev. 417, 428 (1943).

17. Quoted in Charles P. Curtis, *Lions Under the Throne* 281 (1947).
18. Clark, supra note 16 at xix. "Government by a self-designated elite—like that of benevolent despotism or Plato's philosopher kings—may be a good form of government for some, but it is not the American way." Myres McDougal and Asher Lans, "Treaties and Congressional-Executive or Presidential Agreements: Interchangeable Instruments of National Policy," 54 Yale L. J. 534, 578 (1945).

9

Epilogue

INCREASINGLY academicians acknowledge the fact of judicial governance and that it is without warrant in the text or history of the Constitution. In a review of Chief Justice Richard Neely's *How Courts Govern America,* Martin Shapiro notes the progress of "political jurisprudence" and its acceptance by academic constitutional lawyers. Central to this school of thought is "the position that courts are and must be engaged in politics,"[1] more plainly, the making of final policy decisions that the Constitution reserves to the people and their representatives. That is "How Courts Gov-

---

1. Martin Shapiro, "Judge as Statesman, Judge as Pol," *New York Times,* Nov. 22, 1981, Book Review Sec. 7, 42. In consequence, activists wander in a jungle of moral philosophy theories that cannot be traced to the Constitution. See Symposia: 42 Ohio St. L. J. 1 (1981); 56 N.Y.U. L. Rev. 259; 90 Yale L. J. 955 (1981).

ern America." In 1964 Shapiro, meeting the call for honest avowal
that the Court was deciding what it thinks good for the country
rather than enforcing what the Constitution demands, wrote that
"It would be fantastic indeed if the Supreme Court ... were to
disavow publicly the myth on which its power rests,"[2] that is, the
myth that it is enforcing constitutional requirements rather than
its own predilections.[3] The "fantastic" has all but come to pass. If
the Court has yet publicly to confess that it is in fact engaged in
governing America, its apologists now openly espouse such governance. Neely's book, Shapiro observes, "will serve the good purpose of exposing a wider audience to the notion that courts are
and ought to be political actors,"[4] for example, to overrule long-
standing residence restrictions on welfare for indigent migrants
embodied in the statutes of forty states[5] (burdening New York
and Florida, for example, with support of a flood of immigrants),
to overturn death penalty statutes of centuries-old provenance.
But Shapiro signs off on an equivocal—can it be skeptical—note:
"even more important, however, may be the message that judges
think they are truly wonderful people, far more capable of governing America than the rest of us."[6]

Who but the activists have sedulously fostered that delusion?
The Court, they trumpeted, was the keeper of the national conscience,[7] the undefiled font of national morality. Robert Cover

2. Martin Shapiro, *Law and Politics in the Supreme Court* 27 (1964).

3. A Warren Court admirer, Anthony Lewis, wrote that "Earl Warren is
the closest thing that the United States has had to a Platonic Guardian,
dispensing law from a throne without any sensed limits of power except
what is seen [by him] as the good of society." Lewis, "A Man Born to Act,
Not to Muse," *New York Times Magazine,* June 30, 1968, in Leonard Levy,
The Supreme Court under Earl Warren 151, 161 (1972).

4. Supra note 1 at 42; see also Berger *G/J* 416.

5. Raoul Berger, "Residence Requirements for Welfare and Voting: A
Post-Mortem," 42 Ohio St. L. J. 853 (1982).

6. Supra note 1 at 42.

7. Arthur S. Miller counsels us to regard the Court as the "national conscience." A. S. Miller and R. F. Howell, "The Myth of Neutrality in Constitutional Adjudication," 27 U. Chi. L. Rev. 661, 689 (1960); Eugene

thrusts aside "the self-evident meaning of the Constitution" in favor of an "ideology" framed by a nonelected, life-tenured bench.[8] No activist, so far as I could find, attempts to tie this power to a grant by the Constitution.[9] Louis Lusky blandly accepts the Court's "assertion of power to revise the Constitution";[10] and Paul Brest is driven to challenge the assumption "that judges or other public officials were bound by the text or original understanding of the Constitution,"[11] an admission that the Constitution does not confer power to govern on the judiciary; it must be drawn out of thin air.

Brest has recorded his Pilgrim's Progress. In 1977 he heatedly cast me out of the society of scholars because my *Government by Judiciary* necessarily challenged "the entire network of constitutional decisions underlying our *legal commitment* to racial equal-

---

Rostow, "The Democratic Character of Judicial Review," 66 Harv. L. Rev. 193, 208 (1952). Paul Freund observed, "It would be a morally poor country indeed that was obliged to look to any group of nine wise men for ultimate moral light and leading, much less a group limited to men drawn from one profession, even from that of law." Paul A. Freund, *On Law and Justice* 35 (1968).

8. R. M. Cover, Book Review, *New Republic,* Jan. 14, 1978, 26, 27.

9. Paul Brest, "The Fundamental Rights Controversy: The Essential Contradictions of Normative Scholarship," 90 Yale L. J. 1063, 1087 n. 152 (1981), states that activist "claims of authority from the original understanding tend to be conclusory and oblique," "perfunctory at best." But John Hart Ely considers that the framers of the Fourteenth Amendment issued an "open and across-the-board invitation to import" into it extraconstitutional considerations. Supra Chapter 5, note 98. He himself regards the "privileges or immunities" clause as "quite inscrutable," and the "equal protection" clause as "also unforthcoming with details." J. H. Ely, *Democracy and Distrust* 98 (1981). How can the framers' unmistakable determination to exclude suffrage be overcome by "inscrutable" language; how can "inscrutable" language be construed as an "invitation" to reverse that clear intention, much less to curtail the power not delegated by the States and reserved to them by the Tenth Amendment?

10. Louis Lusky, Book Review, 6 Hastings Con. L. Q. 403, 408 (1979).

11. Paul Brest, "The Misconceived Quest for the Original Intention," 60 B.U. L. Rev. 204, 224 (1980).

ity."[12] My study detailed proof that the framers of the Fourteenth Amendment *clearly excluded* suffrage from its scope, as Brest now admits,[13] so that the "one person, one vote" decision reversed the framers and amended the Constitution. The framers' exclusion of suffrage constituted a large gap in our "legal commitment to racial equality." Michael Perry, who did not permit his dedication to activism to blind him to unpalatable facts, perceived that "the legislative history of the fourteenth amendment clearly discloses that the Framers did not mean for the amendment to have any effect on segregated schools or on segregation generally." In reading "the principle of the moral irrelevance of race" into the amendment, Perry continues, "the Court does not enforce a value judgment the Framers made but, instead, makes and enforces a value judgment of its own."[14] To pivot analysis on the benign result of

12. Paul Brest, "Berger v. Brown et al.," *New York Times,* Dec. 11, 1977, Book Review sec., p. 11; but compare infra note 14.

13. The "adopters of the equal protection clause probably intended it not to encompass voting discrimination at all." Brest, supra note 11, at 234 n. 115.

14. Perry 292. An activist, Nathaniel Nathanson, concluded that the view that the Fourteenth Amendment "would not require school desegregation . . . was quite conclusively demonstrated by Alexander Bickel . . . Mr. Berger's independent research and analysis confirms and adds weight to those conclusions." Nathanson, Book Review 56 Tex. L. Rev. 579, 581 (1978). Another activist, Henry Abraham, considers that "Any genuinely objective, factual and rigorous examination of the debates and history of the framing of the Fourteenth Amendment demonstrates that the authors and supporters of that provision specifically rejected its application to segregated schools and the franchise." Abraham, Book Review, 6 Hastings Con. L. Q. 467 (1979). Nevertheless, Brest asserted that, "excluding apologists for racism"—a nice McCarthean touch—"Berger is almost alone in arguing that the Court erred in Brown v. Board of Education," Brest, supra note 12 at 11.

Consider, too, Brest's solution—"broad constitutional guarantees require the Court to discern, articulate and apply values that are widely and deeply held by our society." Brest, id. at 44. Yet he concedes that "the nation was not ready to eliminate [segregation] in the 1860's," id. at 11, and admits that an amendment "in the mid-[19]50's to require school desegregation"

Brown, as Brest does,[15] when the issue is the Court's *authority to set aside the will of the people,* is to premise that the end justifies the means; it is to postulate, in the words of Randall Bridwell, that "the assertion of correctness of the *results* reached by the newly claimed judicial power is tantamount to a demonstration of their legitimacy," that "the Court's claim to power is a *fait accompli;* it is unrealistic [and heretical] to presume it reversible."[16]

After his 1980 conclusion that judges are not bound by the Constitution, Brest examined activist rationalizations for the judicial exercise of extraconstitutional power. Now he notes that "The judges and scholars who support judicial intervention usually acknowledge that the ['fundamental'] rights at stake . . . are not specified by the text or original history of the Constitution," but they argue that "the judiciary is *nonetheless authorized*" to protect "these rights which can be discovered in conventional morality or derived from the principles of philosophy and adjudication."[17] They do not of course locate that authorization in the Constitution, the source of all power. The courts are creatures of the Constitution and enjoy only such power as it confers. Brest acknowledges that "Fundamental rights adjudication is open to criticisms that it is not *authorized* and not *guided* by the text and

---

would have failed. Brest, supra note 11 at 230. Ely also doubts that "opinion nationwide . . . had moved [by 1954] to the point of condemning 'separate but equal schooling.' " J. H. Ely, *Democracy and Distrust* 66 (1980). How then did *Brown* effectuate "widely and deeply held values"? How can Brest distill a "legal commitment to racial equality" from such facts?

15. Brest mistakenly deduces that I share his result-oriented approach: "Berger's condemnation of fundamental rights adjudication *is incidental* to an attack on virtually every significant decision under the Fourteenth Amendment—including Brown v. Board of Education." Brest supra note 9 at 1087. Unlike Brest, I did not start with a desired result, but sought out the historical facts, and unflinchingly followed where they dictated, whether or not they collided with my inclinations.

16. Randall Bridwell, "The Scope of Judicial Review: A Dirge for the Theorists of Majority Rule?" 31 S. Car. L. Rev. 617, 632 (1980), emphasis in the original.

17. Brest, supra note 9 at 1064.

original history of the Constitution.[18] Perry more forthrightly states that "There is no plausible textual or historical justification for constitutional policymaking by the judiciary—no way to avoid the conclusion that noninterpretive review . . . cannot be justified by reference either to the text or to the intention of the Framers of the Constitution"[19]—the thesis of my book.

Brest begins his search with "seven representative scholars who favor one or another form of fundamental rights adjudication," notices that they espouse theories revolving around divergent concepts and sources of "morals,"[20] and concludes that, even if "general principles can be found in social consensus or derived by moral reasoning, the application of these principles is highly indeterminate and subject to manipulation. The point is partially illustrated by disagreements among theorists employing essentially the same methodology . . . Even when the scholars are in substantial agreement, however, their conclusions are not obviously determined by their sources and methods,"[21] suggesting that they are derived from their own predilections. In short, Brest concludes that "no defensible criteria exist" whereby to assess "value-oriented constitutional adjudications."[22] Of such is the Heavenly City of Legal Philosophers. For them it is of little consequence that, as Alexander Bickel and Jesse Choper stress, "the procedure of judicial review is in conflict with the fundamental principles of democracy—majority rule under conditions of political freedom,"[23] that the reservation by the Tenth Amendment to the

18. Id. at 1087. For a critique of judge-made "minority" rights, see Raoul Berger, "Paul Brest's Brief for an Imperial Judiciary," 40 Md. L. Rev. 1, 18–22 (1981).

19. Perry, supra note 14 at 275.

20. Brest, supra note 9 at 1067–1089. "The fundamental rights controversy," Brest remarks, "is concerned with [judicially] constraining the majority acting through their legislatures," id. 1105, more plainly, with the judicial takeover of government.

21. Id. at 1089.

22. Id. at 1065.

23. Id. at 1065, 1068. The "proponents of fundamental rights adjudication," Brest notes, "scarcely address the issue" of countermajoritarianism. Id. at 1100.

States of power not delegated cannot be overcome by glosses of "inscrutable" terms based on conflicting theories of "morals."[24] Such activist rationalizations afford a pitiful foundation for the Court's invalidation of centuries-old death penalties which confessedly runs counter to the people's desires.

This is not to call Brest "a Daniel come to judgment"; rather, he cries out "a plague on both your houses" and seeks to demonstrate that "the alternative strategies of judicial review proposed by the critics cannot withstand the same kind of criticisms they levy against fundamental rights adjudication."[25] For this, Brest examines the views of Robert Bork, John Hart Ely, and myself. Let me focus on his attack on my views. It is dispiriting to find that my prior refutation of his criticism has not deterred him from repeating his misrepresentations of my position.[26] That goes beyond

24. Brest himself observes that "because of its *indeterminacy*, the [equal] protection clause does not offer much guidance in resolving particular issues of discrimination based on race." Brest, supra note 11 at 232. But see supra Chapter 5, text accompanying notes 71–82. Compare Brest's 1977 query: "Should the *unqualified* language of the equal protection clause nevertheless be read to insulate those discriminatory practices—including school segregation—that the nation was not ready to eliminate in the 1860's." Brest, supra note 12 at 11. His deceased colleague, Herbert Packer, better understood that "the new 'substantive equal protection' has under a different label permitted today's Justices to impose their prejudices in much the same manner as the Four Horsemen [of the pre-1937 Court] once did." Packer, "The Aim of Criminal Law Revisited: A Plea for a new Look at 'Substantive Due Process,' " 44 S. Cal. L. Rev. 490, 491–492 (1972).

25. Brest, supra note 9 at 1065.

26. This is mystifying. For Brest now acknowledges the several theses of my book, namely, that suffrage was not granted by the Fourteenth Amendment, infra note 35; that desegregation could not have won popular approval either in the 1860s or in 1954; supra note 14; that judicial creation of rights not embodied in the Constitution is unauthorized, supra text accompanying note 18; that activist arguments to the contrary are merely propaganda for desired results, infra text accompanying note 60. His critique of my views is therefore merely mud-slinging, the more since he patently has been influenced by them.

the issue of his credibility. Given academe's current infatuation with judicial activism,[27] he owes a duty both to scholarship and to the people to state an opponent's view honestly and fairly. Instead he flails away at strawmen of his own devising.

"For Berger," he begins, "the *only* relevant question is how the adopters of the Fourteenth Amendment would have decided a particular case in 1868"; this he labels "strict intentionalism."[28] In my rebuttal of his earlier, identical charge, I wrote:

> My core thesis ... was that the framers of the amendment *un-mistakably excluded* suffrage from its scope, a position that Brest labels as "moderate originalist"; for such the "sources are conclusive *when they speak clearly.*" When, however, he turns to me, he aligns me with the "strict intentionalists" who "determine how the adopters would have applied a provision to a given situation ..." I am no soothsayer; and given the clear exclusion of suffrage there was no occasion to consider how the framers "would have" applied a non-existent provision."[29]

His "only relevant question" puts words in my mouth; for me, how the framers "would have" decided issues of suffrage and segregation was a glaring irrelevancy because they *did* in fact decide to exclude both.

Next Brest states that Berger "is not concerned with their [the framers'] interpretive intentions (the canons of construction by

27. Brest notes that "In contrast to the profusion of articles supporting fundamental rights of adjudication, the scholarly literature contains relatively few unsympathetic analyses," Brest, supra note 9 at 1067.

It was not ever thus; compare Henry Steele Commager's scathing criticism of the pre-1937 Court, Commager, "Judicial Review and Democracy," 19 Va. L. Q. Rev. 417 (1943); compare Lochner v. New York, 198 U.S. 45 (1905); see supra Chapter 5, text accompanying notes 141–142. Brest notes that *"Lochner* remains an embarrassment for proponents of fundamental rights adjudication and cause for skepticism about the practice." Brest, supra note 9 at 1086.

28. Brest, supra note 9 at 1090.

29. Berger, supra note 18 at 26.

which they intended their provisions to be interpreted).''[30] In my earlier rebuttal, I pointed out that

> Senator Charles Sumner, well aware that the great majority of the Senate opposed his extreme abolitionist views, yet stated that if the meaning of the Constitution "in any place is open to doubt, or if words are used which seem to have no fixed signification [for example, equal protection], we cannot err if we turn to the framers . . .'' This was confirmed by confreres who also sat in the 39th Congress. And such views were summarized by a "unanimous Senate Judiciary Committee report, signed by Senators who had voted for the Thirteenth, Fourteenth, and Fifteenth Amendments in Congress," the subject being the fourteenth amendment:
>
>> A construction which should give the phrase . . . a meaning different from the sense in which it was understood and employed by the people when they adopted the Constitution, would be as unconstitutional as a departure from the plain and express language of the Constitution in any other particular. *This is the rule of interpretation* adopted by all commentators on the Constitution, and in all judicial expositions of that instrument.[31]

It is therefore Brest, not myself, who shuts his eyes to "the canons of construction by which [the framers] intended their provisions to be interpreted." And it is misleading to say that *"If they adverted to the matter at all,* the adopters more likely intended a textualist approach such as the 'plain meaning' rule.''[32]

Brest also condemns my unconcern "with the level of abstraction on which [the framers] intended their provisions to be read—for example, whether they intended only to establish general principles or, at the other extreme, to bind future interpreters on each issue that might arise under the provision.''[33] No "level of abstraction" can dispose of the brute fact that the framers un-

30. Brest, supra note 9 at 1090.
31. Berger, supra note 18 at 30.
32. Brest, supra note 9 at 1090.
33. Id.

mistakably excluded suffrage. Brest's "beloved mentor," Justice Harlan, found that the evidence for this exclusion is "irrefutable and remains unanswered."[34] That the framers excluded suffrage Brest now admits.[35] Brest's resort to "levels of abstraction" only blurs the facts, when they are not completely lost to sight. Ely refers to the "understandable temptation to vary the relevant tradition's level of abstraction to make it come out right."[36] To recur to my core concern, the corollary of the framers' exclusion of suffrage—the genus—is that they meant "to bind future interpreters on each [suffrage] issue that might arise under that provision."

Brest further muddies the waters by charging that "Berger's indifference to interpretive intent [that is, interpretive canons], and the intended level of abstraction undermine the very premise of his theory—the obligation of fidelity to the adopter's intention—by confusing their intentions with their mere personal *views*."[37] Can it be that this simple dichotomy—intentions/personal views—escaped the sharp eye of Brest's "beloved mentor," Justice Harlan? In truth, Brest's dichotomy shatters on the fact—earlier drawn to his attention—that "During the pendency of ratification, radical opposition to readmission of Tennessee because its constitution excluded Negro suffrage was voted down in the House 125 to 12. A similar proposal by Senator Sumner was voted

34. Supra Chapter 2, text accompanying note 67. Brest's more seasoned colleague Gerald Gunther considered the Reynolds decision to the contrary "illegitimate." Supra Chapter 5 note 92.

35. The "adopters of the equal protection clause probably intended it not to encompass voting discrimination at all." Brest, supra note 11 at 234 n. 115. The "adopters would probably have disapproved of all the Court's modern voting rights decisions." Id. at 234.

Brest's view that the clause *embodied* "an ideal—of racial equality," Brest, supra note 12 at 11 (compare supra note 14), is at war with his recognition that "those who adopted the Amendment were not ready to make good on its promise." Id. He chides them for not reading *their* handiwork as he would.

36. J. H. Ely, *Democracy and Distrust* 61 (1981).

37. Brest, supra note 9 at 1090, emphasis in the original.

down 34 to 4,"[38] striking evidence that the framers *voted* their "intention," that their "personal views" merged into an overwhelming consensus. Against this background, Brest's insistence that "we cannot determine the adopter's interpretive intent"[39] exhibits willful blindness to the incontrovertible, central fact that suffrage was excluded. Such are the costs of clinging to a predetermined result, be the facts what they may.

Brest also seeks to impeach the reliability of my historical survey: "The academic response to Berger has focussed on his analysis of the equal protection clause, arguing that it is methodically and factually problematic." For this he cites Aviam Soifer's "Critique of Raoul Berger's History,"[40] neglecting to mention that Michael Perry and Randall Bridwell have rejected Soifer,[41] ignoring my point-by-point refutation of Soifer,[42] which a renowned historian wrote me "demolished" him, and making no mention of a considerable body of academic opinion, which Perry was at pains to collate, that endorses my history.[43] In truth, Brest's citation of Soifer

38. Berger, supra note 18 at 31. This vote reflected the will of the people: "Negro voting in the North was out of the question." William Gillette, *The Right to Vote: Politics and the Passage of the Fifteenth Amendment* 32 (1965); see also supra Chapter 5, text accompanying notes 84–92.

39. Brest, supra note 9 at 1090.

40. Id. at 1087.

41. For Perry, see infra note 43; Bridwell, supra note 16 at 621 n. 11, dismissing Soifer's *"ad hominem* and pejorative approach," revealing "an inability to formulate a position of substance."

42. Raoul Berger, "Soifer to the Rescue of History," 32 S. Car. L. Rev. 427 (1981). For other examples of Brest's inveterate "one-sidedness," see Berger, supra note 18 at 34–35. Although John Burleigh disagrees with my view of the Court's role, he considers that my book "not only raises the right questions, but is also carefully documented and rigorously argued, at once learned, illuminating, and challenging." John Burleigh, "The Supreme Court vs. the Constitution," The Public Interest 151, 152–153 (Special Winter Supp. 1978). "Berger's uncomfortable and unfashionable analysis is an important one. It will not do, as some have already done, to brush it aside in a peremptory manner." Henry Monaghan, "The Constitution Goes to Harvard," 13 Harvard C. R.–C. L. Rev. 117, 124 (1978).

43. "For examples of commentary generally accepting Berger's history—though not necessarily the constitutional theory Berger marries to

is a gratuitous diversionary slur for, as Perry points out, "nowhere in his entire essay does Soifer take issue with Berger's central claim that neither the 1866 act nor the fourteenth amendment were intended to affect suffrage or segregation," facts which Brest himself acknowledges.[44] Such one-sided citations befit a high-school debate, not a scholarly attempt to sift out the facts on a momentous issue.

It is also misleading to state that "only Berger rests his case exclusively on the lack of authorization."[45] Philip Kurland, for one,

---

that history—*see* Abraham, *'Equal Justice Under Law'* or *'Justice at Any Cost'?—the Judicial Role Revisited Reflections on* Government by Judiciary: The Transformation of the Fourteenth Amendment, 6 Hast. Const. L.Q. 467 (1979); Alfange, *On Judicial Policymaking and Constitutional Change: Another Look at the 'Original Intent' Theory of Constitutional Interpretation,* 5 Hast. Const. L. Q. 603 (1978); Beloff, *Book Review,* London Times Higher Educ. Supp., April 7, 1978, at 11, col. 1; Bridwell, *Book Review,* 1978 Duke L.J. 907; Gunther, *Book Review,* Wall St. J., November 25, 1977, at 4, col 4; Kay, *Book Review,* 10 Conn. L. Rev. 801 (1978); Kommers, *Book Review,* Rev. of Pol. 409, 413 (July, 1978); Lynch, *Book Review,* 63 Cornell L. Rev. 1091–93 (1978); Nathanson, *Book Review,* 56 Tex. L. Rev. 579, 581 (1978); Perry, *Book Review,* 78 Colum L. Rev. 685 (1978). *See also* Bridwell, *The Scope of Judicial Review: A Dirge for the Theorists of Majority Rule,* 31 S. Car. L. Rev. 617 (1980). For generally effective rebuttals by Berger to criticisms of his history, *see* Berger, *'Government by Judiciary': Judge Gibbons' Argument Ad Hominem* 59 B.U. L. Rev. 783 (1979) (responding to Gibbons, *Book Review,* 31 Rutgers L. Rev. 839 (1978); Berger, *The Scope of Judicial Review: An Ongoing Debate,* 6 Hast. Const. L. Q. 527 (1979) (responding to various articles in a Symposium, 6 Hast. Const. L. Q. 403 (1979)); Berger, *Government by Judiciary: John Hart Ely's 'Invitation,'* 54 Ind. L.J. 277 (1979) (responding to Ely, *Constitutional Interpretivism: Its Allure and Impossibility,* 53 Ind. L.J. 399 (1978); Berger, *The Scope of Judicial Review and Walter Murphy,* 1979 Wis. L. Rev. 341 (1979) (responding to Murphy, *Book Review,* 87 Yale L.J. 1752 (1978); Berger, *Government by Judiciary: Some Countercriticism,* 56 Tex. L. Rev. 1125, 1136–45 (1978) (responding to Clark, *Book Review,* 56 Tex. L. Rev. 947 (1978); Berger's rebuttals to criticisms of his constitutional theory are much less effective in my view." Perry 285. But compare Brest's charge that Berger "persistently distorted [the data] to support his thesis." Brest, supra note 12 at 44.

44. Perry 285, n. 100; for Brest, see supra notes 13, 14.

45. Brest, supra note 9 at 1087.

wrote that "the most immediate constitutional crisis of our present time" is "the usurpation by the judiciary of general governmental powers on the pretext that its authority derives from the Fourteenth Amendment."[46] If activist judicial review is *not authorized,* as Brest now acknowledges,[47] it is of no moment that "only Berger" cries out that the Emperor wears no clothes. "What makes a thing true," as Sidney Hook wrote, "is not who says it, but the evidence for it."[48]

My call to respect the limited role the Framers assigned to the judiciary is not, I submit, "subject to the same kind of criticism" as is "levied against fundamental rights adjudication"; it is not merely an "alternative strategy of judicial review";[49] it is not a "theory" spun out of thin air as is activist theorizing. Rather, as Brest's activist colleague, Thomas Grey, observed, it represents a view that is "of great power and compelling simplicity . . . deeply rooted in our history and in our shared principles of political legitimacy. It has equally deep roots in our constitutional law."[50] It is a view that proceeds from the Framers' unequivocal canon, oft-repeated and never questioned by the Supreme Court, that *all* power

46. Letter to Harvard University Press, August 15, 1977. On my core issue, suffrage, Justice Harlan declared: "When the Court disregards the express intent and understanding of the Framers, it has invaded the realm of the political process to which the amending procedure was committed, and it has violated the constitutional structure which it is its highest duty to protect." Oregon v. Mitchell, 400 U.S. 112, 203 (1970), dissenting in part.

47. Supra text accompanying note 18.

48. Sidney Hook, *Philosophy and Public Policy* 121 (1980).

49. Supra note 25.

50. Thomas C. Grey, "Do We Have an Unwritten Constitution?" 27 Stan. L. Rev. 703, 705 (1975). Respecting the rule, drawn from Marbury v. Madison, that the textual language "is to be understood in exactly the sense intended by those who wrote, proposed, and ratified it without reference to changed circumstances," Richard S. Kay wrote, it "is a narrow application of what continues to be orthodox constitutional theory, generally espoused by the Court itself." Kay, "Preconstitutional Rules," 42 Ohio St. L. J. 187, 196 (1981). "Critics of interpretivism, who typically, of course, are defenders of noninterpretivism, achieve nothing by pretending that interpretivism is not a forceful theory." Perry 278.

must be drawn from the Constitution. Activist theorizing, on the other hand, is a very recent phenomenon, seeking to justify judicial exercise of ungranted power by moral theories that have no constitutional roots in order to undergird judicial governance that supports activist aspirations.[51] To argue that such academic web-spinning is in equipoise with constitutional history and unbroken Supreme Court pronouncements to the contrary, is to exhibit the admittedly tendentious nature of activist advocacy.[52]

Throughout Brest and his ilk ignore that we are dealing with a question of *power*,[53] that under a written Constitution which limits power, the question must always be: where is the power conferred.[54] Power cannot be supplied by academic theorizing from premises that have no constitutional roots.[55] Brest would escape from the weakness of activist theorizing by reliance on the courts' *"competence,* on the special contributions they make to the

51. Leonard Levy referred to arguments "of comparatively recent vintage, raising the suspicion that the arguments have been concocted to rationalize a growing satisfaction with judicial review among the liberal intellectuals and scholars." Levy, ed., *Judicial Review and the Supreme Court* 24 (1967).

52. Infra text accompanying note 61.

53. As Willard Hurst stated, "When you are talking about Constitutional law, you are talking about the balance of power in a community." Hurst, "The Role of the Constitutional Text," in Edmond Cahn, ed., *Supreme Court and Supreme Law* 64, 68 (1954).

54. Supra Chapter 5, text accompanying note 1. Thomas Gerety refers to "an important convention . . . simply that there must be a text for any assertion of the power of judicial review. Going without a text is like going naked . . . to say that the judge has no text is to say that he has no authority at all. *Writtenness* plays a central part in our constitutional tradition." Gerety, "Doing Without Privacy," 42 Ohio St. L. J. 143, 145 (1981).

55. I concur with John Hart Ely that if a principle is not rooted in the Constitution, "it is not a constitutional principle and the Court has no business imposing it," that the Court "is under an obligation to trace its premises to the charter from which it derives its authority." Ely, "The Wages of Crying Wolf: A Comment on Roe v. Wade," 82 Yale L. J. 920, 949 (1873).

quality of our social life."[56] This is an apology for self-conferred judicial power. Expertise does not confer power; and if it did, it cannot be left to the expert to determine that he is the best fitted to rule. That would make him the judge in his own cause.[57]

Still less is that determination left to academe. Nor does the record of the Court inspire confidence that it knows better than the people what will best contribute "to the quality of our American life,"[58] to decide against their will, for example, that death penalties must be hobbled. From Mill to Sidney Hook, elitist pretensions to know better than the people themselves what is for their good have been suspect.[59] Wiser than academe, Judge

56. Brest, supra note 9 at 1102. Arthur S. Miller, a perfervid activist, considers that judges have not been prepared "for the task of constitutional interpretation." Few have "the broad-gauged approach and knowledge" essential "to search for and identify the values that should be sought in constitutional adjudication." A. Miller, Book Review, 6 Hastings Con. L. Q. 487, 500, 507 (1979). And the Justices labor under the grave disadvantage of employing the "faulty" "adversary system as a means of settling public policy," "faulty on at least three scores—the competence of the personnel, an inability to know the consequences of adverse decisions and the flow of information to the judges." Miller, id. 508, 509.

Owen Fiss, on whom Brest relies, acknowledges that "in terms of personal characteristics [judges] are no different from successful businessmen or politicians. Their capacity to make a specific contribution to our social life derives not from any personal traits or knowledge but from the definition of the office in which they find themselves and through which they exercise power." Fiss, "The Supreme Court, 1978 Term: Foreword: The Forms of Justice," 93 Harv. L. Rev., 1, 12 (1979). On this theory, it is not expertise but the chance elevation to the "office" that endows them with unique power to divine the nation's needs—a form of transubstantiation. On the other hand, Miller considers that the "search" "takes a different type of mind from that usually evident in the legal profession." Martin Shapiro observes that the judge is insulated "from technological expertise by a legal education that leaves him absolutely ignorant of the workings of industrial society." Supra note 1 at 7.

57. For more extended analysis, see Berger, supra note 29 at 7–10.

58. For the Court's poor track record, see supra Chapter 8, note 17.

59. For J. S. Mill, see supra Chapter 8, text accompanying note 16; for Hook, Chapter 6, text accompanying note 63.

Learned Hand did not want to be ruled by "Platonic Guardians,"[60] the haphazard product of swirling politics. Activist defense of such rule needs to be viewed against Brest's plea to academe "simply to acknowledge that most of our writings [about judicial review] are not political theory but advocacy scholarship—amicus briefs ultimately designed to persuade the Court to adopt our various notions of the public good."[61] Hallelujah!

60. Learned Hand, *The Bill of Rights* 73 (1958). Myres McDougal wrote, "Government by a self-designated elite—like that of benevolent despotism or Plato's philosophers . . . is not the American way." Myres McDougal and Asher Lans, "Treaties and Congressional-Executive or Presidential Agreements: Interchangeable Instruments of National Policy," 54 Yale L. J. 181, 577–578 (1945).

61. Brest, supra note 9 at 1109. Bridwell earlier commented that "shorn of imposing rhetorical trappings, it is obvious that modern scholarship normally consists of nothing more than a declared consensus in favor of particular results," serving "as a polling place for the 'intellectual elite' in which the options to avoid democracy are proposed and approved." Bridwell, supra note 16 at 655–656.

Appendix A
"Equal Protection of the Laws"

THE "equal protection" clause deserves some further comment because, as Herbert Packer concluded, "the new 'substantive equal protection' has under a different label permitted today's Justices to impose their prejudices in much the same manner as the Four Horsemen [of the pre-1937 Court] once did."[1] The keynote was sounded by Justice Frankfurter, the apostle of judicial "self-restraint." Frankfurter, his then law clerk, Alexander Bickel, indicated, "was a moving force" in the decision of *Brown v. Board of Education,* the desegregation case, as is borne out by such facts as have already come to light.[2] At his behest Bickel prepared a study of the legislative history of the Fourteenth Amendment, which Frankfurter deemed so impressive that he had it printed for distribution to the other Jus-

---

1. Herbert Packer, "The Aim of Criminal Law Revisited: A Plea for a New Look at 'Substantive Due Process,' " 44 S. Cal. L. Rev. 490, 491–492 (1971).
2. Bickel 33; for details see Berger *G/J* 128–133.

tices.[3] Bickel decided, "It is impossible to conclude that the 39th Congress intended that segregation be abolished,"[4] a deduction he repeated in 1962.[5] My own subsequent study convinced me that the framers intended to *exclude* segregation.[6] Herewith some additional evidence that they tied equal protection to the limited goals they adopted in the Civil Rights Act of 1866, which they incorporated in the Fourteenth Amendment.

Time and again sweeping proposals in the 39th Congress to abolish *all* discriminations were rejected.[7] James Wilson, chairman of the House Judiciary Committee and sponsor of the Civil Rights Bill in the House, explained that the words "civil rights" did not mean that black "children shall attend the same schools. These are not civil rights."[8] At the outset Thaddeus Stevens, the Radical leader, submitted to the Joint Committee a proposal that "*All* laws, state or national, shall operate impartially and equally on all persons." But in summing up in favor of the Fourteenth Amendment, he sadly confessed that while he had hoped to remodel "all our institutions as to have freed them from every vestige of . . . inequality of rights . . . that *no* distinction would be tolerated . . . this bright dream has vanished."[9] The Joint Committee chairman, Senator William Fessenden, told the framers, "We cannot put into the Constitution, owing to existing prejudices and existing institutions, an entire exclusion of all class distinctions,"[10] as the exclusion of suffrage alone demonstrates. Then

3. Kluger, *Simple Justice* 653 (1976).

4. Id. 654.

5. The framers did not intend "to forbid the states to enact and enforce segregation statutes." They "did not intend or expect then and there to outlaw segregation, which, of course was a practice widely prevalent in the North." Alexander Bickel, *The Least Dangerous Branch* 100 (1962).

6. Berger, *G/J* 117–133; Raoul Berger, "The Fourteenth Amendment: Light from the Fifteenth," 74 Nw. U. L. Rev. 311, 326–331 (1979).

7. For citations, see Berger *G/J* 163–164.

8. *Globe* 1117.

9. Ben Kendrick, *The Journal of the Joint Committee of Fifteen on Reconstruction* 46 (1914); *Globe* 3148.

10. *Globe* 705.

there is the fact that in an early version of the Amendment provision was made for *both* "the same political rights and privileges and ... equal protection in the enjoyment of life, liberty, and property,"[11] testimony that "equal protection" was not deemed to comprehend "political rights and privileges," but was confined to "life, liberty, and property." When the words "political rights and privileges" were deleted, leaving "equal protection" standing alone, the latter patently did not include the elided "political privileges," illustrating the framers' unwillingness to proceed beyond protection of the right to exist.[12]

Throughout the debates on the Civil Rights Bill, which, it will be recalled, secured only the "equal benefit of all laws for security of person and property," the framers interchangeably referred to "equality," "equality before the law," and "equal protection," but always in the circumscribed context of the rights enumerated in the Bill. So, Samuel Shellabarger of Ohio said, "whatever rights as to each of these *enumerated* civil (not political) matters the States may confer upon one race ... shall be held by all races in equality ... It secures ... *equality of protection* in those enumerated civil rights."[13] In *Reiche v. Smythe* the Court held that if two acts are *in pari materia,* "it will be presumed that if the same word be used in both, and a special meaning were given to it in the first act, that it was intended that it should receive the same interpretation in the latter act, in the absence of anything to show a contrary intention."[14] That "special meaning" was equal pro-

11. Alexander Bickel, "The Original Understanding and the Segregation Decision," 69 Harv. L. Rev. 1, 31 (1955).

12. "Early drafts of the Fourteenth Amendment employed language sufficiently broad to bar racial discrimination with respect to political rights; but the ultimate decision to protect [only] interests in 'life, liberty, and property' seems to have reflected hesitation over wide spread extension of political rights to Negroes." E. L. Barrett, P. W. Burton, and John Honnold, *Constitutional Law: Cases and Materials* 804 (2d ed., 1963).

13. *Globe* 1293; for other citations, see Berger *G/J* 169–171.

14. 80 U.S. (13 Wall.) 162, 165 (1871).

tection for the civil rights "enumerated" in the Civil Rights Act, no more.[15]

15. Bickel concluded that, "The Senate Moderates, led by Trumbull and Fessenden, who sponsored this [civil rights] formula, assigned a limited and well-defined meaning to it," namely, "the right to contract," to own property and "also a right to equal protection in the literal sense of benefitting equally from the laws for the security of person and property." Bickel supra note 10 at 56; for more detailed discussion, see Berger *G/J* 166–192.

Appendix B
Congressional Contraction of Judicial
Jurisdiction: An Addendum

A S this study was about to go to the printer my attention was drawn to an article by Lawrence Sager, "Foreword: Constitutional Limitations on Congress' Authority to Regulate the Jurisdiction of the Federal Courts" (November 1981).[1] It is a full-scale, densely packed, 77-page attack on the conventional learning. Necessarily comment must be limited.

Sager maintains that Article III "contains a direct, self-executing grant of jurisdiction . . . to the Supreme Court," a proposition he regards as "well settled,"[2] citing among other cases *Durousseau v. United States* and *The "Francis Wright."*[3] But Congress, he notes,

1. 95 Harv. L. Rev. 17.
2. Id. 23–24.
3. Id. 24 n. 17. These cases are discussed supra Chapter 7, text accompanying notes 22–24. To these may be added Daniels v. Railroad Co., 70 U.S. (3 Wall.) 250, 254 (1866): "But it is for Congress to determine how far, within the limits of the capacity of this Court to take, appellate juris-

has "never chosen to act as if the Supreme Court's jurisdiction were self-executing," beginning with the Judiciary Act of 1789 wherein it "assumed the statutory voice of affirmatively granting the Court jurisdiction."[4] This was enacted by the First Congress, in which sat a substantial number of members "who had served in the Convention,"[5] who were doubtless familiar with its aims, and whose construction of the Constitution is ranked very high. Chief Justice Marshall, himself a member of the Virginia Ratification Convention, declared that the Judiciary Act was in execution of "The *power they possessed* of making exceptions to the appellate jurisdiction."[6] Such decisions are described by Sager as "Congress acts as though it were giving the Court jurisdiction . . . and ordinarily the court has no occasion to take umbrage at this pretense," a "polite ritual."[7] It had such an "occasion" in *Ex parte McCardle* and meekly repeated Marshall's pronouncement.[8]

Sager reiterates that

> Congress has always understood the exceptions clause to permit
> it to subtract legal issues and cases from the Article III jurisdic-
> tion of the Supreme Court.

---

diction *shall be given,* and when conferred, it can be exercised only to the extent and in the manner prescribed by law. In these respects it is wholly a creature of legislation."

4. Supra note 1 at 24–25.

5. The First Congress, Charles Warren observed, was "almost an adjourned session" of the Federal Convention. Charles Warren, *Congress, the Constitution and the Supreme Court* 99 (1925).

6. Quoted supra note 1 at 25.

7. Id.

8. For continuing recognition of McCardle, see supra Chapter 7, note 23. Charles Fairman observed that "To the Court it was an everyday truth that its appellate jurisdiction was bounded by the Acts of Congress . . . Over the years the Court unhesitatingly cited *McCardle* to the point that the repeal of a court's jurisdictional grant, without a saving clause, cut off its power to decide. There seemed to be no question that, as Justice Frankfurter wrote in 1949, 'Congress . . . may withdraw appellate jurisdiction once conferred . . .' [I]n 1962 Justice Harlan repeated that proposition [Justice Brennan and Stewart concurring]." 6 Charles Fairman, *History of the Supreme Court of the United States* 495, 511 (1971).

The Court itself has shared this understanding. In no opinion has the Court taken a contrary view. Indeed, in the pertinent opinions, the Court displays almost unseemly enthusiasm in discussing Congress' power to lop off diverse heads of the Court's article III jurisdiction.[9]

Manifestly Sager undertakes a formidable task in disposing of an unbroken stream of such pronouncements. And he overlooks the need for dealing with judicial usurpation.

He inveighs against "prejudice to judicially protected *rights*," against burdening "the exercise of a *constitutional* right."[10] But many, if not most, of the "rights" fashioned by the Warren-Burger Courts, activists concede, are "actually supraconstitutional," not derived from "the text or original understanding."[11] They are unauthorized judicial constructs. Nowhere was the Court empowered to create extraconstitutional rights.[12] Seven hundred years ago Dante perceived that "The usurpation of a right does not create a right."[13] In effect, Sager would insulate

9. Supra note 1 at 32.

10. Id. 70.

11. Supra Chapter 7, text accompanying notes 52–53.

12. In the First Congress, James Jackson said: "we must confine ourselves to the powers described in the constitution, and the moment we pass it, we take an arbitrary step towards a despotic government." 1 *Ann. Cong.* 489. There, too, Alexander White, who had participated in the stormy Virginia Ratification Convention, referred to the "specifically enumerated powers" for "particular purposes only," and said, "If these powers are insufficient . . . it is not within our power to remedy. The people who bestowed them must grant further powers . . . This was the ground on which the friends of the Constitution supported the Constitution . . . [otherwise] the Constitution would never have been ratified." Id. 514–515. See also supra Chapter 5, text accompanying note 1.

Ely, who regards the Ninth Amendment as "open-ended," *Democracy and Distrust* 33–34 (1981), stated: "One thing we know to a certainty from the historical context is that the Ninth Amendment was not designed to grant Congress authority to create additional rights, to amend Article I, Section 8 by adding a general power to protect rights." Id. 37. Much less did the Framers empower the courts thus to diminish the rights reserved to the States.

13. Will Durant, *The Age of Faith* 1063 (1950).

these judge-made rights and make the Court the judge of its own usurpation.[14] Nor does he examine the impact of §5, which designedly conferred jurisdiction to enforce the Fourteenth Amendment on Congress, not the Court, in order to exclude the Court from decision of "political" issues such as *Dred Scott*.[15]

If decisions such as those dealing with school prayer, abortion, and death penalties, are indeed in excess of the authority of the Court, it is not easy to conclude that despite the unqualified text—"exceptions and regulations"—Congress is disabled from curtailing such usurpations in the interest of restoring self-government.

14. Jurisdictional limitations, Sager urges, would "seriously reduc[e] the capacity of the entire legal system to adjudicate and enforce ['constitutional rights'] fairly." Supra note 1 at 70.

15. Supra Chapter 7, text accompanying notes 57–76.

Bibliography

BOOKS

Adams, Henry. *John Randolph* (Boston, Houghton Mifflin, 1882).

Adams, Samuel. *Writings,* ed. Harry Alonso Cushing, 4 vols. (New York, G. P. Putnam's Sons, 1904-1908).

Allen, C. K. *Law in the Making,* 6th ed. (Oxford, Clarendon Press, 1958).

Avins, Alfred. *The Reconstruction Amendments' Debates* (Richmond, Virginia Commission on Constitutional Government, 1967).

Bacon, Matthew. *A New Abridgment of the Law,* 3d ed., 4 vols. (London, 1768).

Bailyn, Bernard. *The Ideological Origins of the American Revolution* (Cambridge, Mass., Belknap Press of Harvard University Press, 1967).

Barnes, Harry E. *The Repression of Crime: Studies in Historical Penology* (Montclair, N.J., Patterson Smith, 1969).

Barrett, Edward L., Jr., Paul W. Burton, and John Honnold. *Constitu-*

tional Law: Cases and Materials, 2d ed. (Brooklyn, Foundation Press, 1963).

Barrington, Boyd C. *The Magna Charta and Other Great Charters of England,* 2d ed. (Philadelphia, William J. Campbell, 1900).

Bedau, Hugo A. *The Courts, The Constitution, and Capital Punishment* (Lexington, Mass., Lexington Books, 1977).

———— *The Death Penalty in America,* rev. ed. (Garden City, N.Y., Doubleday Anchor Books, 1967).

Berger, Raoul. *Congress v. The Supreme Court* (Cambridge, Mass., Harvard University Press, 1969).

———— *Government by Judiciary: The Transformation of the Fourteenth Amendment* (Cambridge, Mass., Harvard University Press, 1977).

———— *Impeachment: The Constitutional Problems* (Cambridge, Mass., Harvard University Press, 1973).

Berlin, Isaiah. *Personal Impressions* (New York, Viking, 1981).

Berns, Walter. *For Capital Punishment: Crime and the Morality of the Death Penalty* (New York, Basic Books, 1979).

Bickel, Alexander M. *The Least Dangerous Branch: The Supreme Court at the Bar of Politics* (Indianapolis, Bobbs-Merrill, 1962).

———— *The Supreme Court and the Idea of Progress* (New York, Harper & Row, 1970).

Black, Charles L., Jr. *The People and the Court* (New York, Macmillan, 1960).

Brest, Paul. *Processes of Constitutional Decisionmaking: Cases and Materials* (Boston, Little, Brown, 1975).

Brinton, Crane, John B. Christopher, and Robert Lee Wolff. *A History of Civilization,* 2 vols. (New York, Prentice-Hall, 1955).

Cahn, Edmond, ed. *Supreme Court and Supreme Law* (Bloomington, Indiana University Press, 1954).

Cardozo, Benjamin N. *The Nature of the Judicial Process* (New Haven, Yale University Press, 1921).

Chitty, Joseph. *Collection of Statutes,* 2 vols. (London, W. Benning, 1828).

Commager, Henry Steele, ed. *Documents of American History,* 2 vols., 7th ed. (New York, Appleton, 1963).

Corwin, Edward S. *The Doctrine of Judicial Review: Its Legal and Historical Bases and Other Essays* (Princeton, Princeton University Press, 1914; rpt. Gloucester, Mass., Peter Smith, 1963).

——— *The Twilight of the Supreme Court: A History of Our Constitutional Theory* (New Haven, Yale University Press, 1934).

Cox, Archibald. *The Role of the Supreme Court in American Government* (New York, Oxford University Press, 1976).

Curtis, Charles P., Jr. *Lions Under the Throne* (Boston, Houghton Mifflin, 1947).

Devlin, Sir Patrick. *Trial by Jury* (London, Stevens, 1956).

Donald, David. *Charles Sumner and the Rights of Man* (New York, A. A. Knopf, 1970).

Douglas, William O. *The Court Years, 1939–1975: The Autobiography of William O. Douglas* (New York, Random House, 1980).

Durant, Will. *The Age of Faith* (New York, Simon and Schuster, 1950).

——— *Caesar and Christ* (New York, Simon and Schuster, 1944).

Dusinberre, William. *Henry Adams, The Myth of Failure* (Charlottesville, University Press of Virginia, 1980).

Earle, Alice M. *Curious Punishments of Bygone Days* (1896; rpt. Montclair, N.J., Patterson Smith, 1969).

Elliot, Jonathan. *Debates in the Several State Conventions on the Adoption of the Federal Constitution,* 2d. ed, 4 vols. (Washington, D.C., 1836).

Elliott, Ward E. Y. *The Rise of a Guardian Democracy.* (Cambridge, Mass., Harvard University Press, 1974).

Elton, G. R. *England Under the Tudors* (London, Methuen, 1955).

Ely, John Hart. *Democracy and Distrust: A Theory of Judicial Review* (Cambridge, Mass., Harvard University Press, 1980).

Fairman, Charles. *Mr. Justice Miller and the Supreme Court* (Cambridge, Mass., Harvard University Press, 1939).

——— *Reconstruction and Reunion, 1864–1878,* vol. 6 of *History of the Supreme Court of the United States* (New York, Macmillan, 1971).

Farrand, Max. *The Records of the Federal Convention of 1787,* 4 vols. (New Haven, Yale University Press, 1911).

The Federalist (New York, Modern Library ed., 1937).

Forsyth, William. *History of Trial by Jury* (London, J. W. Parker and Son, 1852).

Frankfurter, Felix. *Law and Politics,* ed. Archibald MacLeish and E. F. Prichard (New York, Harcourt Brace, 1939).

——— *Of Law and Life and Other Things That Matter: Papers and Addresses of Felix Frankfurter, 1956–1963,* ed. Philip B. Kurland (Cambridge, Mass., Belknap Press of Harvard University Press, 1965).

—— *Of Law and Men,* ed. Philip Elman (New York, Harcourt Brace, 1956).

Freedman, Max, ed. *Roosevelt and Frankfurter: Their Correspondence, 1928-1945* (Boston, Little, Brown, 1968).

Freund, Paul A. *On Law and Justice.* (Cambridge, Mass., Belknap Press of Harvard University Press, 1968).

Gillette, William. *The Right to Vote: Politics and the Passage of the Fifteenth Amendment* (Baltimore, Johns Hopkins University Press, 1965).

Goodhart, A. L. *English Law and the Moral Law* (London, Stevens, 1953).

Gray, Anchitell. *Debates of the House of Commons, 1667-1674* (London, Henry & Cave, 1763).

Gunther, Gerald, ed. *John Marshall's Defense of McCulloch v. Maryland* (Stanford, Stanford University Press, 1969).

Hamilton, Alexander. *The Papers of Alexander Hamilton,* ed. H. C. Syrett and J. E. Cooke (New York, Columbia University Press, 1962).

—— *Works,* ed. H. C. Lodge, 12 vols. (New York, Knickerbocker Press, 1904).

Hand, Learned. *The Bill of Rights* (Cambridge, Mass., Harvard University Press, 1958).

—— *The Spirit of Liberty,* ed. Irving Dillard (New York, Knopf, 1952).

Hirsch, H. N. *The Enigma of Felix Frankfurter* (New York, Basic Books, 1981).

Holdsworth, William S. *History of English Law,* 12 vols. (London, Methuen, 1903-1938).

Holmes, Oliver Wendell, Jr. *Collected Legal Papers* (New York, Harcourt Brace, 1920).

Hook, Sidney. *Philosophy and Public Policy* (Carbondale, Southern Illinois University Press, 1980).

Howell's State Trials (Cobbett's Collection), 33 vols. (London, R. Bagshaw, 1809-1826).

Hughes, Charles Evans. *Addresses of Charles Evans Hughes, 1906-1916,* 2d ed. (New York, G. P. Putnam's Sons, 1916).

—— *The Supreme Court of the United States: Its Foundation, Methods and Achievements, an Interpretation* (New York, Columbia University Press, 1928).

Hyman, Harold M. *A More Perfect Union* (New York, Knopf, 1973).

———— ed. *New Frontiers of the American Reconstruction* (Champaign, University of Illinois Press, 1966).

Jackson, Robert H. *The Struggle For Judicial Supremacy: A Study of a Crisis in American Political Power* (New York, Knopf, 1941).

Jefferson, Thomas. *Writings,* ed. P. L. Ford, 10 vols. (New York, Putnam, 1892–1899).

Jones, Harry W., ed. *Political Separation and Legal Continuity* (Chicago, American Bar Association, 1976).

Kalven, Harry, Jr., and Hans Zeisel. *The American Jury* (Boston, Little, Brown, 1966).

Kent, James. *Commentaries on American Law,* 9th ed. (Boston, Little, Brown, 1858).

Kluger, Richard. *Simple Justice* (New York, Knopf, 1976).

Kurland, Philip B. *Politics, the Constitution and the Warren Court* (Chicago, University of Chicago Press, 1970).

———— *Watergate and the Constitution* (Chicago, University of Chicago Press, 1978).

Levy, Leonard W. *Against the Law: The Nixon Court and Criminal Justice* (New York, Harper & Row, 1974).

————, ed. *Judicial Review and the Supreme Court* (New York, Harper & Row, 1967).

———— *Judgments: Essays in American Constitutional History* (Chicago, Quadrangle, 1972).

———— *The Supreme Court under Earl Warren* (New York, Quadrangle, 1972).

Lusky, Louis. *By What Right?* (Charlottesville, Va., Michie/Bobbs-Merrill 1975).

McIlwain, Charles H. *Constitutionalism: Ancient and Modern,* rev. ed. (Ithaca, N.Y, Cornell University Press, 1947).

McKechnie, William S. *Magna Carta: A Commentary on the Great Charter of King John* (Glasgow, J. Maclehose, 1905).

McRee, G. J. *Life and Correspondence of James Iredell,* 2 vols. (New York, Appleton, 1857–1858).

Madison, James. *Writings,* ed. G. Hunt, 9 vols. (New York, Putnam, 1900–1910).

Malden, Henry Elliot, ed. *Magna Carta: Commemoration Essays* (London, Royal Historical Society, 1917).

Mendelson, Wallace, ed. *Felix Frankfurter: The Judge* (New York, Reynal, 1964).

Mill, J. S. *On Liberty* (London, Longmans, Green, 1867).

Monnet, Jean. *Memoirs* (Garden City, N.Y., Doubleday, 1977).

Montesquieu, Charles de. *The Spirit of the Laws,* trans. M. de Secondat (Philadelphia, 1802).

O'Brien, F. William. *Justice Reed and the First Amendment* (Washington, D.C., Georgetown University Press, 1958).

Parliamentary Debates, H. L. vol. 268 (5th Series) (London, Hansard, 1965).

Perry, Richard L. *Sources of Our Liberties* (1959; rev. Chicago, American Law Foundation, 1978).

Poore, Ben P. *Federal and State Constitutions, Colonial Charters,* 2 vols. (Washington, D.C., Government Printing Office, 1877).

Prettyman, E. Barrett, Jr. *Death and the Supreme Court* (New York, Harcourt Brace & World, 1961).

Radzinowicz, Leon. *History of the English Criminal Law and Its Administration from 1750,* 4 vols. (London, Stevens, 1948–1968).

Redish, Martin H. *Federal Jurisdiction: Tensions in the Allocation of Judicial Power* (Charlottesville, Va., Michie/Bobbs-Merrill, 1980).

Richardson, James O. *Compilation of the Messages and Papers of the Presidents, 1789–1897,* 10 vols. (Washington, D.C., Government Printing Office, 1897).

Shapiro, Martin. *Law and Politics in the Supreme Court* (New York, Free Press of Glencoe, 1964).

Smith, Page. *John Adams,* 2 vols. (Garden City, N.Y., Doubleday, 1962).

Smith, Paul H., ed. *Letters of Delegates to Congress, 1774–1789,* 7 vols. (Washington, D.C., Library of Congress, 1976–1981).

Smith, Sydney. *Selected Writings,* ed. W. H. Auden (New York, Farrar, Straus, 1956).

Stampp, Kenneth M. *The Peculiar Institution* (New York, Vintage Books, 1956).

Stephen, James F. *History of the Criminal Law of England,* 3 vols. (London, Macmillan, 1883).

Story, Joseph. *Commentaries on the Constitution of the United States,* 5th ed., 2 vols. (Boston, Little, Brown, 1905).

Warren, Charles. *Congress, the Constitution and the Supreme Court* (Boston, Little, Brown, 1925).

Washington, George. *Writings,* ed. J. C. Fitzpatrick, 39 vols. (Washington, D.C., Government Printing Office, 1940).

Wharton, Francis. *State Trials of the United States during the Adminis-*
trations of Washington and Adams (Philadelphia, Carey and Hart,
1849).

Wilson, James. *Works,* ed. R. G. McCloskey, 2 vols. (Cambridge,
Mass., Harvard University Press, 1967).

Wood, Gordon. *The Creation of the American Republic, 1776–1787*
(Chapel Hill, University of North Carolina Press, 1969).

Wright, Charles. *Federal Courts* (St. Paul, Minn., West Company,
1963).

ARTICLES

Abraham, Henry J. Book Review, 6 Hastings Constitutional Law
Quarterly 467 (1979).

Alexander, Larry A. "Modern Equal Protection Theories: A Metatheoretical Taxonomy and Critique," 42 Ohio State Law Journal 3
(1981).

Alfange, Dean. "On Judicial Policymaking and Constitutional
Change: Another Look at the 'Original Intent' Theory of Constitutional Interpretation," 5 Hastings Constitutional Law Quarterly
603 (1978).

Benedict, M. L. "To Secure These Rights: Rights, Democracy and Judicial Review in the Anglo-American Heritage," 42 Ohio State Law
Journal 69 (1981).

Berger, Raoul. "Bills of Attainder: A Study of Amendment by the
Court," 63 Cornell Law Review 355 (1978).

——— "Congressional Contraction of Federal Jurisdiction," 1980
Wisconsin Law Review 801.

——— "Constructive Contempt: A Post-Mortem," 9 University of
Chicago Law Review 602 (1942).

——— "Ely's 'Theory of Judicial Review,'" 42 Ohio State Law Journal 87 (1981).

——— "The Fourteenth Amendment: Light from the Fifteenth," 74
Northwestern University Law Review 311 (1979).

——— "From Hostage to Contract," 35 Illinois Law Review 154
(1940).

——— "Incorporation of the Bill of Rights in the Fourteenth
Amendment: A Nine-Lived Cat," 42 Ohio State Law Journal 435
(1981).

———— " 'Law of the Land' Reconsidered," 74 Northwestern University Law Review 1 (1979).

———— "The Ninth Amendment," 66 Cornell Law Review 1 (1980).

———— "Paul Brest's Brief for an Imperial Judiciary," 40 Maryland Law Review 1 (1981).

———— "Residence Requirements for Welfare and Voting: A Post-Mortem," 42 Ohio State Law Journal 853 (1981).

———— "Soifer to the Rescue of History," 31 South Carolina Law Review 427 (1980).

Bickel, Alexander M. "The Original Understanding and the Segregation Decision," 69 Harvard Law Review 1 (1955).

Black, Charles L., Jr. "The Presidency and Congress," 32 Washington and Lee Law Review 841 (1975).

Bork, Robert J. "Neutral Principles and Some First Amendment Problems," 47 Indiana Law Journal 1 (1971).

Brest, Paul. "Berger v. Brown et al.," New York Times, December 11, 1977, Book Review, section 7.

———— "Foreword: In Defense of the Antidiscrimination Principle," 90 Harvard Law Review 1 (1976).

———— "The Fundamental Rights Controversy: The Essential Contradictions of Normative Constitutional Scholarship," 90 Yale Law Journal 1063 (1981).

———— "The Misconceived Quest for the Original Understanding," 60 Boston University Law Review 204 (1980).

Bridwell, Randall. "The Federal Judiciary: America's Recently Liberated Minority," 30 South Carolina Law Review 467 (1979).

———— "The Scope of Judicial Review: A Dirge for the Theorists of Majority Rule?" 31 South Carolina Law Review 617 (1980).

Burleigh, John. "The Supreme Court vs. the Constitution," 50 The Public Interest 151 (Special Winter supplement 1978).

Commager, Henry Steele. "Judicial Review and Democracy," 19 Virginia Quarterly Review 417 (1943).

Cover, Robert M. Book Review, New Republic, January 14, 1978, p. 26.

Cox, Archibald. "The Effect of the Search for Equality Upon Judicial Institutions," 1979 Washington University Law Quarterly 795.

Curtis, Charles P. "Review and Majority Rule," in Cahn, ed., Supreme Court and Supreme Law 170 (1954).

Dix, George E. "Appellate Review of the Decision to Impose Death," 68 Georgetown Law Journal 97 (1979).

Douglas, William O. "Stare Decisis," 49 Columbia Law Review 735 (1949).

Ely, John Hart. "Constitutional Interpretivism: Its Allure and Impossibility," 53 Indiana Law Journal 399 (1978).

―――― "Foreword: On Discovering Fundamental Values," 92 Harvard Law Review 5 (1978).

―――― "The Wages of Crying Wolf: A Comment on Roe v. Wade," 82 Yale Law Journal 920 (1973).

Fairman, Charles. "Does the Fourteenth Amendment Incorporate the Bill of Rights?" 2 Stanford Law Review 5 (1949).

Fiss, Owen. "The Supreme Court, 1978 Term: Foreword: The Forms of Justice," 93 Harvard Law Review 1 (1979).

Friendly, Henry J. "The Bill of Rights as a Code of Criminal Procedure," 53 California Law Review 929 (1965).

Gangi, William. "Judicial Expansionism: An Evaluation of the Ongoing Debate," 8 Ohio Northern University Law Review 1 (1981).

Gerety, Thomas. "Doing Without Privacy," 42 Ohio State Law Journal 143 (1981).

Goebel, Julius. "Ex Parte Clio," 54 Columbia Law Review 450 (1954).

Goldberg, Arthur J., and Alan M. Dershowitz. "Declaring the Death Penalty Unconstitutional," 83 Harvard Law Review 1773 (1970).

Granucci, Anthony. " 'Nor Cruel and Unusual Punishments Inflicted': The Original Meaning," 57 California Law Review 839 (1969).

Grey, Thomas C. "Do We Have an Unwritten Constitution?" 27 Stanford Law Review 703 (1975).

Gunther, Gerald. "Some Reflections on the Judicial Role: Distinctions, Roots and Prospects," 1979 Washington University Law Quarterly 817.

Hart, Henry M., Jr. "The Power of Congress to Limit the Jurisdiction of the Federal Courts: An Exercise in Dialectic," 66 Harvard Law Review 1362 (1953).

Hazeltine, H. D. "The Influence of Magna Carta on American Constitutional Development," in Malden, ed., Magna Carta: Commemoration Essays 180 (1917).

Henkin, Louis. " 'Selective Incorporation' in the Fourteenth Amendment," 73 Yale Law Journal 74 (1963).

Horwitz, Morton J. "The Emergence of an Instrumental Conception of American Law, 1780–1820," in 5 *Perspectives in American History* 287 (1971).

Hurst, James Willard. "The Process of Constitutional Construction," in Cahn, ed., *Supreme Court and Supreme Law* 55 (1954).

——— "The Role of the Constitutional Text," in Cahn, ed., *Supreme Court and Supreme Law* 64 (1954).

Hutchinson, Dennis. "Unanimity and Desegregation Decisionmaking in the Supreme Court, 1948–1958," 68 Georgetown Law Journal 1 (1979).

Isenbergh, Max. "Thoughts on William O. Douglas' *The Court Years: A Confession and Avoidance*," 30 American University Law Review 415 (1981).

Jaffe, Louis L. "The Court Debated—Another View," *New York Times* Magazine June 5, 1960, in Levy, ed., *The Supreme Court under Earl Warren* 199 (1972).

——— "Was Brandeis an Activist: The Search for Intermediate Premises," 80 Harvard Law Review 986 (1967).

Jones, Harry W. "The Common Law in the United States: English Themes and American Variations," in Jones, ed., *Political Separation and Legal Continuity* 91 (1976).

Kaufman, Irving R. "Congress v. the Court," *New York Times* Magazine, September 20, 1981, p. 44.

Kauper, Paul G. "The Supreme Court: Hybrid Organ of State," 21 Southwestern Law Review 573 (1967).

Kay, Richard. "Preconstitutional Rules," 42 Ohio State Law Journal 187 (1981).

Kelly, Alfred H. "Clio and the Court: An Illicit Love Affair," 1965 Supreme Court Review 119.

——— "Comment on Harold M. Hyman's Paper," in Hyman, ed., *New Frontiers of the American Reconstruction* 41 (1966).

Kurland, Philip B. "Brown v. Board of Education Was the Beginning," 1979 Washington University Law Quarterly 309.

Kutler, Stanley, Book Review, 6 Hastings Constitutional Law Quarterly 511 (1979).

Lewis, Anthony, "A Man Born to Act, Not to Muse," *New York Times* Magazine, June 30, 1968, in Levy, ed., *The Supreme Court under Earl Warren* 151 (1972).

Lusky, Louis. Book Review, 6 Hastings Constitutional Law Quarterly 403 (1979).

McDougal, Myres, and Asher Lans. "Treaties and Congressional-Executive or Presidential Agreements: Interchangeable Instruments of National Policy," 54 Yale Law Journal 185, 585 (1945).

Miller, Arthur S. Book Review, 6 Hastings Constitutional Law Quarterly 487 (1979).

—— and Ronald F. Howell. "The Myth of Neutrality in Constitutional Adjudication," 27 University of Chicago Law Review 661 (1960).

Monaghan, Henry P. "The Constitution Goes to Harvard," 13 Harvard Civil Rights–Civil Liberties Law Review 117 (1978).

—— "Professor Jones and the Constitution," 4 Vermont Law Review (1979).

Nathanson, Nathaniel. Book Review, 56 Texas Law Review 579 (1978).

Neal, Phil C. "Baker v. Carr: Politics in Search of Law," 1962 Supreme Court Review 252.

Packer, Herbert. "The Aim of Criminal Law Revisited: A Plea for a New Look at 'Substantive Due Process,' " 44 Southern California Law Review 490 (1971).

—— "Making the Punishment Fit the Crime," 77 Harvard Law Review 1071 (1964).

Perry, Michael J. "Interpretivism, Freedom of Expression and Equal Protection," 42 Ohio State Law Journal 261 (1981).

—— "Noninterpretivist Review in Human Rights Cases: A Functional Justification," 56 New York University Law Review 278 (1981).

Polsby, Daniel. "The Death of Capital Punishment? Furman v. Georgia," 1972 Supreme Court Review 1.

Ratner, Leonard G. "Congressional Power Over the Appellate Jurisdiction of the Supreme Court," 109 University of Pennsylvania Law Review 157 (1960).

Richardson, H. G., and G. O. Sayles. "Parliament and Great Councils in Medieval England," 77 Law Quarterly Review 213 (1961).

Rostow, Eugene V. "The Democratic Character of Judicial Review," 66 Harvard Law Review 193 (1952).

Sager, Lawrence. "Foreword: Constitutional Limitations on Congress' Authority to Regulate the Jurisdiction of the Federal Courts," 95 Harvard Law Review 17 (1981).

Sandalow, Terrance. "Judicial Protection of Minorities," 75 Michigan Law Review 1162 (1977).

Shapiro, Martin. "Judge as Statesman, Judge as Pol," *New York Times,* November 22, 1981, Book Review, section 7.

Thayer, James Bradley. "The Origin and Scope of the American Doctrine of Constitutional Law," 7 Harvard Law Review 129 (1893).

Wechsler, Herbert. "The Courts and the Constitution," 65 Columbia Law Review 1001 (1965).

Wheeler, Malcolm. "Toward a Theory of Limited Punishment II: The Eighth Amendment after *Furman v. Georgia,"* 25 Stanford Law Review 62 (1972).

Wigmore, John H. "A Program for the Trial of Jury Trial," 12 Journal of American Judicature Society 166 (1929).

Zeisel, Hans. "Race Bias in the Administration of the Death Penalty: The Florida Experience," 95 Harvard Law Review 456 (1981).

Ziskind, Martha Andes. "Judicial Tenure in the American Constitution: English and American Precedents," 1969 Supreme Court Review 135.

MISCELLANEOUS

Annals of Congress, vol. 1 (1789), 2d ed. (Washington, D.C., Gales & Seaton, 1834, print bearing running head "History of Congress").

Annals of Congress, vol. 2 (1791).

Congressional Globe, 39th Congress, 1st Session (1866).

——— 41st Congress, 3d Session (1871).

——— 42d Congress, 1st Session (1871).

Journal of the Continental Congress, 1774–1789, vol. 1, 1774 (Washington, D.C., Government Printing Office, 1904).

Report of the Joint Committee on Reconstruction, June 8, 1866 (39th Congress, 1st Session); reprinted in Avins, *The Reconstruction Amendments' Debates* 94 (1967).

Senate Report No. 21, 42d Congress, 2d Session (January 25, 1872); reprinted in Avins at 573.

Statutes

Act of April 30, 1790, §21 (1st Congress, 2d Session, Chapter 9), 1 United States Statutes at Large 117.

1 Mary, 1st Session, Statute I, c. 1 (1552).

General Index

Abbott, Jack Henry, 176
Abolition of death penalty, abolitionists, 114, 176, 178; efforts
   of, 4–7, 58, 74; understanding
   of Framers, 61, 68; importance
   of *Weems* for, 72–73, 113; argument's points, 119, 122, 127:
   Justice Marshall's argument,
   124; rejected by States, 125: and
   standards in sentencing, 141;
   and death penalty for rape, 149;
   view of Court's powers,
   173–174; and life imprisonment,
   177
Abraham, Henry, 24, 83, 97, 192;
   on 14th Amendment and school
   segregation, 184
Act of April 30, 1790, 43, 47, 48,
   49, 63, 113, 148
Act of March 3, 1825, 148
Acton, Lord, 64
Adams, Abigail, 14
Adams, Henry, 78
Adams, Samuel, on clear terms, 75
Agca, Mehmet Ali, 176

Aiding and abetting issue, 150–151
Alaska, 124
Alexander, L. A., 9
Alfange, Dean, 24, 192
Amendment process: power of,
   7–8, 49, 58, 59, 60, 61, 66, 71,
   78, 89, 123, 156, 175; "cumber-
   some," 7, 153–154; change in
   death penalty obtainable by,
   72
Amercement, 30–31, 33
American Friends Service Commit-
   tee, 178
Amsterdam, Anthony G., on Su-
   preme Court members, 142
Anglo-Saxon laws, 30–31
Annan, Noel, on government
   knowing what people want, 126
Appellate jurisdiction of Court, 91,
   155, 158–167, 201–203
Appellate review, 137–138
Arizona, 140
Articles of Confederation, 94
Atlanta, Ga., 56
Attaint, 137

217

Index of Cases